Spain

at its best

ABOUT THE AUTHOR

Robert S. Kane's initial writing stint was as editor of the [Boy Scout] *Troop Two Bugle* in his native Albany, New York. After graduation from Syracuse University's noted journalism school, he did graduate work at England's Southampton University, first making notes as he explored in the course of class field trips through the Hampshire countryside. Back in the U.S., he worked, successively, for the *Great Bend* (Kansas) *Daily Tribune, Staten Island Advance, New York Herald Tribune,* and *New York World-Telegram & Sun* before becoming travel editor of, first, *Playbill,* and later *Cue* and *50 Plus.* His byline has appeared in such leading magazines, such as *Travel & Leisure, Vogue, House & Garden, Atlantic, Harper's Bazaar, Family Circle, New York, Saturday Review,* and *Modern Bride;* and such newspapers as the *Newark Star-Ledger, New York Post, New York Daily News, New York Times, Los Angeles Times, Chicago Sun-Times, Boston Globe, San Diego Union, Dallas Morning News, San Francisco Examiner,* and *Toronto Globe & Mail.* And he guests frequently, with the subject travel, on TV and radio talk shows.

Africa A to Z, the first U.S.-published guide to largely independent, post-World War II Africa, was the progenitor of his acclaimed 14-book *A to Z* series, other pioneering volumes of which were *Eastern Europe A to Z,* the first guide to the USSR and the Soviet Bloc countries as seen through the eyes of a candid American author, and *Canada A to Z,* the first modern-day, province-by-province guide to the world's second largest country. His current *World at Its Best* series includes two volumes (*Britain at Its Best* and *France at Its Best*), tapped by a pair of major book clubs, and a third (*Germany at Its Best*) that's a prize-winner.

Kane, the only American authoring an entire multi-volume travel series, has the distinction of having served as president of both the Society of American Travel Writers and the New York Travel Writers' Association, and is a member, as well, of the National Press Club (Washington), P.E.N., Authors Guild, Society of Professional Journalists/Sigma Delta Chi, and American Society of Journalists and Authors. He makes his home on the Upper East Side of Manhattan.

Robert S. Kane

Spain
at its best

 PASSPORT BOOKS

Trade Imprint of National Textbook Company
Lincolnwood, Illinois U.S.A.

BY **ROBERT S. KANE**

The World at Its Best Travel Series
BRITAIN AT ITS BEST
FRANCE AT ITS BEST
GERMANY AT ITS BEST
HAWAII AT ITS BEST
HOLLAND AT ITS BEST
ITALY AT ITS BEST
LONDON AT ITS BEST
PARIS AT ITS BEST
SPAIN AT ITS BEST
SWITZERLAND AT ITS BEST

A to Z World Travel Guides
GRAND TOUR A TO Z: THE CAPITALS OF EUROPE
EASTERN EUROPE A TO Z
SOUTH PACIFIC A TO Z
CANADA A TO Z
ASIA A TO Z
SOUTH AMERICA A TO Z
AFRICA A TO Z

Published by Passport Books, Trade Imprint of National
Textbook Company, 4255 West Touhy Avenue,
Lincolnwood, Illinois 60646-1975.
Manufactured in the United States of America.
Library of Congress Catalog Card Number: 87-62828

890 ML 9 8 7 6 5 4 3 2 1

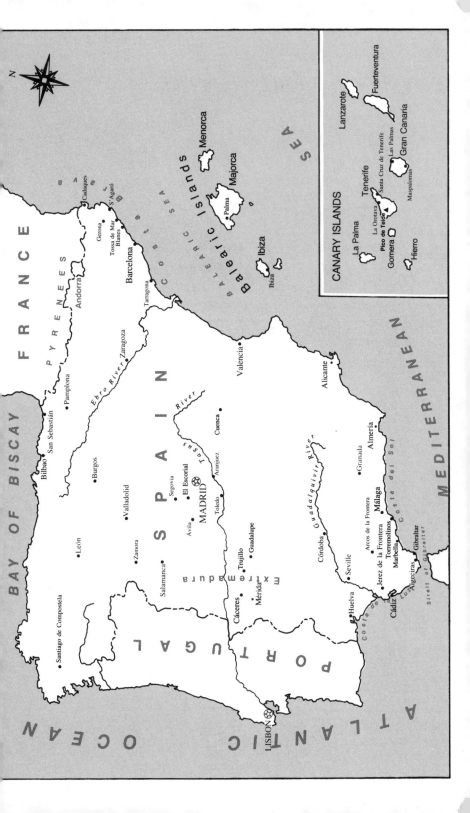

For Bunny Brower

Contents

Foreword

America's Second Homeland

Roots to Spain? Our national sense of Hispanic consciousness becomes increasingly well defined. Hispanics have come to constitute the nation's fastest growing community. Concurrently, the contemporary Kingdom of Spain has emerged as one of Europe's favored vacationlands, and the American traveler is increasingly curious about it.

Well and good. But what of the transatlantic Spanish Connection vis-à-vis ties to Britain—the country from which we acquired not only a national language but a broad range of cultural manifestations? There is no question of the enormity of our debt to British cousins. But surely it is worth considering that well into the last century, Spanish America comprised most of the New World—all of South America save Brazil, Central America in toto, Mexico as well. The massive Louisiana Territory embracing much of the center of North America, which was briefly French before it was purchased by the U.S.A., had for long been Spanish. California reverted to Mexico before it became American in the mid-nineteenth century. Florida, originally larger than it is now, remained Spanish until the mid-eighteenth century. We tend to forget that Ponce de León was not only the legendary seeker of the fountain of youth, but earlier governor of a territory now flying the Stars and Stripes (Puerto Rico), and a fellow explorer (on the second voyage) with Columbus.

Even today, the beautiful Spanish language is our second, widely spoken in New Mexico, California, Texas, Florida, and in the north as well, especially in New York, where I live. Language, though, is but one of our bonds with Spain. Others become discernible when we cross to the land from which the conquistadores and the priests came so many centuries back.

Some of us beeline, once in Madrid, for the Museo de América, for tangible evidence of the culture we share. Others—many fewer—journey to Extremadura near the Portuguese frontier, to experience the somnolent cities from which the explorers set off, later returning to retire. Or we continue south to coastal Huelva, with still additional historic American associations.

Actually, all Spain emerges as an instant evocation of the heritage that's crossed the Atlantic. With the yoke of the Franco oppression of three and a half decades well behind it, this ancient land has emerged—more effortlessly than many observers dared dream—a responsible constitutional monarchy. There are strikes. There is inflation. There are isolated acts of terrorism. But by and large, the transformation from totalitarianism to democracy has been extraordinarily smooth and sensible. All this while more visitors than ever before come for respite. Northern Europeans seek warmth and sunshine. New Worlders, while never averse to gentle climate, are after manifestations—cultural, artistic, architectural, gastronomic—of Spain's western hemisphere legacy.

What I attempt to facilitate in these pages is a discovery—or in the case of many travelers, a rediscovery—of the most visitworthy of Spanish destinations. There is a substantial chapter on Madrid—almost twice as thick as the next longest. On the other hand, I make no attempt to hide admiration for Barcelona, the touristically overlooked second city, nor the third city, Valencia, almost terra incognita to New Worlders. I do not neglect favored destinations like Toledo, Seville, and Granada. The Costa del Sol, Majorca, and Ibiza sunspots are accorded their due, as are the Canaries—where winter weather can be iffier—and the Costa Brava, which is more a French-Spanish than American destination.

In between there are chapters on places moderately familiar—Segovia and Córdoba, to name two—and only vaguely known to many of us, like, say, Salamanca and Valladolid, Santiago de Compostela and La Coruña, Cuenca and Ávila, Burgos, and the small but charming cities of still-somnolent Extremadura, edging the frontier with Portugal.

In this book, the format is essentially as it has been in my other guides: enough background to make newcomers feel acquainted, city by city, area by area; followed by my own candid evaluations—never, I hope, too detailed as to put one off—of places that I've enjoyed visiting (and not only from without); hotels, restaurants, and cafés—categorized by me as *Luxury, First Class,* and *Moderate* to give you an idea of cost and ambience—in which I've enjoyed eating or pausing for a drink or snack.

No matter occasional irritants in the Spanish travel scene—relatively limited open-hours at museums (Madrid's celebrated Prado is the country's most generous, in this important respect), virtually ubiquitous admission tabs to cathedrals; and a near-national aversion to fluency in foreign languages, once one veers from beaten paths. The point is that Spain will always be a satisfying land for a holiday; too many of its own people and others—Phoenicians, Carthaginians, Romans, Visigoths, Moors, Jews—have made rich contributions over the centuries. The Spaniards, proudly and appreciatively, have allowed much of this handiwork to remain. As Americans, no matter our own personal backgrounds, we owe Spain enough to want to experience firsthand the origins of its gifts to us. Now, more than ever before, on-scene exploration is the way.

ROBERT S. KANE

Spain
A Mini A to Z

ADDRESSES: National Tourist Office of Spain branches in North America are at 665 Fifth Avenue, New York, New York 10022; 845 North Michigan Avenue, Chicago, Illinois 60611; San Vicente Plaza Building, 8383 Wilshire Boulevard, Los Angeles, California 90211; Casa del Hidalgo, St. Augustine, Florida 32084; 4800 The Galleria, Houston, Texas 77056; and 60 Bloor Street West, Toronto, Ontario, Canada M4W3B8. Home base for the Secretaría General de Turismo: Calle María de Molena 50, Madrid. Within Spain, the local tourist office—*Oficina de Turismo*—is the traveler's best friend; addresses of these appear in chapters following.

BREAKFAST to Spaniards is nothing more than a breaking of the night's fast, and minimally, by means of coffee—usually *café con leche* (mixed with milk)—or tea, served with uninteresting bread and rolls, butter and jam, and occasionally orange juice. The better category the hotel, the less likely *desayuno* (breakfast) is to be included in the room rates. But all hotels, even the simplest, serve it in rooms. Easiest extra to order, again no matter the hotel category, is a boiled egg—with which you'll be served salt but no pepper unless you specify. In better places you may order your eggs scrambled or fried, and with bacon or ham. If breakfast is not included in your hotel room rate, and you want to save money, have it in a nearby *cafetería* or bar, as many Spaniards do, standing at a counter. Order the Madrileños favorite pick-me-up, a cup of hot *chocolate con churros*, these last finger-shaped fritters that are designed for dunking; or coffee with a split hard roll, toasted and buttered; simply ask for *pan tostado*.

BULLFIGHTS are Spain's *fiesta nacional*, although *aficionados* have, in recent seasons, begun to lament—and publicly, in the press—a lowering of standards that some critics attribute to the excessive number of spectators who are undiscerning, unknowledgeable foreign tourists applauding even substandard matadors and bulls. Bullfights are generally a Sunday afternoon (and sometimes Thursday) diversion from late spring through early fall. No. 1 ring, kingdom-wide, is Madrid's Plaza Monumental de las Ventas, but those of Barcelona and the major Andalusian cities like Seville and Granada, not to mention the historic ring in little Ronda, are considered big league, too. Not that *plazas de toros* are limited to these places. Rare is the Spanish town—however small—without a ring. As you travel, watch for colorful posters advising of dates. Even a modest fight is a spectacle. The tourneys are preceded by a musically accompanied parade of resplendently attired *toreros*, or bullfighters. The bullfighter who kills the bull, the *matador*, is assisted by *picadores* (mounted warriors who stab or "pick" at the bull) and *banderilleros* (who plant darts in the bull's shoulders). The bullfight consists of three parts, or *suertes*. In the first, *suerte de picar*, the *picadores* lance the bull between the shoulder blades. The *banderilleros* try to plant darts around these wounds in the second part of the fight, *suerte de banderillear*. Finally, in *suerte de matar*, the *matador* attacks the bull alone, first with the *muleta*, or cape, until he can execute the death blow with the *estoque*, a short sword.

BUSES, in areas of the country where train service has not kept pace with the times, have become popular because they are faster than the competition, and can be more comfortable. Which is hardly to say that they are lightning-like. (Stops along the way can be frequent.) Still, an extensive network more or less covers the kingdom. By and large, the long-distance bus is air-conditioned, with reclining seats and, on some routes, a screen

over the driver's head, for video presentations. Like train personnel, those in the bus industry—at ticket-windows and on
board—do not speak foreign languages. Rest stops are made on
longer runs, and stations are minimally attractive.

CASINOS are found throughout the country, something like a
score strong, with new ones popping up, the better to swell coffers with tourist dollars, although Spaniards are estimated to
provide about half their patronage. You must be 21, and pay a
fairly steep admission fee to enter; games include roulette,
blackjack, chemin de fer, and craps. Locations range from resorts (like Marbella and Majorca) to big cities (such as Barcelona
and Valencia).

CATHEDRALS in Spain are unique in the world in that—no
matter their architectural or artistic significance, their size or lack
of it, their celebrity or obscurity—they mostly charge admission
fees. (The local faithful, who know where the side doors are,
enter to pray for free.) Museums and artistic monuments
throughout Spain charge also, although most churches that are
not cathedrals do not. So far as my researches (and receipts!) indicate, Cartuja on Majorca (where George Sand and Chopin
wintered) and Barcelona's Fundación Joan Miró are the priciest
of Spain's museums.

CLIMATE: Not even winter is all that cold, with Madrid temperatures rarely below the 20s (Fahrenheit) and usually going into
the 50s, whereas the Costa del Sol ranges at that time from the
40s to the 60s—too cold to swim, but mild. Only region I avoid in
winter—having tried it once—is the Canary Islands, whose
highly touted "eternal springtime" did not work out that way, at
least for me. You may ski in the Sierra Nevada, near Granada,
cold-weather months into spring, which, Spain-wide, are invariably delightful. Madrid in May averages 50 to 75, and the Costa
del Sol is even warmer. Summer—Spain's major tourist season,
country-wide—is hot. August in Madrid sees temperatures
ranging from the mid-60s to 90; somewhat higher on the Costa
del Sol. Autumn can be rainy in November but earlier on is gen-

erally most agreeable. October averages low 40s to mid-60s in Madrid, mid-50s to high 70s on the Costa del Sol.

CLOTHES: Spaniards—especially urban Spaniards—know style and grooming. (Spain's perfumes, toilet waters, and after-shave lotions are arguably Europe's best, after France's. And its fine soaps rank with those of France and England.) Dress as you would at home in this temperate land where seasonal variations are much like ours—changeable to some degree. Be as informal as you like during the day, unless of course you're a business person meeting with Spanish colleagues. Be dressier—especially if the occasion is at all festive—in the evening, especially in big cities and better resort hotels. Have a raincoat and collapsible umbrella along, regardless of season.

CONSERJES are concierges, the chaps who not only take care of keys and mail in hotels, but are equipped with the latest intelligence on hours of museums and monuments, trains, planes, and the like.

CREDIT CARDS (*tarjetas de crédito*) are widely accepted. Both American Express and Diners Club are strong. Of the bank cards, Visa appears to be more popular than MasterCard. Still, acceptance is not universal, especially in the case of restaurants you may want to try that are away from larger cities or resorts.

CUSTOMS: Entering Spain: Generally, quick, polite, and easy, with a verbal declaration invariably acceptable. Nondutiable personal effects include two still cameras and a movie camera, with 10 rolls of film for each; portable radio and tape recorder (so long as they look used—and not for sale or to be given as a gift), sports gear, "reasonable quantities" of cigarettes and tobacco, a bottle each of liquor and wine. (Spanish table wines and most Spanish brandies are not expensive but sherry most definitely is, as are imported spirits. Stock up in supermarkets—*supermercados*—which are indeed super.)

Returning to the United States: Each individual may bring back $400 worth of purchases, duty-free. That is allowable once every 30 days, provided you've been out of the country at least 48 hours. If you've spent more than $400, you'll be charged a flat 10 percent duty on the next $1,000 worth of purchases. Remember, too, that antiques, duly certified to be at least 100 years old, are admitted duty-free, and do not count as part of your $400 quota; neither do paintings, sculptures, and other works of art, of any date, if certified as original; it's advisable that certification from the seller or other authority as to their authenticity accompany them. Also exempt from duty, but as a part of the $400 quota: one quart of liquor. And—this is important—there is no restriction on how much one may bring in beyond the $400 limit, so long as the duty is paid.

DEPARTMENT STORES AND SHOPS: The former are the most sensible sources of purchases, souvenirs to requisites; one is sure that prices are realistic: the very same that hard-working, budget-conscious Spaniards themselves are paying. There are two country-wide chains: El Corte Inglés (The English Cut, if you want a translation) and Galerías Preciados. Also worthy of your consideration: the government chain of handicraft shops—range is furniture to pottery, carpets to silver—under the umbrella of the Empresa Nacional de Artesanía; they're called Artespaña. I bring these stores—and others I've scouted—to your attention in the shopping sections of chapters following, on major cities. Note that you may receive as much as ten percent tax rebate on purchases of more than 10,000 Spanish pesetas, using a special form (available in department stores) that is submitted to Spanish customs upon exiting the country. Stores—especially the bigger and more important ones—have details.

DRIVING: Car-rental firms are ubiquitous. If you want to use your American license, authorities recommend that you ask the Spanish Consulate nearest you to give you a Spanish translation of it, just in case you're asked to show it to a police officer who doesn't read English. Or travel with an international driving license; local auto clubs have details on how to obtain these.

ELECTRIC CURRENT: Mostly 220 volts D.C., but you still come across 110 volts D.C. occasionally, as well as 120 volts A.C. Take with you an adapter and a set of plugs with the various size prongs likely to be found in Spanish hotel-room walls, so that you can use your American blow-dryer and other appliances. Your local hardware shop can help.

FACIAL TISSUE: Take along your own. Generally, only luxury hotels (there are some exceptions) provide them. But they're easy to find in stores, when you run out.

FLAMENCO is Spain's emotional safety valve; the bittersweet dances, songs, and guitar music that, at their best, are a major art form. Flamenco—of Andalusian, not gypsy—origin is for an intimate café, not a big theater's stage. The performance is rarely good if close rapport has not been established between performers and audience. A typical company (each of whose members is traditionally garbed; wasp-waisted men in black, women in flounced, polka-dotted gowns) includes the ever-so-important guitarist, one or two male dancer-singers, several female dancer-singers, and a mature woman who not only sings and dances but is as well the good-natured den mother of the group. In larger companies there are additional *bailadores* (dancers), *cantadores* (singers), and *jaleadores* (clappers of the rhythm) as well. Generally, price of admission—rather steep—includes an initial drink. Quality of companies varies; better ones are increasingly rare.

FOOD: Spaniards, when it comes to the matter of Americans identifying their cuisine with that of Mexico, have the patience of *santos*. Mexicans, because of their country's historic association with Spain, eat some Spanish dishes. But Mexican food is essentially derivative of the cuisine of the Mexican Indians. Spain has no Indians. Spanish food is Spanish, at once subtle, uncomplicated, and very often delicious. Sauces, not common, are simple. Broiled or roasted meat—lamb, mutton, veal, beef, sometimes kid—are popular. Cod—*bacalao*—is perhaps the major fish, but there are a number of others more to Americans' tastes, sole (*lenguado*) and trout (*trucha*) most deliciously. And seafood—clams, squid, crab, mussels, crayfish—play important roles. Vegetables are more interesting in salads than as cooked dishes, although artichokes and eggplant are well prepared. French fries are the most frequently encountered accompaniment to meats.

Poultry is only fairly common. Game—partridge in particular, but quail and rabbit, too—is eaten more frequently in Spain than in any other country I know, save Britain. Soups can be excellent; *gazpacho*, an uncooked blend of tomatoes, oil, peppers, onions, and seasonings, served chilled, is a summer treat. *Tapas*, bite-size appetizers served with drinks, constitute Spanish food at its most amusing: olives and almonds of course, but tidbits like fried mussels, tiny fritters known as *buñuelitos*, mini-turnovers called *empanadillas*. Classic Spanish dessert is the caramel custard, *flan*, not unlike France's *crème caramel*. Fresh fruit—never turn down figs—is a common dessert. Ice creams and sherbets are popular and satisfying. *Manchego*—best when rock-hard and crumbly—is the premier cheese. Most celebrated dish is named for the two-handled metal pan it's cooked in: *paella*, with its saffron-flavored rice base blanketed with a mix of chicken, red peppers, shellfish, green peas for color, sometimes snails to be speared with toothpicks. Spaniards are not big butter eaters; they cook with excellent olive oil. Bread and rolls often look like those of France and Italy but only rarely are as tasty. In the chapters following, I recommend personally sampled restaurants in the *Luxury, First Class,* and *Moderate* categories, often indicating regional specialties you'll want to try; they appear in order of my personal preference.

GEOGRAPHY: We tend to underestimate Spain's area. Nearly 39 million Spaniards inhabit an area of close to 200,000 square miles, equalling the size of Colorado and Wyoming combined, and there are 42 cities with populations exceeding 100,000. If you forget the minuscule principality of Andorra in a Pyrenées valley, it's bordered by but two countries: France to the north, and Portugal—with which it unequally shares the Iberian peninsula, Spain occupying 85 percent—to the west. And water: there's a bit of Atlantic on the southwest, an extension of the Atlantic—the Bay of Biscay, or *Vizcaya*, as it's called in Spanish—in the north, with considerable stretches of the Mediterranean, both on the south coast and the east. The continent of Africa is a near-neighbor; nowhere indeed is it closer to Europe than at the Strait of Gibraltar, which is eight miles at its narrowest point. Spain is essentially a giant of a plateau, if hardly without topographical variety: notably the peaks of the Pyrenees that form its border with France, and mountain ranges in the center, extending southerly as a dramatic backdrop to the Costa del Sol resorts. There are a trio of principal rivers—Guadalquivir in the south, Tagus in the center, Ebro to the northeast—none of which is a geographical household word abroad, in the manner of, say, the Seine or the Thames. Offshore Spain—not neglected within these covers—embraces the Atlantic's Canary Islands and the Mediterranean's Balearic Islands.

GOVERNMENT: Spain is a very modern constitutional monarchy. The present constitution, ratified only in 1978, provides for it to be governed by the king as head of state, and the Cortes, or Parliament, with the prime minister—representing the political party victorious in general elections—in power for four years. The two houses of Parliament are the *Congreso de los Diputados* (with 350 members) and the *Senato* (with 208 members)—all elected by universal suffrage. The constitution grants considerable autonomy to 17 regions, or autonomous communities, to wit: Catalonia, Basque Country, Galicia, Andalucía, Valencia, Extremadura, Canary Islands, Aragón, Balearic Islands, Castille-León, Castille–La Mancha, Navarra, Asturias, Madrid, Murcia, La Rioja, and Cantabria. And the regions are subdivided into 50 provinces.

HISTORY is capsulized within, chapter by chapter, with Madrid—the capital—understandably accorded more detail than other cities and areas. The idea is to provide just enough perspective to enrich your visit. Suffice it to say, at this point, that—following the routing of the Moors and the unification of the kingdom in the late fifteenth century—Spain has been ruled by several dynasties whose reigns have been occasionally interrupted by commoners. The royal pair we know so well—thanks to their dispatch of one Christopher Columbus to our shores—Isabella I (of Castile) and her husband, Ferdinand II (of Aragón), controlled a united kingdom, and have gone down in history as *Los Reyes Católicos*—The Catholic Kings. They were succeeded by a clutch of Austrian-Low Countries-related Hapsburgs, starting with their daughter, Joanna the Mad, who gave birth to the great Emperor Charles V, and her husband, Philip the Handsome. Charles's celebrated son was the same Philip II who married England's Bloody Mary (the second of four wives). But there were three later Hapsburgs: Philip III, who developed Madrid into a proper city; Philip IV, whom we know best thanks to Velázquez's portraits of him and his family; and Charles II, who preceded the early eighteenth-century, French-origin Bourbon reign.

There were an even half-dozen Bourbon—or *Borbón*—kings. Again we thank a painter—this time, Goya—for our familiarity with that dynasty's Charles III. Napoleon's brother Joseph usurped the Spanish throne for five early nineteenth-century years (1808–13), to be followed by two monarchs of the first Bourbon Restoration—Ferdinand VII and the second Isabella— Spain's counterpart of England's Victoria; the era took her name for design and furniture, not to mention politics. Isabella II reigned till 1868.

A little-remembered elective monarchy followed, for a half-decade, with the First Republic's four presidents succeeding. In 1874 Bourbons returned, in the persons of Alfonso XII (Isabella II's son), and Alfonso XIII—the last pre-Civil War king (he abdicated and fled into exile in 1931). The ill-fated Second Spanish Republic spanned but eight years, during which time Francisco Franco's fascist insurgents wrested the democratic government from the Loyalist Republicans—while the world mostly looked on, offering precious little Loyalist aid. Upon Dictator Franco's death, totalitarian Spain reverted to the monarchy, with Alfonso XIII's grandson, Juan Carlos I, ascending the long-dormant throne to preside—as a constitutional monarch (see *Royal Family*, below) with the government headed by a prime minister—over a remarkably smooth transition to democracy. There have, to be sure, been problems. Long-repressed labor, now represented by politically strong unions, asserts itself by means of frequent strikes. Inflation is a problem. And regional politics became complex, with Basque terrorist attacks the principal offenses, and increased status for regional languages like Basque and Catalán, among the accomplishments.

HOTELS AND PARADORES: *About the hotels in this book:* I have either lived in or thoroughly inspected the hotels carefully selected for evaluation in these pages. I disregard complexities and inconsistencies of the official Spanish star system and have divided hotels (and restaurants) into the three price groups I employ in all of the books of my *World at Its Best* series: *Luxury, First Class,* and *Moderate.* Bear in mind that I am fussy. In towns of any size and cities, I favor *centrally situated* hotels, including suburban, exurban and country hotels only when they are exceptional and will be of interest to travelers with cars. All hotels in my *Luxury* and virtually all in my *First Class* categories have television and mini-bars (stocked with liquor, wine, soft drinks, and sometimes snacks—for purchase) in all rooms, as well, of course, as private baths and (except possibly in the north where it is not anything like as essential as in the center and south), air-conditioning. My *Moderate* category hotels are, by and large, *better*-Moderate, very often with TV and/or mini-bars, with baths attached to most or all rooms (I indicate the proportion in each case) and frequently with air-conditioning.

Hotels operated by top-rank United States-based chains are, oddly enough, relatively rare in Spain. Indeed, I can come up with but two: Madrid's Castellana *Inter-Continental* and Majorca's Son Vida *Sheraton.* A number of individually owned hotels are, however, affiliated with Arizona-based *Best Western International.* Italy's *Ciga Hotels* and Britain's *Trusthouse Forte* are on scene. Paris-headquartered *Relaix et Châteaux* (whose U.S. representative is David B. Mitchell Co., 200 Madison Avenue, New York, N.Y. 10016) has a clutch of Spanish affiliates, and there's a group of all-Spain leaders in the luxury field—elected by their hard-to-please confrères—of appropriately-titled, New York–headquartered *Leading Hotels of the World* (Head office, 747 Third Avenue, New York, N.Y. 10017).

Of the American hotel representation companies, hands down leader with respect to Spanish hotels is Spanish-born Antonio Alonso's *Marketing Ahead, Inc.* (Head office: 433 Fifth Avenue, New York, N.Y. 10016), which acts on behalf of some 250 hostelries—grand to modest—including the eighty-plus links of the Spanish Government-owned *parador* chain (below).

And there are a number of Spanish chains, including *Husa, Interhoteles, Meliá, Sol,* and *Tryp.*

About paradores: These are a remarkable chain of inns—many in deftly refurbished castles, palaces and convents that date back centuries, others in new albeit traditionally designed and furnished structures—found throughout the kingdom. More are in rural than urban areas. They are good value, with respect both to guest rooms (always with white-tiled private baths) and the authentically Spanish meals (regional specialties are featured often) in their invariably attractive restaurants. Although their staffs (even including managers) rarely speak foreign languages, *paradores* are mostly smashing to look upon, especially when occupying sumptuously situated and furnished quarters of great age. At most, room capacity is limited: a *parador* with, say, 35 or 40 rooms is a biggie, so that you must book as much in advance as possible, either via your travel agent or directly, through the *Paradores de España* section of Marketing Ahead, Inc. (address above).

HOURS: Meals, first. They're late. Simpler places like snack-bars and coffee shops—in Spain called *cafeterías,* albeit not usually self-service—are conveniently open nonstop throughout the day. But proper restaurants shutter until 1 P.M. when *almuerzo* (lunch) is served, with Spaniards drifting in for the midday meal as late as 2 or even 3 P.M. The long afternoon and early evening hours are punctuated, nutritionally, by a snack or *merienda* and/or aperitifs with *tapas,* the bite-size nibbles that always accompany drinks in Spain. Then, along about 10 P.M.—and as late as 11 P.M.—Spaniards sit down to *cena* (dinner). Now, then, there's no need for visitors to have the evening meal that late. Most restaurants open as early as 8 P.M. and in the resort areas—Majorca, Costa del Sol, the Canaries (where there can be more foreigners than natives)—that is the usual dinner hour in hotels. I repeat: popularly priced *cafeterías* are open nonstop the day and evening long.

Which brings us to open-hours for museums and other sight-seers' destinations. Madrid's Prado and Real Academia de Bellas Artes and Granada's Alhambra have nonstop weekday hours 9 A.M.–7 P.M. But by and large, museums and other important monuments—palaces, cathedrals, art-filled churches—shutter for lunch, reopening in mid-afternoon, until early evening. Ask your hotel concierge for free, locally published what's-on booklets that have current schedules. Or inquire at local tourist information offices. But don't forget that tourist offices, like everything in Spain save hotels, restaurants, and big department stores, *close for lunch, usually from 1 to 4:30 P.M.*, and reopen until 8. Banks are open 9 A.M. to 2 P.M. weekdays, 9 A.M. to 1 P.M. Saturdays.

HOUSEKEEPING: Señor Clean is on-scene. Spain is spotless. Rare—very rare indeed—is the hotel (rooms, baths, public spaces) that doesn't glisten. Ditto restaurants, *cafeterías*, bars. Spaniards are compulsive housekeepers.

IBERIA, Spain's international airline, links New York, Chicago, Los Angeles, and Miami—in the U.S.—with Madrid, Málaga, Barcelona and (in summer) Santiago de Compostela; and flies transatlantic, as well, between Montreal, in Canada, and Spain. It operates an extensive domestic network within Spain, flies throughout Europe, not to mention much of the rest of the world, to a total of more than 90 cities in more than half a hundred countries. Spain's second airline, Aviaco, flies domestically, along with Iberia; their routes do not always duplicate each other. Pan American and Trans World also serve Spain.

ITINERARIES/TOUR OPERATORS: First-time visitors choose Madrid, and possibly Toledo, Seville, and Granada on a round-Europe package. Or they'll opt for an around-Spain package visiting those cities, along perhaps with the Costa del Sol. Barcelona, the No. 2 city, is too often neglected, and so for that matter is most of the rest of the kingdom. At least by newcomers to the European scene. Many tour operators package tours of Spain. Among those with a variety of Spanish packages—and this is a partial group—are *Extra Value Travel, Go Go Tours, Hartours, Inc., International Weekends, M.I. Travel, Petrabax USA, and Worldventures*—all U.S. companies; and *Hispanidad Holidays, Marsans, Meliá Tours, and Viajes Ecuador*—all Spain-headquartered firms. Returnees like to pick and choose, and stay on-scene for longer periods, to explore lesser-known cities like Salamanca, Santiago de Compostela, Valladolid, and Valencia—to name but four. That's where this book should help. Along with the counsel of a travel agent for the booking of packages or the planning of individually tailored tours—ideally one whose credentials include membership in the prestigious American Society of Travel Agents (ASTA).

LANGUAGES: Spanish is more often than not called Castilian, or *Castellano* by Spaniards, after the region where it originated and developed into one of the planet's most beautiful tongues. It is, of course, the universal language of the kingdom. However, regional languages—Catalán (a venerable tongue of the Romance group), in Catalonia, with variations in Majorca and Valencia; Galician in the northwest; and Basque in the northern Basque provinces—are on an equal legal footing, and you must expect to see menus in these languages, not to mention other printed material and signs—including street signs, especially in Catalonia—as well. Most uptight and rigid about the employment of the regional languages—over Castellano—are Catalonians and Basques; most relaxed, Majorcans and Valencians. English is the most widely spoken foreign language. But, take note: *Away from big cities and major resorts, English is not all that widely spoken.* In Barcelona and the Costa Brava, French is commonplace. German—especially on the Costa del Sol, Majorca, Ibiza, and the Canaries—is No. 3. Whatever Spanish you can muster will, believe me, prove helpful; at the very least carry an English-Spanish dictionary and/or a phrase book, such as *Just Enough Spanish*, published by Passport Books; or study the language in advance of departure with Passport's *Just Listen 'n Learn Spanish*, a three-cassette-and-textbook kit.

MONEY: Unit of exchange is the peseta. It comes in 1-, 2½-, 5-, 25-, 50-, and 100-peseta coins; and 100-, 500-, 1,000-, and 5,000-peseta bills. Your hotel will, of course, change money. But best rates are obtained in the banks, at which you absolutely must present your passport when making a transaction. Keep the bulk of your funds in traveler's checks; the $20 and $50 denominations are the most convenient.

PASSPORTS: Necessary for admission to Spain, and to be presented to U.S. Immigration upon your return. Apply at U.S. Department of State Passport Offices in a dozen-plus major cities (look under U.S. Government in the telephone directory) or—in smaller towns—at the office of the clerk of a federal court; and, so long as the practice obtains, at certain post offices. Allow three to four weeks, especially for a first passport (valid for ten years), for which you'll need a pair of two-inch-square photos, proof of identity, and birth certificate or other proof of citizenship. There's a $42 fee (subject to change) for first passports; renewals are cheaper. If you're in a hurry when you apply, say so; Uncle Sam will usually try to expedite. Upon receipt of this valuable document, sign your name where indicated, fill in the address of next of kin, and keep with you—*not packed in a suitcase*—as you travel. In case of loss, contact local police, nearest U.S. Embassy or Consulate, or Passport Office, Department of State, Washington, D.C. 20524

POLICE: London Bobbies have nothing on Spanish policemen when it comes to courtesy. There are exceptions to the rule, but invariably when you ask a cop a question—anywhere in Spain—more often than not he'll greet you not only with a smile but a salute. How about that?

RATES: Carefully selected *hotels* on the pages following (which I've either lived in or have thoroughly inspected) and *restaurants* (where I've eaten) are categorized by me as *Luxury, First Class,* or *Moderate,* which translate pretty much into what those terms connote in the U.S. as regards cost, convenience, and accommodations.

R.E.N.F.E. —pronounced *"ren-fay"*—is the Spanish language acronym for the national railway system. There are two classes: first and second. And, in addition, there are super expresses— Talgo by name—on important routes (Madrid-Barcelona, for example), which require a supplement to the regular first-class fare. Generally, if your run will be just a couple of hours, second class is adequate. If longer, choose first, and—if your budget will allow it—Talgo; Talgo cars have reclining seats, arranged as they

are in American trains rather than in European-style compart-
ments. Generally, trains are equipped with snack bars—at which
sandwiches, cookies, and drinks are sold—and, in certain instances, full-fledged restaurant cars. Inquire about such amenities before you book so you're not stuck with a lemon; many still
exist. In any event, do as Spaniards do: take food along—a package of cookies, fruit, a chocolate bar—for sustenance en route.
By and large, Spanish railway personnel—though polite—speak
only Spanish, both in stations and on trains. And inquire locally
as to whether long-distance buses (see above) might not be more
appropriate for the run in question than trains; this is often the
case.

ROYAL FAMILY: Spain's contemporary rulers are not nearly as
well known abroad as are, for example, those of Britain. Which is
hardly to imply they shouldn't be. This is among the more interesting royal families of Europe.

By the time he ascended the throne as Dictator Francisco
Franco's successor in 1975, Prince Juan Carlos de Borbón—
grandson of the last pre-Civil War king, Alfonso XIII, and son of
the then pretender, popularly known as Don Juan, Count of
Barcelona—had been designated Prince of Spain and successor
to the headship of state with the title of king, by the Spanish Parliament, or Cortes, voting 49 to 19 (with 9 abstentions) on a proposal of Franco's. On July 19, 1984, Juan Carlos became acting
Head of State when Franco fell ill, and after Franco's death, he
was proclaimed king on November 22, 1975. Surely his
success—he is popular throughout the realm, where people rec-
ognize him as a unifier—must be partially attributed to his extraordinary education. No modern monarch has been better
schooled. And it has paid off: he has successfully restored the institution of a constitutional monarchy, which had atrophied for
four and a half decades—in a highly democratic state which had
been a repressive dictatorship.

Born in Rome in 1938, Juan Carlos studied, variously, in
Switzerland, Portugal, and Spain (which he visited for the first
time at the age of 10), where his alma maters included the
Zaragoza Military Academy and the University of Madrid, and
where, in the 1960s, he undertook a systematic training program

in every major government ministry and an intensive travel program which took him—with his wife, former Princess Sophie of
Greece, whom he married in Athens in 1962—to every region of
Spain. He is fluent not only in the Romance languages akin to
Spanish—French, Italian, and Portuguese—but English, as well,
while Queen Sofía converses in her native Greek, her adopted
Spanish, as well as English, French, and German. Popular like
her husband, she has a diploma in pediatrics, is a knowledgeable
student of archeology, and takes a special interest in the problems of the mentally handicapped.

Juan Carlos and Sofía do not live in Madrid's vast Palacio Real
(it is used for ceremonial purposes) but rather in the smaller
Palacio de la Zarzuela, away from the center, and originally built
in the seventeenth century as a hunting lodge for King Philip IV.
(It was during this period that one-act operettas of the kind seen
today in Madrid theaters were first performed in its court theater,
taking their name—Zarzuela—from the name of the palace.)

The king and queen have three children: two princesses (the
Spanish term is *infanta*), Elena (born in 1963) and Cristina (born
in 1964), and a prince, or *infante*, Felipe (born in 1968). Prince
Felipe, being groomed as the future King Philip V, was declared
Prince of Asturias (traditional title conferred upon heirs to the
throne, in the manner of Britain's Princeship of Wales) in 1977.
He studied at a coed school at home, in Canada, and at Zaragoza
Military College, likes sailing and science, and has been fulfilling
royal engagements—abroad as well as in Spain—since 1983.

SHOWERS: My hat is off to the Spanish plumbing industry.
Bathrooms of Spanish hotels, luxury to budget, are invariably
equipped with the kind of showers Americans like: attached to
the wall, with a wide nozzle. And shower curtains—so often absent in Continental European hotels, where showers are attached to rubber hoses that run wild when turned on.

TAXIS are set off rather elegantly by the coat of arms of the city
in which they operate. When they're open for business, you'll
observe a sign—*Libre* (free). In cities, they're metered, unless
they're the big limousines—*gran turismos*—sometimes encountered in the vicinity of the luxury hotels, and best avoided. Nor

usually are taxis in resort areas metered, more's the pity; agree on fare before setting off.

TIPS: Tipping is not a problem in Spain; it should not be done to excess. Service is included in restaurant bills, but if you're pleased, add an additional five to 10 percent. Tip taxi drivers—on metered rides only—five percent. Give baggage porters in air and rail terminals the equivalent of fifty cents per bag; likewise, hotel bellmen. Leave hotel concierges the equivalent of a dollar of two per day—*only* if they've performed personal services. If hotel chambermaids have been helpful, beyond making up your room regularly, leave a token tip.

WINES, by Max Drechsler: Spanish table wines deserve to be better known by Americans—especially those of us traveling in the country of origin, where they can be so easily sampled.

Best wines come from the northeast, close to France, from the district called Rioja; top Riojas compare favorably with some of France's fine Bordeaux. The Rioja region breaks down into Rioja Alta, south of the Ebro River with the city of Haro its headquarters, producing excellent reds (*tintos*) and whites (*blancos*); Rioja Baja, whose main town is Logroño, producing *tintos* that are good but coarser and higher in alcohol than the Rioja Altas; and Rioja Alavesa, north of the Ebro River, producing many fine *tintos*, whose lightness and clarity cause them to be called *clarete* (a term sometimes used, also, with light wines from Valencia).

Wines of southern and central Spain, chiefly red, tend to be undistinguished, which is not to say they're not acceptable; they are, especially considering their low cost, and you'll drink them often as the house wines of restaurants, served in carafes. (Valdepeñas, a dry *tinto*, is the restaurant carafe favorite in Madrid.) Wines from the east—mainly the Barcelona and Valencia regions—are considerably better than those of the center, and more expensive.

Herewith a selection worth seeking out in restaurants or supermarket shelves:

Vega Sicilia— a superb dry red, one of Spain's very best, high in price and difficult to find.

Peñafiel—full-bodied dry red and like Vega Sicilia (above), from near Valladolid in the north.

All Riojas— both *tinto* and *blanco*—are invariably excellent; producers include Marqués de Riscal, Marqués de Murrieta, Marqués de Cáceres, López de Heredia, Bodegas Bilbaínas, Paternina.

Clarete— a dry red from Valencia; Calderón is a good label.

"Green" wines—Chacolí (a crisp dry white, sharp on the tongue) from the Basque coast; Albarino del Palacio (a dry and flowery white) from Galicia.

Xampan—the Spanish for champagne; sparkling wines that come from around Barcelona; Cordoniú is a leading label.

Vino común or Vino corriente—These are terms for regional wines, both *tinto* and *blanco*; they're usually served in carafes, sometimes in bottles; always try them.

Jerez—or sherry—is Spain's universally beloved aperitif wine; further details in Chapter 9.

2

Aranjuez
*A Kingdom's History
in a Palace*

BACKGROUND BRIEFING

To term Aranjuez Spain's Versailles—as, indeed, Alexandre Dumas did on a nineteenth-century visit—might be to exaggerate. But not all that much. This little Tagus River town, an oasis smack in the center of the harsh Castile plain, with Madrid a scant 25 miles due north, has been a favorite with Spanish royals—the present king and queen so far excluded—for something like half a millennium.

No less a ruling pair than Ferdinand and Isabella put Aranjuez on the monarchial map when they took up residence in a palace built especially for them. That was in the fifteenth century. Later, Emperor Charles V—who enjoyed hunting in its woods—enlarged the palace, and his son Philip II—no doubt remembering that Aranjuez was where he endured a childhood bout of chicken pox—tore down the building and had the pair of architects whom he was later to commission to design El Escorial (Juan Bautista de Toledo and Juan de Herrera) replace it. The Renaissance saw half a dozen Palacio Real de Aranjuez fires—and rebuildings. What one sees today, as regards the palace, is a history-drenched rococo structure to the taste, by and large, of the eighteenth-century kings. The surrounding parklike gardens are quite the loveliest such in Spain, and there are, as well, a couple of surprises of no little import.

Whereas Versailles depicts the history of but three royal

French reigns, Aranjuez—though far less distinguished as regards architecture, interior design, and furnishings—is an easy-to-take history lesson on the royal houses of Spain from the discovery of America to our own era.

Which is no mean succession of rulers. Consider: Aranjuez's residents have included Ferdinand and Isabella of the pre-Hapsburg dynasty; the Hapsburg Holy Roman Emperor, Charles V; his builder-warrior-politician-ascetic son, Philip II; later Hapsburgs like the much-painted Philip IV; the Bourbons, including Philip V (a grandson of France's Louis XIV), the enlightened Charles III, and Charles IV, who abdicated in favor of his son, Ferdinand VII, at Aranjuez; the nineteenth-century reigns of Isabella II and the last two Bourbon Restoration monarchs, who occupied the throne before the Second Republic and the tragic Civil War of the 1930s: Alfonso XII and Alfonso XIII—grandfather of the reigning monarch, Juan Carlos.

ON SCENE
Lay of the Land: Aranjuez's similarity to Versailles extends even to geography in that it is a brief commute from the capital, revolves around a palace set in a vast formal park, and has an ancillary play-palace to complement the big house, with a bonus of museums.

Trains from Madrid no longer pull directly into the main vestibule of the palace to the very foot of its grand staircase (which was the case during rail buff Isabella II's reign), but the railroad station is conveniently close—follow Calle de Toledo to Plaza de Armas at the palace entrance. The *Parterre*, an elegant formal garden, French-designed in the eighteenth century, flanks the palace to the rear, while *Jardín de la Isla*—laid out by Philip II in the Renaissance manner of the sixteenth century—occupies an island framed by the Tagus River to the north.

Aranjuez's largest park, *Jardín del Príncipe*, dates, like the Parterre, to the eighteenth century, and lies to the east with the river its northern flank and Calle de la Reina to its south. *Real Casa del Labrador*, the Laborer's Palace, on the order of the auxiliary Trianon mansions at Versailles, is set in the Príncipe garden, as is *Casa de Marinos*, an oddball museum, of which more later.

Nonroyal, nonpalatial *Aranjuez* is south of the parks. Walk east along Calle del Príncipe to the *Church of San Antonio*, a classic-style specimen of eighteenth-century rococo; to the south—and from the same elegant era—is a municipal theater, a legacy of Charles III that is one of the most underappreciated and most charming in Spain.

Palacio Real: The royal palace's main entrance is through arches in the statue-surmounted, four-story central block, flanked by circular towers, from which lead newer wings. State rooms are mostly eighteenth century as regards furnishings; most spectacular—missed on no account—is the *Salón de Porcelana*, a tribute to the Spanish genius for tilework, with walls and ceiling in white porcelain, garlanded throughout in ebullient rococo style. The throne room—site of the palace's only abdication, that of Charles IV in the early nineteenth century—is crystal-chandeliered with Brussels tapestries flanking the royal chairs. The chapel is in gold and white with sculpted angels and ceiling frescoes. Paintings throughout are by the Neapolitan baroque master, Luca Giordano, reflecting the period when Spaniards were kings of Naples. The royal bedrooms are worth viewing, but the most amusing chamber of the lot is the *Salón de Fumar*, where titled gents left the ladies after dinner for cigars, in an opulent mock-Moorish setting inspired by Granada's Alhambra.

Museum of Court Dress: You start off with a bang—a make-believe throne room of their Catholic Majesties, Ferdinand and Isabella. Hapsburg Dynasty rooms include representations of Queen Joanna the Mad—Juana la Loca—and hubby Philip the Handsome; their eminent son, Emperor Charles V; Charles's melancholy offspring, Philip II, and his second wife, England's Bloody Mary Tudor; and Philip IV, immortalized by the paintings of Velázquez. Move along to the Spanish Bourbons' galleries with white-wigged kings, their ladies in elaborate, French-inspired brocades. The mid-nineteenth century decades of Isabella II's rule—the romantic-era decades still styled Isabelline by the Spaniards—are handsome, with portraits of the queen and her king-consort, Francisco de Asís, all about. Still other rooms are devoted to royal fans: the *abanicos*, which no people are more skilled at making than the Spaniards; royal children and their playthings; royal courtiers—ladies- and gentlemen-in-waiting—and what they wore. And on into the twentieth century, with an entire room devoted to King Alfonso XIII's duds.

Real Casa del Labrador—at the far east end of Jardín del Príncipe, flanking the Tagus River—was a case of the Spanish royal house of the late eighteenth century imitating Queen Marie Antoinette's Le Petit Trianon, the mini-palace at Versailles. The Laborer's Cottage is, of course, no such thing. Indeed, a case can be made for its interiors considerably surpassing those of the parent palace. Neoclassic, the casa embraces a central pavilion flanked by wings behind an extraordinary façade, whose score-plus of pillars and buttresses are surmounted by busts of Roman emperors and mythologic deities. The billiard room—yes, billiard room—is one of the kingdom's most resplendent interiors, with a richly frescoed ceiling, walls surfaced in silk printed in a Pompeian motif, and a knock-'em-dead gold-and-white billiard table.

Casa de Marinos: Royals are indubitably attracted to water. (Even presidents of the United States had an official yacht—FDR through Nixon.) Spanish monarchs have always liked to go sailing during their stays at Aranjuez. And they liked to do it in style. One of them—the first Bourbon king, Philip V—built this boathouse for the monarchial vessels; it's a beauty, as are the boats within it.

SETTLING IN
Hotel Infantas (Calle Infantas 4): Hardly anyone stays the night in Aranjuez these days. (Most visitors are excursionists from Madrid.) But these simple digs are as adequate as any in town; two score rooms, some with baths. Breakfast only. *Moderate.*

DAILY BREAD
Casa Pablo (Calle Hermanos Guardiola 20). "Paul's House" has a traditional look and an appetizing fixed-price menu. *Moderate.*

La Mina (Príncipe 21) is central—just east of the palace—with old-school ambience, and fare adequate for a midday pick-me-up. *Moderate.*

INCIDENTAL INTELLIGENCE ══════════════

Twenty-five miles south of Madrid, Aranjuez is a made-to-order day or half-day excursion from the capital. The wonder is that but a relative handful of foreign visitors go. (Madrileños—especially on Sundays—more than compensate.) Easiest way is via half-day bus tours. Mind, though, these are expensive. Much more highly to be recommended is a do-it-yourself excursion by train—there are departures hourly or more often the day long—from Madrid's downtown Atocha station. Travel time is a half hour, and upon arrival you move at your own speed, looking at what *you* want for as long as you want. *Further information:* Oficina de Turismo de Aranjuez, Plaza Santiago Rusiñol.

3

Ávila
*Mysticism
and the Middle Ages*

BACKGROUND BRIEFING

If it does not typify Spain at its cherriest, Ávila compensates with an evocation—almost tangible—of what Middle Ages life must have been like in a small city on the Castilian plain.

There was, to be sure, an Ávila of even earlier times. Romans made of it a military outpost a couple of millennia back. Some five centuries later, Visigoths settled in, in the course of their Spanish conquest. But Ávila's still-standing trademark—its encircling walls—was not to come until the eleventh century, the work of ruling Christian nobles, as part of a campaign to extricate the town from Moorish domination. Still later, the walls served the city in its efforts to remain aloof from the pan-Spanish designs of Emperor Charles V. At about the same time, the mid-1500s, a locally born Carmelite nun—later to become St. Teresa of Ávila—led bold reforms in her order, collaborating with still a second locally born saint, John of the Cross.

The continuing presence of the remarkable walls—there are no others quite like them in all of Europe—and the pervasiveness of the buoyant, uncompromising mysticism of St. Teresa—each formidable in its way—combine to create Ávila's contemporary personality. No other small Spanish city—population is about 40,000—makes a stronger, more distinctive, more immediately discernible impact, in as little time as the course of a day's excursion.

ON SCENE

Lay of the Land: Ávila revolves around appropriately named Plaza Santa Teresa, the busy principal square just west of the walls that encircle the ancient city. The *Church of San Pedro* is on the square's west flank, and Calle San Segundo, lined with shops and cafés, connects Plaza Santa Teresa with Plaza de la Catedral. *Casa de los Deanes*—the Provincial Museum—is at the northern trip of Plaza Italia, east of the Cathedral. An entire row of venerable and quite splendid Gothic palaces, each with serene patios beyond their gates, lines Calle López Núñez, below the northern side of the city walls, and south of the *Convent of the Encarnación*—where Teresa spent much of her life as a nun. The *Church of San Vicente*, most important after the Cathedral, lies just beyond the walls at their northeast corner, opposite the gate that takes its name.

Las Murallas: They deserve more than a cursory glance; Ávila's walls are unique in Europe; no others are so intact. Virtually unrestored, they're a 1,000-year-old testament to the engineering and architectural skills of the Middle Ages, reminiscent of those of Visby on the Swedish island of Gotland; a century older than those—much rebuilt—of Carcassonne in France. And, like the walls of England's York, they have a walkway built into inner parapets, so that one can promenade from within. More than 30 feet in height, the walls completely enclose the old town, embracing 88 stunning towers and nine handsomely arched gateways. Climb up and tread their walkway (entrance is from Plaza de Calvo Sotelo). Then proceed—by car or cab, since it's a fairish walk from the center—to the stone cross framed by four Doric columns at the northwest edge of town. It's called *Los Cuatro Postes* and affords the definitive perspective of the city.

Santa Teresa's convents: Pope Paul VI, in 1970, singled out Ávila's St. Teresa as a Doctor of the Church—the first woman so designated. Described variously as bright, determined, charming, boundlessly energetic, and with a razor-sharp intellect, Teresa not only formed her own Discalced, or Barefoot, reform branch of the Carmelites. The inner visions she experienced led her into mysticism, and she became a writer of stature. Her works—*The Way of Perfection, Interior Castle,* and an auto-biography—continue to be celebrated for literary style as well as theologic content. *San José Convent,* which she founded in 1562, still operates. But her activity even extended to the male religious orders. With her collaborator, Juan de la Cruz, later sainted like herself, and named, as well, a Doctor of the Church—she founded monasteries, and was a mentor in matters spiritual to this man who was imprisoned and tortured for his articulate opposition—in poems like *Songs of the Soul*—to the lethargic clergy of the Reformation period.

Teresa's Ávila embraces a quartet of convents, each visitable. *Convento de Santa Teresa* (Plaza de la Santa) is more a memorial to Teresa than one of the places where she lived or worked, with an elaborate chapel built on the site of the room in which she is be-lieved to have been born. The baroque convent church, adjacent, contains relics, including the crucifix that legend says she held at her death. *Convento de Nuestra Señora de Gracia* (Calle Señora de Gracia, at Plaza Santa Teresa) is where Teresa studied. One can visit the sacristy, which was her schoolroom. Pop into the chapel; there's a lovely altarpiece. *Convento de San José* (Calle del Duque de Alba) is the first convent founded by Teresa—with the help of a brother and sister—in 1562, and still, amazingly after all these centuries, with Teresian mementos. These include the stone desk at which she worked, a belt, personal writings, even a flute she played. *Monasterio de la Encarnación* (Calle de la Encarnación) is—if you must make a choice among the quartet of Teresa's convents—the most interesting to most tourists. It's where she lived and worked for about three decades, and it now is a mu-seum with the convent kitchen just as it was in her time, and a nun's cell as it was before she imposed her austerities. It was in this convent that San Juan de la Cruz visited Santa Teresa, and where they formulated joint activities.

Cathedral (Plaza de la Catedral): Overshadowed by the walls and the Teresian convents, Ávila's Cathedral is a sleeper. Square-towered—its silhouette dominates the low skyline—it is a Romanesque-Gothic-Renaissance meld, with a vaulted nave, ravishing altarpiece, brilliantly carved choir, lovely chapels, and—a bonus for which one wants to allot enough time—a museum of assorted treasures, not the least of which is a portrait of a knight by El Greco.

Church of San Vicente (Puerta de San Vicente) is a Romanesque masterwork with its two bell towers a trademark, and a capacious interior—somberly handsome—that contains the 900-year-old tomb of the saint for which the church is named. St. Vincent's martyrdom is portrayed on the sculpted façade.

Convento de Santo Tomás (Calle Santa Fe) is worth the necessary excursion from the center. This is a fifteenth-century Dominican monastery, nobly proportioned, that has historic associations, the most notable of which is its use as headquarters by Ferdinand and Isabella when they visited Ávila. Indeed, the Catholic monarchs were fond enough of St. Thomas to select it as the burial site for their only son, Prince Juan, who died at the age of 19. But there is more: not one or a pair but a trio of cloisters and—masterpiece of the complex—a painted altar that in and of itself makes an Ávila visit worthwhile.

Museo Provincial de Bellas Artes (Plaza de Nalvillos) has an inspired setting: a Renaissance mansion that originally saw service as official residence of deans of the nearby Cathedral. The *Casa de los Deanes* masterwork is a triptych by the Flemish Primitive Hans Memling. Almost—but not quite—anticlimactic, after the Memling, are collections of Spanish ceramics and furniture.

SETTLING IN
Hotel Valderrábanos (Plaza de la Catedral 6) is one of the finest small-city hotels in Spain, an originally fifteenth-century palace (the founding noble family's crest remains above the entrance) deftly transformed into a 73-room inn of considerable panache. Rooms are handsome, the dining room—one of the best restaurants in town—and bar/lounge likewise. *Luxury.*

Parador Nacional Raimundo de Borgoña (Calle Marqués de Canales de Chozas 16) is not among the most beautiful in the kingdom-wide chain of government-run inns. Nor is it among the ancient structures that have been converted to *paradores*. Still, though contemporary, the style is traditional. The restaurant is, like that of Hotel Valderrábanos above, a town leader (don't miss the score-plus of *entremeses*—hors d'oeuvres—at lunch, and order the local Monte-Peraldo wine). Thirty rooms. Central. *First Class.*

Hotel Rey Niño (Plaza de José Tome 1) is a small, simple house, with a core-of-town location and two dozen rooms, not all with private bathrooms. Breakfast only. *Moderate.*

DAILY BREAD
El Rastro (Plaza del Rastro 1): After the restaurants of the top two hostelries, Ávila has relatively little to offer, culinarily. El Rastro has the virtue of being central, with a traditional ambience, and adequate fare. *Moderate.*

INCIDENTAL INTELLIGENCE

Madrid is some 60 miles southeast, and if you can't visit Ávila on a proper overnight visit, go for a day's excursion—of your own making—from the capital. *Further information:* Oficina de Turismo de Ávila, Plaza de la Catedral 4.

4

Barcelona
*Underappreciated
Número Dos*

BACKGROUND BRIEFING

If they do not always have the last laugh, the relatively unheralded Second Cities of the planet go quietly about the business of making more of the money that has, in many instances, made possible the amenities that make them so visitable. Milan, for example, makes no attempt to compete with Rome for international eminence; it is secure in the knowledge that it's the source of much of Italy's economic prowess. The same is true of America's Los Angeles vis-à-vis New York. Toronto—until it recently overtook Montreal in population—contented itself as Canada's No. 2. And so it goes, right along to Barcelona, the ancient Mediterranean metropolis that is Spain's greatest port.

I say "ancient" advisedly. By the time long-somnolent backwater Madrid finally became a proper royal seat as recently as the sixteenth century (I refer you to the Madrid chapter), Barcelona was long since a sophisticated and thriving center, mellowed and molded by an extraordinary mix of cultures, beginning with the distant Carthaginians, whose powerful Barca family is traditionally credited with being the source of the city's name.

Barcelona thrived, later, as a Roman colony, as a profitable commerce evolved on the Mediterranean between the colonial port and the motherland. Economic progress continued with Christian Visigoths out of Germany, who entered the city in 415 A.D. Then, Moors swept out of North Africa in the eighth century. Unlike elsewhere in Spain, they did not remain all that long. No less a warrior king than Charlemagne routed them in the early ninth century.

Charlemagne's victory was followed by the establishment of a Spanish state—the March it was called—that eventually became self-governing after 874 A.D. under the series of generally competent counts of Barcelona. Not content with the city alone, the counts successfully battled the Arabs, coming out lords of all Catalonia and eventually marrying into the throne of the adjacent kingdom of Aragón.

Eventually, the Aragonian kings and the counts of Barcelona were one and the same, with Barcelona the royal seat. Crown cachet did it no harm, as its port's commerce expanded, and its coffers filled. This medieval wealth subsidized not only the fine and applied arts—an entire museum is today devoted to the Barcelona school of the Middle Ages—but Barcelona also flourished as a manufacturing and banking center.

Politics and war intruded—there were repeated invasions from next-door France, not to mention the pan-Spanish policies of the kingdom united in the fifteenth century by Ferdinand and Isabella, while the city and surrounding Catalonia clung to their language and customs.

As it became richer, Barcelona became bolder, ethnically separatist from, and politically more progressive than the rest of Spain.

There was, for example, a short-lived Catalonian republic just before World War II—with Barcelona its capital. During the Spanish Civil War the city was Loyalist headquarters until 1938–1939, when it fell to Francoist troops. Post-World War II years saw it become wealthy—this is where most of Spain's money is made—and increasingly pro-Catalonian politically. Today's Barcelona is Spain's most Continental European city—buoyant, amusing, modish, and proud of the Catalonian culture, speaking its language (usually in preference to Spanish, which—fortunately for us foreign visitors who invariably are unversed in Catalán—remains a co-official tongue), cooking its delicious food, and acting as a repository of rich cultural treasures, in its capacity as capital of the Region of Catalonia.

ON SCENE

Lay of the Land: Barcelona is big. Mainly, but not exclusively, one wants to concentrate on its relatively compact historic core, a monument-rich district leading inland from a square called Plaza Puerta de la Paz, which punctuates the harborfront boulevard named for Columbus—Paseo de Colón—and with a statue of the explorer atop a towering, fountain-based column that could be called a giant counterpart of a similar monument to the very same Cristoforo Colón—on Columbus Circle in New York. The Columbus statue straddles the southern tip of a verdant promenade, the Ramblas, that cuts through Old Barcelona, skirting the Cathedral and other landmarks of its medieval-era Barrio Gótico district, until it reaches Plaza de Cataluña, perhaps best described as a kind of Iberian Trafalgar Square.

By the time it's reached Plaza de Cataluña, the Ramblas—centered with book and flower stalls and alfresco cafés and lined by aged palaces, hotels, restaurants, and shops, and at all times of day and night people-packed—has had five names, beginning at the harbor as Rambla Santa Mónica, and continuing in a northerly direction as Rambla Capuchinos, Rambla San José, Rambla Estudios, and Rambla Canaletas. *Una rosa* by any *nombre*: call it by the collective Las Ramblas, and you can't go wrong.

Its terminal, Plaza de Cataluña, signals the northern frontier of Old Barcelona, and is the core of Shopper's Barcelona (the department stores are here and on the adjacent pedestrians-only street, Puerta del Angel). Directly north is Gran Vía. An extension of the Ramblas—Rambla de Cataluña—extends from the northern fringe of Plaza Cataluña to still another principal thoroughfare which, because it runs in a diagonal direction from northwest to southeast, is called La Diagonal. Plaza de Francisco Macías, the square that intersects it at Calle de Urgel, is worth remembering because it marks the progression of the city, begun as modern Barcelona at Plaza de Cataluña, to new, *very* modern Barcelona, continuing north all the way—if you want to ascend via funicular for a bird's-eye view of city and sea—to Monte Tibidabo.

Gain the city by train and you arrive at *Estación del Norte*, just east of the historic core, or very contemporary *Estación de Santos*,

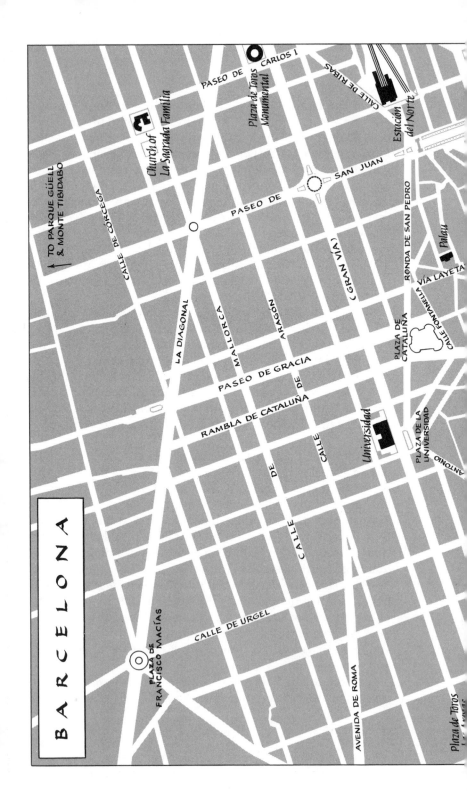

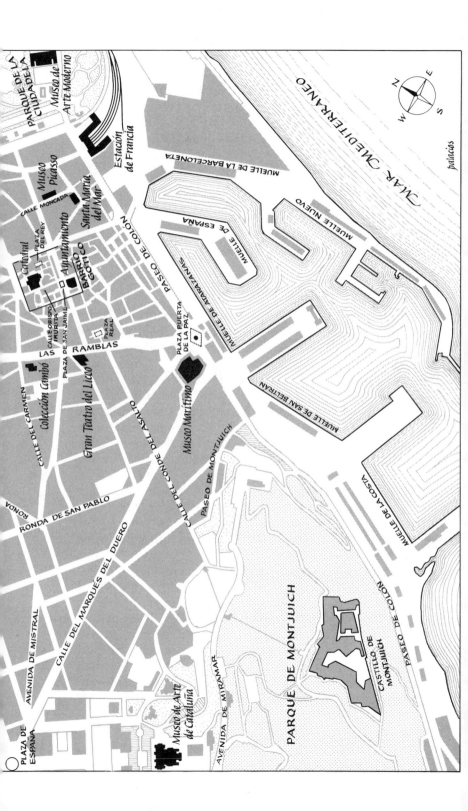

PARQUE DE LA CIUDADELA

Museo de Arte Moderno

Estación de Francia

Museo Picasso

CALLE MONCADA

Santa María del Mar

Catedral

PLAZA DEL REY

Ayuntamiento

BARRIO GÓTICO

Colección Cambó

CALLE DEL CARMEN

LAS RAMBLAS

CALLE OBISPO IRURITA

CALLE DE SAN JAIME

PLAZA DE SAN JAIME

PLAZA REAL

Gran Teatro del Liceo

RONDA

RONDA DE SAN PABLO

CALLE DEL CONDE DEL ASALTO

Museo Marítimo

PLAZA PUERTA DE LA PAZ

PASEO DE COLÓN

MUELLE DE LA BARCELONETA

MUELLE DE ESPAÑA

MUELLE NUEVO

MUELLE DE ATARAZANAS

MAR MEDITERRÁNEO

palacios

MUELLE DE SAN BELTRÁN

PLAZA DE ESPAÑA

AVENIDA DE MISTRAL

CALLE DEL MARQUES DEL DUERO

PASEO DE MONTJUICH

AVENIDA DE MIRAMAR

Museo de Arte de Cataluña

PARQUE DE MONTJUICH

CASTILLO DE MONTJUICH

MUELLE DE LA COSTA

PASEO DE COLÓN

N W E S

northwest of the center. The city is not limited to the green of the Ramblas and Monte Tibidabo. Another northern park—*Güell* by name—is notable as the site of a museum dedicated to the turn-of-century Barcelona architectural genius, Antonio Gaudí. And there are additional museums of consequence in an additional pair of parks, flanking downtown. *Parque Montjuich* to the west is the site not only of the world-class *Museo de Arte de Cataluña*, but of a museum-school founded by—and full of the works of—the late contemporary painter Joan Miró, while the *Parque de la Ciudadela*, just east of downtown, is the site of both the *Museo de Arte Moderno* and the zoo.

REQUISITE MONUMENTS

The Cathedral (Calle del Obispo Irurita in downtown's Barrio Gótico) is, along with the Museo de Arte de Cataluña and the Museo Picasso (in the museums section, below) and the Gaudí-designed *Sagrada Familia Church*, Barcelona at its most visit-worthy. The Cathedral comes as a surprise in this city that has so much else going for it. Visitors who haven't pondered Barcelona's past—as a royal capital, Middle Ages through to Renaissance—are startled not only by the Gothic detail of its façade (make a point of inspecting at least two of the entrance doors and its magnificently vaulted central nave) but by the quality of its art. If Barcelona Cathedral is not quite on a level with the bishops' seats of Toledo, Burgos, Seville, and Santiago de Compostela, it certainly ranks with those of, say, León, Salamanca, and Palma de Majorca. And in what other cathedral—anywhere—are you going to encounter pet geese padding about in the cloister?

The cloister's main door dates from a Romanesque-era cathedral. But it is otherwise mostly Gothic, with a wealth of chapels—on three of its four sides—and, beyond, a museum brimming with luminous paintings and altars, Romanesque through rococo. Back in the Cathedral proper, you want to give the choir some attention. Blocking the nave, as one goes forward from the entrance—in the usual manner of Spanish cathedrals—its carved-wood stalls—a couple score all told—are backed by painted coats of arms and surmounted by exquisite spires, miniatures, it would seem, of the central Cathedral steeple that pierces the Barcelona sky.

Barrio Gótico, the choicest area, architecturally, in the core of town, is at its most sublime in the case of the Cathedral (above). But you will want to admire the façades of its houses, linger in its squares, step inside its museums (see the museums section below), churches, and public buildings.

Start at Plaza de San Jaime, a broad quadrangle wherein is concentrated the power of both the city and provincial governments, in palaces facing each other. The façade of the *Ayuntamiento,* or city hall, fools you. It is sober mock-classic out of the baroque era, and so you're surprised to find within that the broadly arched, severely stone-walled *Salón de Ciento* is Gothic. Another great chamber, *Salón de las Crónicas,* is more contemporary, its high walls occupied by monochromatic murals by this century's José María Sert, whose work visitors to New York's Rockefeller Center know from the still-to-be-seen Sert originals in the lobby at 30 Rockefeller Plaza.

The old *Diputación,* formerly provincial government headquarters, is graced with a picture-book fifteenth-century patio—named Naranjas for its orange trees—and a number of ravishing rooms within (including a chapel), leading from a Gothic staircase.

Another square, Plaza del Rey, is dominated by arched windows of the somber stone slab of a tower that could be out of a surrealistic Giorgio de Chirico painting. Other sides of the square contain the *Chapel Royal of Santa Águeda,* small and severely Gothic, with a luminous altar; *Palacio Real Mayor,* with a fourteenth-century hall—often the site of concerts—called *Salón de Tinell,* and striking because of the half-dozen severe semicircular arches that support its ceiling; *Archivo de la Corona de Aragón,* a Renaissance mansion whose royal archives are for scholars, but whose patio is worth a moment if only to observe the carved-wood ceiling enclosing the staircase leading from it; and last, a sixteenth-century townhouse, *Casa Padellás,* now sheltering the city's historical museum, which I recommend with enthusiasm in the museums section below; along with two other downtown museums, one devoted to Pablo Picasso on a magnificently medieval street, Calle Montcada; and the other devoted to works of Federico Marés, occupying a Middle Ages palace, displaying its Middle Ages sculpture.

Church of Santa María del Mar (Plaza de Santa María) is, after the Cathedral, Barcelona's most beautiful church: a gigantically scaled Gothic wonder, with a pair of slender towers framing its rose window.

La Lonja (Plaza de Antonio López) is Stock Exchange in Spanish, and a feature of a number of Spanish cities, most especially Valencia. Barcelona's multi-period *Lonja* is not up to some of the others, but its main hall is strikingly visitable, with a fine beamed ceiling.

Church of La Sagrada Familia (Calle Mallorca): Turn-of-century architect Antonio Gaudí's most famous monument, this still-uncompleted church with its irregular, oddly embellished, needle-thin towers, is not the easiest of this Barcelona master's works to love. Still, you owe it to yourself to try. There is no question but that Gaudí's erratic variations on Romanesque-Gothic motifs are worth pondering. It is easier to like his more Art Nouveau-related civil architecture—a gatehouse that could be of gingerbread at the entrance to Parque Güell, and houses about town—you'll know they're Gaudí—including *Casa Batlló* (Paseo de Gracia 43) and *Casa Vicens* (Calle Carolinas 24).

Monasterio de Montserrat (Montserrat) is a good day's excursion—some 35 miles—northwest of the city. This is a favorite destination of Spaniards and other Europeans. Many of them are pilgrims, whose mission is to pray before the so-called *Black Madonna*, possibly dating to the twelfth century, in a chapel of an even older Benedictine monastery that was virtually destroyed by early nineteenth-century French troops, and has been rebuilt. Still other visitors make the excursion because getting there—over hairpin-curve highways leading into the mountains—is at least half the fun, with the other half the views from on high, once arrived, not only from the main monastery (whose boys' choir has a history going back centuries and sings at one or two masses daily), but from half a dozen additional points in the neighborhood. There are regularly scheduled tour-bus excursions from the city.

Pueblo Español (Parque de Montjuich) had respectable enough origins. It was part of Barcelona's celebrated 1929 international exhibition; embracing some four score buildings surrounding half a dozen plazas, the idea was to demonstrate variations, by region, of traditional Spanish architecture. But in a country brimming with original architecture dating back to the Roman-esque, one wonders about the need for these copies, now being put to such blatant commercial use. You pass through the main gate—Puerto de Ávila—into small Plaza Castellana, which leads to vast Plaza Mayor, where there's a folk-art museum, and lanes leading to other parts of the village. Artisans demonstrate their crafts, à la Colonial Williamsburg. And there are shops, res-taurants, and cafés all about.

REQUISITE MUSEUMS

Museo de Arte de Cataluña (Parque Montjuich): It is a toss-up as to which is the greater museum city: Barcelona or Madrid. Both are all-Europe leaders in this enviable regard. It's only that in the case of Barcelona, visitors are unprepared for such an em-barrassment of choices and earmark too little time. If one must choose a single museum, there is no doubt as to which. The Catalonian, occupying a preposterous and pretentious monster of a pavilion—*Palacio Nacional de Montjuich*, left over from the 1929 international exhibition—offers a unique concentration of medieval Catalonian art. No matter that the artists' names are unfamiliar to the nonspecialists among us. Their work—in an extensive series of high-ceilinged galleries—is searing. The museum's trademark exhibit, a massive and majestic Christ giv-ing His blessing, called simply *Pantocrator*, was painted 900 years ago. A carved-wood crucifixion—*Majestad Batlló*—is equally old, and painted in still-luminous pastels. Walk through slowly, steeping in the beauty of altars and framed portraits from, say, Balthazar on horseback, through the Virgin Mary with St. John, on to a red-capped and pensive St. George by the best known of the Catalonians, Jaime Huguet. With a bonus of apses. Yes, entire apses of medieval churches and chapels transported intact to the museum from remote mountain villages, the better for us to see their frescoed walls. And, to be noted as you walk through—a museum—within the museum—of exquisite Catalonian ceramics over the centuries, with its own shop selling reproductions.

Museo Picasso (Calle Montcada 15): Málaga-born (and not neglected in that city's Museo de Bellas Artes, as I report in the Costa del Sol chapter of this book), Picasso moved to Barcelona with his family in 1895, at the age of 14, when his father came to take a job teaching art. They lived in the neighborhood of the palace-lined street, Calle Montcada, in one of whose mansions the Picasso Museum makes its home. A visit here is a triple-threat treat. The street is an aesthetic pleasure in and of itself. (If one of its houses—No. 12—that shelters an amusing museum of costumes is open, do go in.) The medieval palace with Gothic-arched patios housing the Picasso collection is still another major monument. Finally, the master's works. Visitors who remember the museum from earlier years are incredulous at how its holdings have increased. (Gifts—some from the artist—and purchases are the reason for this.) The collection totals more than 1,000 paintings and drawings, not to mention ceramics, engravings, sketchbooks, notebooks, and Picasso-illustrated books. Range is broad—childhood, student days, the Blue Period, cubism and neoclassicism, on through to the later years. Very early work—doctor and nursing nun attending a hospital patient, a food-and-floral still life—is fascinating because it seems so atypical. As one moves along (there are nearly two score galleries on two floors), a more familiar Picasso emerges: slim, brush-cut *Harlequin*; Cannes through a balconied window; the white dove that became Picasso's trademark; the master's interpretation of Velázquez's *Las Meninas*. Allow enough time.

Museo Gaudí (Parque Güell): The Barcelona architect, whose Sagrada Familia Church and other works are called to your attention earlier on, is the subject of a museum in the city park that's the site of some of his buildings. Seeing Gaudí buildings is enough for most Barcelona visitors. Real *aficionados*, though, may want to delve further, by means of a look at plans, scale models, and other Gaudiana. Hours are even more limited than at most Spanish museums.

Colección Cambó (La Diagonal 686, in Palacio de Pedralbes [below]): Art museums in Spain with non-Spanish work in quantity are a rarity. Madrid's Prado is the major exception in this regard, with Seville and Valencia's Museos de Bellas Artes secondary ones. Colección Cambó is still another, albeit on a considerably smaller scale. Señor Cambó, who gave half a hundred Old Masters to the city of Barcelona before he died just after World War II, had superb taste. The paintings break down into five groups—Italians, including a lovely Lippi *Madonna and Child* and a pair of joyous Tiepolos, Flemings and Dutch— with the range Massys through Rubens, French—portraits by Fragonard and de la Tour, on to Cranach and Gainsborough, with the Spanish representations hardly minimal: splendid Goyas, among others.

Museo de la Historia de la Ciudad (Plaza del Rey): Don't let that dry-as-dust title keep you out of sixteenth-century Casa Padellás, one of the more sumptuous of the Barrio Gótico palaces, and chockablock with bits and pieces of old Barcelona: ceramics of the prehistoric Iberians, mosaics from the Roman period, Moorish swords, Jewish religious objects, Romanesque paintings, Gothic architectural fragments, on through the Renaissance and baroque epochs into the rococo, and the early nineteenth-century French occupation. Europe is full of municipal historic museums; this is one of the best on the Continent. That in Madrid, on the other hand, is so dull as not to be worth visiting. And note well: two outstanding Barrio Gótico interiors earlier recommended—the Chapel of Santa Águeda and the Salón de Tinell, being immediate neighbors of the museum—are passed through in the course of a museum tour.

Fundación Joan Miró (Parque de Montjuich): It's nice when a painter grows rich enough in his lifetime to fund the construction of a smashingly handsome building to shelter both an art school and a collection of his own globally celebrated works. The foundation's quarters—a poured-concrete variation on traditional Mediterranean architectural themes—represent contemporary Spanish architecture at its boldest. Against stark white walls, big canvasses, riveting and vivid, bring you up to date on the evolution of the abstract Miró style from, say, the 1940s on into late work preceding Miró's death in 1983. There's a cafetería on the premises.

Museo Marítimo (Puerto de la Paz): The setting here—a carefully restored medieval shipyard called *Atarazanas Reales*—is at least as striking as the collection. This is a stadium-sized stone environment, with arched ceilings high enough to easily accommodate such exhibits as large-as-life sailing vessels from earlier centuries. But there may be more here than you want to absorb—ship models and cannons, anchors and flags, maps and compasses.

Museo Arqueológico (Parque de Montjuich) is an appropriately classic-style pavilion, sheltering extraordinary souvenirs of ancient Barcelona, Roman most especially—and most brilliantly. You're not going to see finer mosaics anywhere in Spain, nor for that matter more perfectly preserved architectural fragments: two sides of a little temple, for example, with half a dozen Corinthian columns supporting a graceful pediment; glass, pottery, sculptures, too.

Museo Federico Marés (Calle de los Condes de Barcelona 8): Though without the range of subject matter and the broad appeal of the Museo de Historia de la Ciudad (above), this Barrio Gótico museum occupies still another patio-centered mansion of old. It brims with medieval sculpture, dramatically placed against a background of somber stone walls.

Museo de Arte Moderno (Parque de la Ciudadela): The thrust here is Catalonian art, nineteenth and twentieth centuries. There are thirty galleries—paintings, drawings, sculpture—on two floors of a rambling building that goes on and on and on. No

Picassos, mind you. But many worthy works by names mostly unknown to us.

The pair of Pedralbes museums can confuse. They are near each other, both in the northwest section of town, and conveniently taken in during an outing to Monte Tibidabo, the earlier-mentioned peak accessible by funicular (and with an amusement park), that overlooks the city. The senior Pedralbes museum, *Monasterio Pedralbes* (Plaza del Monasterio), is an early Gothic complex, with fine stained glass in its church, a beautiful cloister, enclosed by three levels of sculpture-filled galleries, and—special treat, this—a group of murals by a fourteenth-century genius named Ferrer Bassa. *Palacio de Pedralbes* (La Diagonal) is of our own era: It went up in the 1920s as a Barcelona residence for Alfonso XIII, last king before the Spanish Civil War of the 1930s and grandfather of King Juan Carlos. Have a look at its rather grand state rooms, mock-Renaissance in style, with the furnishings and art objects Italian in origin. There's also a collection of antique coaches, on the grounds. The opulent Pedralbes furnishings constitute part of Barcelona's *Museo de Artes Decorativas*—its Decorative Arts Museums—whose other on-site exhibits include a superb grouping of Spanish eighteenth-century furniture. (The Pedralbes also houses Barcelona's sadly underappreciated Fine Arts Museum—*Colección Cambo*—which I single out in an earlier paragraph.)

SETTLING IN
Hotel Ritz (Gran Vía 688): The Ritz is special, embracing 202 suites and rooms in a gracious Belle-Epoque building that went up in 1911, when architects and designers did not stint on opulence. The high-ceilinged, main-floor public spaces—a vast lounge for conversation with or without drink, coffee, or tea; a handsome restaurant noteworthy enough to warrant later comment—are a joy. Service is a pleasure. Indeed, I don't know of a hotel staff in Spain—reception, restaurant, bars, room-service, chambermaids, and most especially concierges—that surpasses that of the Ritz. Nor can its central situation be improved upon. All that was lacking, until relatively recently, was much-needed refurbishing. Now, though, that has been largely

put to rights—and in splendid fashion. Public spaces—most spectacularly the great oval of a lounge, its pilastered walls of palest gray and its massive glass ceiling framing a newly installed marble floor—stand out. Just as in the lounge, restaurant and bars, where historic original furnishings were restored, renewed and reupholstered rather than replaced, so have they been retained—along with turn-of-century mantelpieces, brass lighting fixtures, wall sconces, even bedside and desk lamps—in the redecorated rooms and suites, where only elderly bathrooms have been replaced; new baths are marble-sheathed, with counter sinks and new shower and other fittings. The refurbishing, though, has been meticulous and long-range, so that by the time you arrive, possibly not every room (or more important, every bath) will have been transformed; specify that you prefer updated accommodations. Member, Leading Hotels of the World. *Luxury.*

Miramar Palace Hotel (Parque Montjuich)—Barcelona's newest luxury house—is all-suite and very grand indeed. Choose one of the royal apartments (each with *five* bedrooms), one of a score of smaller four-bedroom units, or, if you really must economize, a three-bedroom, so-called junior suite; there are 44 of these, and they can be divided into single-chamber doubles. Look of the Miramar Palace is more horizontal than vertical, with its main portion a reconverted classic-style structure that had housed TV studios and to which has been appended a contemporarily styled four-story addition, with svelte locales for dining and drinking among amenities. Views from this elevated situation are striking. But you have to want to be isolated from the core of the city, way atop the eminence which is also the venue of such museums (see above) as Arte de Cataluña, Fundación Joan Miró and Arqueólogico. *Luxury.*

Hotel Presidente (La Diagonal 570) is an agreeably post-World War II skyscraper, quietly and tastefully furnished, well-located, and with a lobby whose compactness belies the generous size of the bedrooms, especially the twins. There are 180 rooms all told, and a convenient restaurant, bar, and swimming pool. *Luxury.*

Hotel Princesa Sofía (Plaza Pío XII) is a 500-room-and-suite stunner, way out in the modish Ciudad Universitaria barrio. I don't know of a more thoughtfully and creatively designed and furnished contemporary hotel in Spain. This flagship of the Husa chain embraces five bars and four distinctive restaurants—from a rooftop restaurant-bar-bôite-cum-dancing to a never-closed *cafetería*. If you're *muy, muy rico* you'll book Suite 1715, out of a James Bond movie. But the standard twins are smart too. Indoor pool. *Luxury.*

Hotel Condes de Barcelona (Paseo de Gracia 75) is surely the most imaginatively striking of the newer Barcelona hotels. Its clever creators bought a turn-of-the-century mansion that was a stellar example of the Art Nouveau style, retained standout architectural and decorative features of its façade, turned its atrium of an entrance hall into a dazzler of a pillared lobby, fashioned a honey of an intimate bar in shades of black (the furnishings) and beige (the walls) and an also small-scaled restaurant-brasserie, the while converting upper floors into accommodations. Standard twins are in tones of peach, with Art Deco accents. Suites are in jet and white. Baths throughout are of marble. The general manager is Miguel Paradela, for long the well-liked No. 2 over at the Ritz. The staff smiles. The location is heart-of-town. Lovely. *First Class.*

Hotel Majestic (Paseo de Gracia 70) is an up-to-the-minute, essentially traditional-style house, with a couple of hundred rooms and suites with especially nice baths (counter sinks, complimentary toothbrushes in case you've forgotten yours), rooftop pool that's a treat in summer, reliable restaurant, and lively bar. Super location. *First Class.*

Hotel Avenida Palace (Gran Vía 605)—enviably well-located at the intersection of Gran Vía and Paseo de Gracia—has been on scene since the century's early decades. And it appears tired. There are just over 210 rooms and suites in undistinguished but comfortable enough traditional style (a general refurbishing would not be out of order), small restaurant and bar, and a reception/concierge staff only partially cordial. Disappointing. *First Class.*

Hotel Royal (Ramblas 117) is a neat-as-a-pin modern house, with close to 110 full-facility rooms, attractive lobby-lounge, bar, and *cafetería* which is, as well, a pizzeria. Central. *First Class.*

Hotel Regente (Rambla de Cataluña 76): Note the address. Rambla de Cataluña is the extension of the principal Ramblas, north of Plaza Cataluña. It has the advantage of being central, while at the same time less frenetic than the main Ramblas. The Regente is Art Nouveau without, stylish modern within. I like it stem (rooftop pool-sundeck) to stern (restaurant-bar), not to mention the pleasant rooms in intervening floors. *First Class.*

Hotel Ramada (Rambla de los Estudios 111) comes through, for me, as the best of the Ramblas houses. This is a no-nonsense, old-fashioned hotel—big and broad-beamed—that's been nicely updated with a restaurant up a flight, a cozy bar-lounge, attractive rooms, and professional service. *First Class.*

Hotel Calderón (Rambla de Cataluña 26): If it has no special cachet, the modern Calderón is not without pluses, including an enviable situation, a rooftop pool, nearly 230 well-equipped rooms and suites, *cafetería* and bar. *First Class.*

Hotel Colón (Avenida de la Catedral 7): How about the Colón's setting, smack in the heart of the Barrio Gótico, opposite the Cathedral? This is a lovely, traditional-style house, with 200 handsome rooms (many of them extra-large), a period-decor subterranean restaurant, and a bar-lounge off the big lobby. *First Class.*

Hotel Sarriá Sol (Avenida de Sarriá 50): Would that the Sarriá Sol was central. Still, business travelers who headquarter here are not put off by being as far north as Plaza de Francisco Macías. There's no doubt that this 21-story hotel is agreeable; some 350 rooms and suites, an interesting mix of places to dine and drink, and a health club. *First Class.*

Hotel Regencia Colón (Calle Sagristans 13) has not quite the charm of its big sister-hotel, the Colón (above). Given its modernity, it can't. Still, the Barrio Gótico location, 50 pleasant rooms with baths, and its restaurant-bar are hardly to be despised. *Moderate.*

Hotel Wilson (La Diagonal 568) is an across-the-street neighbor of the much bigger, much grander Presidente (above). I don't know of any moderate-category hotel in town with lovelier bedrooms than the Wilson's (which total 55). Breakfast only. *Moderate.*

Hotel Rialto (Calle Fernando 42) has the advantage of a Barrio Gótico location, a hundred adequate rooms with bath, *cafetería* and bar. *Moderate.*

Hotel Granvía (Gran Vía 642) is an elderly establishment retaining original architectural details in public spaces but otherwise updated. There are just under 50 rooms. Central. Breakfast only. *Moderate.*

Hotel Astoria (Calle París 203): Up near Plaza de Francisco Macías, just off the Diagonal, the Astoria is an elderly house that's loaded with charm, from the capacious lounge and snack bar leading from it, on through the 100-plus extraordinarily inviting rooms—each behind a door of knotty pine. Breakfast only. *Moderate.*

Hotel Covadonga (La diagonal 596) is a near-neighbor of Plaza de Francisco Macías, with the Barcelona outpost of Sears Roebuck just across the street to make you feel at home. There are just 75 functional—and good-sized—rooms with baths, and a *cafetería*-bar. *Moderate.*

Gran Hotel Cristina (La Diagonal 458) is worth knowing for its location, on the Diagonal, where Rambla de Cataluña intersects it. There are 125 rooms with baths, and a restaurant and bar leading from the small lobby. Withal, more staff smiles are in order. *First Class.*

Hotel Montecarlo (Rambla de los Estudios 124) is a landmark Ramblas mansion converted—not without some éclat—into a hotel. I like the plaid-decor bar that faces the Ramblas more than I do the bedrooms; would that mattresses were firmer. Still, all 75 units have baths. Friendly. Breakfast only. *Moderate.*

Hotel Derby (Calle Loreto 21): It's away from the center, to be sure, on a quiet street off Plaza de Francisco Macías. But the Derby is a winner, with 118 smallish but smart rooms, marble sinks in the baths, inviting lobby, cozy bar, and commendable restaurant. *First Class.*

Hotel Oriente (Ramblas 45) has, to be sure—very sure—seen much better days. Originally eighteenth century, rebuilt in the nineteenth, it retains just enough of its old-school look to remain attractive. You like it even though you wish the beds had new mattresses, and the baths new equipment. Restaurant, bar-café. And the Ramblas out front. *Moderate.*

Hotel Internacional (Ramblas 54) wins you over before you enter: just have a look at its intricately embellished façade of old. Within, the ambience is pleasing, although rooms tend to be prosaic; some have baths. Breakfast only. *Moderate.*

Hotel Zenit (Calle Santaló 8) is away from the center, near the Diagonal, but its 62 small but spotless rooms—all with baths—are desirable if you're on a budget. Breakfast only. *Moderate.*

DAILY BREAD
Beltxenea (Calle de Mallorca 275) occupies the antiques-accented ground floor and exquisitely planted garden-cum-tables, of a lovely townhouse on a quiet street just off Paseo de Gracia. Basque-owned (and with a Basque name that translates as motherland), this is an outstanding class act in a city of many such. You might begin with cream of pumpkin soup or smoked-on-premises northern salmon. A typical entrée—*arroz con almejas en casuelita* blends fluffy rice with flavorfully sauced mussels. Grilled sole is exemplary, likewise tarragon-flavored chicken. If you have dessert, make sure it's a cake or ice cream

that will go well with a blanket of Beltxenea's homemade hot-chocolate sauce. *Luxury.*

Tasca Jacinto (Gran Vía Carlos III 29): I don't know of a better restaurant in Barcelona at which to get an idea of what the robust Catalonian cuisine is all about. This is an eternally busy, unpretentious house; customers are trendy locals who appreciate good food and good value. The menu is limited but delicious. Start with the delectable *chorizo* (sausage) or the special salad. Go on to grilled hake or a ham omelette; cod, *pil-pil* style, or *pulpitos*—tiny octopus simply grilled. *Zarzuela de mariscos*—a seafood stew—is a good Catalonian choice. *Butifarra con judías*—the local sausage—grilled and served with beans, is delicious. So is *escudella de payés*, the Catalonian counterpart of the Madrid boiled dinner, a meat-based soup-stew. For dessert, Catalonia's answer to *flan* custard: *crema Catalana*. Regional wines can be superb: whites from nearby Tarragona, reds from Panadés, for example. Tasca Jacinto is a taxi-ride away from the center in a posh residential quarter. And worth it. Book in advance. *First Class.*

Los Caracoles (Calle Escudillers 14) has been packing them in, heart of downtown, since 1835, the same family—Feliciano—operating it all this time. The setting is a maze of atmospheric rooms, wine barrels against the walls, strings of red peppers hanging from the rafters, tables packed, waiters saucy but smiling. And food absolutely delicious. Specialties are mostly—but by no means entirely—from the sea. *Caracoles* (snails), or *mejillónes* (mussels) to start, perhaps. With a main course of *bullabesa* (Barcelona's answer to Provence's seafood stew, bouillabaisse), a whole chicken roasted on a spit, or a mixed seafood fry. Order a bottle of the house's white wine. Continuous service from 1 P.M. to midnight daily. *Moderate/First Class.*

Reno (Calle Tuset 27) could not contrast more with Tasca Jacinto (above). This is just the ticket for a dressy Barcelona evening, as smart as it is delicious, with the look impeccably maintained post-World War II modern, the service skilled and smiling. Deftly prepared classic French specialties—*bisque de langouste* (crayfish bisque), *carré d'agneau roti aux herbes aromatiques* (herb-flavored roast lamb), *sorbet de framboises au citron* (lemon-scented raspberry sherbet) would be the makings of a memorable meal—are delicious; so is seafood and game. *Luxury.*

Font del Gat (Parque de Montjuich) is at once felicitously situated within the greenery of Barcelona's major downtown park, handsome to look upon both within and (in warm weather) without; and a source of delicious comestibles. A typical lunch or dinner might include a mix of appetizers such as smoked Serrano ham, crayfish with house-made mayonnaise, sausages in glorious variety, and *pan tomate*—course country bread smeared with garlic-accented oil; and continue with a special entrée—the three-fish platter embracing grilled hake, red snapper and cod; with a dessert of assorted sherbets. *First Class.*

Culleretes (Calle Quintara 5) is a downtown oldie, occupying a series of chandelier-illuminated chambers, their walls plastered with signed photos and nineteenth-century murals. The *menú del día* is a good buy. But there is a wide à la carte range, soups and omelettes, meats as well as seafood. Geographical note: You are likely to have difficulty finding the entrance; it's on Calle Fernando Boqueria. *Moderate.*

Hotel Ritz Restaurante (Gran Vía 688): I can't imagine a more romantic setting for lunch than the Ritz. They've refurbished the high-ceilinged restaurant in palest blues and greens; its parquet floors shine and its crystal chandeliers twinkle. The white-gloved staff serves delicious victuals with a flourish. Open with a salad or gazpacho, go on to paella Valenciana—long a Ritz speciality—or still another house favorite, *medallones de tres carnes* (grilled *médaillions* of veal, lamb, and pork). Catalán seafood specialties are excellent. And so are desserts wheeled up on a trolley, pastries especially. Extraordinary cellar. *Luxury.*

7 Puertas (Paseo Isabel 11) is a long-on-the-scene favorite, on the waterfront. This is a cavernous space, illuminated by silk-shaded ceiling lamps, one over each table. The menu matches the ambience: traditional. Ask for the day's specials, perhaps braised partridge or *solomillo*—a thick grilled steak. *First Class.*

Orotava (Calle Consejo de Ciento 335): You forgive excesses—an overabundance of marble, gilt, mirroring and fussy brica-brac—in Orotava's decor) because both fare and service compensate. You even overlook the inconvenience of the unilingual (Catalán) bill of fare because the multilingual serving staff happily translates. Go with the good-value four-course-and-wine menu, opening with the day's soup (*vichysoisse* on a bed of crushed ice is refreshing in summer), continuing with shrimp cocktail in a house-made Russian dressing, with such entrées as expertly-roasted duck, or venison in tandem with the chef's own apple sauce. Choose either a delicate pastry or ice cream to conclude. Good Catalonian wines accompany. Central. The menu is *First Class*; à la carte is *Luxury*.

La Cuineta (Calle Paradis 4) occupies a suite of atmospheric rooms on two floors (main and basement) of a fine Barrio Gótico house; it tastes as good as it looks, and the welcome is cordial. Open with the Cuineta's celebrated fish soup, Catalán spinach (pine nuts and raisins have been added), or an appropriately smallish portion of *paella*. Grills make for excellent entrées—veal steak, or pork filets, for example. And chocolate mousse topped with whipped cream is the indicated sweet. *First Class*.

Agut d'Avignon (Calle Trinidad 3): Don't be put off by the traditional folk decor here. White-walled Agut d'Avignon is classy, favored by affluent locals (you must book ahead), and just a mite pretentious. The food—especially Catalonian specialities like *pollo con gambas*, chicken with giant shrimp—is delicious, the wines top-class. *First Class*.

Soley (Calle Bailen 29) is agreeable for a quiet dinner. This is a smallish, smartish spot, with fairly standard—albeit tasty—fare, a friendly staff, and a tiny bar popular with neighborhood regulars. *First Class*.

Lluria (Calle Roger de Lluria 23) offers original contemporary paintings on the walls and canaries in cages suspended from the ceiling. Basque-costumed waiters serve favorites like *pollo asado* (roast chicken), *entrecôte ternera* (veal steak), and *casuela de pescado* (seafood casserole). *Moderate.*

Finisterre (La Diagonal 469): Animated by locals who know food, Finisterre's specialities are celebrated. The roast duck, I suspect, will be easier for outlanders to experiment with than the *brandada de bacalao*—a mélange of mashed cod, potatoes, milk, and olive oil that tastes better than it sounds. *First Class.*

Casa Costa (Calle de Baluarte 124, at Calle de Juicio) is one of a number of seafood restaurants—unpretentious albeit spotless, and excellent value—overlooking the city's white-sand beach, Playa Barceloneta, a brief taxi ride from the core of town. Casa Costa has two floors (the view is better upstairs), and the menu is exclusively of fresh fish and seafood, with the day's fish-platter the best buy. *Moderate.*

Gorría (Calle de Diputación 421) is a looker of a Basque restaurant. Thousands of bottles of wine line its walls, and there are spectacular displays of food specialties. Concentrate on roasts— prepared in a giant *horno de asados*, or special oven—as entrées; they're delicious. *First Class.*

Tinell (Calle Freneria 8) is indicated for lunch, in the course of a day exploring the Barria Gótico. Smallish, old-school. Order the sausage called *butifarra*, grilled and served with beans. Or the *menú del día. Moderate/First Class.*

Casinet del Barri Gotic (Calle Freneria 6) is still another provider of nourishment, in the *Barri Gotic*, as Barrio Gótico is written in Catalán. More *cafetería* than proper restaurant, available fare ranges from snacks like *churros* (finger-shaped fritters) invariably served with hot chocolate, in which they're dunked, to sandwiches and tasty hot dishes. *Moderate.*

El Corte Inglés (Plaza de Cataluña): This Barcelona outpost of the Spain-wide department chain offers sustenance on the ninth floor in a vast restaurant with both counter and table service. Seat yourself before one of the picture windows for smashing views of the city. The sandwiches are super; consider one of chopped tomatoes and *salchichón de vich*, a tangy sausage. *Menús del día* are sound value. Or order pastry with tea or coffee. *Moderate.* (*Galerías Preciados* department store—the other major—has a restaurant, too, albeit not as attractive as that of El Corte Inglés; location is Puerta del Angel.)

Cafe de la Rambla (Rambla de Cataluña 13), smart modern ambience and friendly staff notwithstanding, proves satisfactory only if you avoid gloopily-sauced meat-and-vegetables plates, concentrating instead on pizza, *bocadillos* (sandwiches on rolls, notably of Serrano ham) and gooey ice cream concoctions. Central and *Moderate.*

Cafe Eivissa (Plaza de Cataluña): An outdoor table in the sunshine is a happy choice for crowd-watching. Variously filled crêpes are specialty. *Moderate.*

New Kansas (Paseo de Gracia 65) is an odd name for a Barcelona *cafetería.* Still, the alfresco tables are pleasant, in the course of a stroll along this fashionable *paseo,* and you might be tempted by a slice of pizza. *Moderate.*

SHOPPER'S BARCELONA
If it is not as elegant as Madrid, smaller but wealthy Barcelona quite holds its own as a shopping center. Principal department stores and popular-priced shops are in and around Plaza de Cataluña, on the Ramblas leading into it, and on pedestrians-only Puerta del Angel, leading from it. Smarter shops are on nearby thoroughfares like Paseo de Gracia and La Diagonal, and in such attractive shopping centers as Paseo de Gracia's *Boulevard Rosa* and *Halley,* La Diagonal's *Diagonal Center,* Rambla de Cataluña's *La Avenida,* and Calle Urgell's *Urgell Center.*

Of the major department stores, *El Corte Inglés* (Plaza de Cataluña) is, in my view, the smarter, with a strategically sited restaurant (recommended above) on nine; women's, men's, children's, and china-glassware-giftware departments on middling floors; souvenirs and colognes on the main floor, and a supermarket in the basement. *Galerías Preciados* (Puerta del Angel) has similarly diverse wares. There's a branch of Madrid's ever-so-pricey *Loewe* (leather, both men's and women's fashions) on Paseo de Gracia. *Centro de Antigüedades* (with 70-plus quality antique shops) is another Paseo de Gracia attraction, as are *Santa Eulalia* (women's and men's clothing), and *Roca* (jewelry). Look also on Rambla de Cataluña for *Todo Para la Mujer* (which, as its title indicates, is for ladies). And amble along La Diagonal, noting such boutiques as *Pertegaz* (women's couture), *Fancy Men* (gents' togs), *Grife y Escoda* (china and glass).

INCIDENTAL INTELLIGENCE

Catalán is, to understate, the preferred official language (with Spanish following), in this Region of Spain, and you'll make its acquaintance on menus, street and other signs, official notices, and the like. If, in a restaurant, you're given a menu in Catalán only, and you'd prefer one in Spanish, just ask; only the most rabid of Catalonian nationalists will refuse you, and in many places, as throughout Spain, menus are also in English, French, and sometimes German. There are two big bullrings, at either end of Gran Vía. *Las Arenas* is at the west end, fronting Plaza de España. *Monumental*, the other *plaza de toros*, is at the Gran Vía's east end, at the corner of Paseo Carlos I. Along with Madrid and the Andalusian cities of Seville and Granada, this is an important bullfight town; try to take one in. Even more so than Madrid, Barcelona is a center—the leading Spanish center, for that matter—for symphonic music, ballet, and opera. Orquesta Municipal de Barcelona is long-established and distinguished; moreover, its home base is a concert hall—shortened by locals from *Palacio de la Música* to *Palau*, the Catalán for palace—that is one of the planet's great Art Nouveau buildings, more so even within than without. The Palau is open only for performances; there are, unfortunately, no daytime inspection hours; address is Calle Amadeo Vives 1. The other major hall—principally for opera and ballet—is *Gran Teatro del Liceo*, a landmark on the Ramblas since it went up in the middle of the last century: the look is elaborate neo-baroque typical of the period throughout Europe, with a seating capacity of some 3,500 in the orchestra, boxes, and half a dozen levels of balconies. Watch the Spanish-language newspaper, *El Correo Catalán*, whose daily events calendar, titled *Cartelera*, will keep you up to date so that you can ask your concierge to help you snag tickets. Barcelona has a well-planned, 4-line *Metro*, or subway, system, one-class, with route maps in all stations. This city is a major air terminus, with transatlantic services from New York—not only by Iberia (via Madrid, where you must, alas, change planes) but by TWA (with no change of plane, via Lisbon). Both Iberia and Aviaco fly from Barcelona to points within Spain, with the former connecting the city to foreign points as well, as do airlines of a number of other countries. Note, too, that Iberia operates a convenient shuttle service between Barcelona and Madrid. The airport is eight miles from the center. Passenger ships link Barcelona with the Balearic islands of Majorca and Ibiza, as well as the Canaries. *Further information:* Patronato de Turismo de Barcelona, Paseo de Gracia 35.

5

Burgos
*More Than
a Great Cathedral*

BACKBROUND BRIEFING
There is something to be said for an out-of-the-way location. Consider Burgos. It is just far enough from Madrid to escape excursionists who beeline from the capital to nearer points like Toledo, Ávila, Segovia, El Escorial, and Aranjuez.

And so, undisturbed by admirers in the mass, it has quietly gone its way, a medium-small northern town with a glory of a cathedral—one of Europe's great ones—its central focus, but by no means its only attribute. Indeed, it is the rest of the core of historic Burgos (some inspectors term it the surprise package of the north, along with Santiago de Compostela) that combines with the Cathedral to present an urban landscape of utter charm.

Look back a bit and one learns, rather surprisingly, that Burgos preceded Toledo (and Toledo preceded Madrid) as the capital of Castile, under the first of the Kings Ferdinand. That was back a thousand years ago, when Spain was divided into a cluster of not-always-amicable kingdoms, despite the presence of a common enemy: the Moors.

It was a son of Burgos who became the greatest of the Moor-fighters. His proper name—Rodrigo Díaz de Vivar—is familiar mostly to Spanish schoolchildren. The rest of the world knows him as El Cid—the Lord Conqueror who vanquished Moorish army after Moorish army in the service first of King Ferdinand I and later of King Sancho II. What is not always remembered is that still a third monarch—Alfonso VI—fearing El Cid's ground-swell strength with the people, expelled him from the kingdom. El Cid was then welcomed by the North African-origin enemy, for whom he fought for almost two decades until, changing sides again, he became the conqueror—and ruler—of Valencia, way south.

His erratic career notwithstanding, El Cid is claimed by Burgos as its most distinguished son. His tomb is in the transept of the Cathedral. There are monuments to him in suburban San Pedro de Cardeña Monastery—where his body was first shipped after he died in Valencia—and downtown points, especially sculptures on Arco de Santa María, near the Cathedral, and Plaza del General Primo de Rivera. The *Church of Santa Águeda* is the scene of the public confrontation with Alfonso VI that led to the Cid's banishment. And Avenida Cid Campeador—the widest street in town—is a modern memorial.

ON SCENE

Lay of the Land: Give Burgos credit for respecting both its history and its geography. The ruins of a medieval castle, atop a hill over its core, have been restored rather than razed. In the core, the Cathedral dominates. (Nothing even approaching a skyscraper has been allowed.) Continuing south, the terrain bordering the Arlanzón River has been preserved as a tree-lined promenade, punctuated by nine bridges—most of them historical monuments in and of themselves (the oldest is twelfth century).

If the railroad station—*Estación del Norte*—is too far from the core to walk (it's on the south bank of the river), the heart of town, north of the Arlanzón, is compact. It works its way around the most central of a cluster of squares—Plaza de Santa María—with the Cathedral on one side and sculpture-decorated *Arco de Santa María* on the other. A waterfront boulevard, Paseo del Espolón, extends from Plaza de Castillo west to Plaza Mayor. All about, there are bits and pieces: of ancient walls, gates, and towers; of venerable streets—San Juan, San Gil, and Fernán González, to name but three; and of pretty parks, from that of the ruined *Castillo*, way on high, to *Parque del Empecinado*, fringing the railway station to the south.

Cathedral (Plaza de Santa María): A pair of slim and lacy Gothic pinnacles—reminiscent of Cologne's—up front; a spunky, chunky tower over a transept flanked by rose windows, the steeples of ancillary churches in an uneven ring surrounding: that is Burgos Cathedral from without. It is No. 3 in size—and architecturally—of the seats of Spanish bishops; not as art-filled as that of Toledo, perhaps; not as sweeping in scale as Seville. But with extraordinary richness of detail.

Burgos Cathedral went up from the thirteenth through the sixteenth centuries. Walk around the exterior before you enter, the better to appreciate the intricate carving that frames not only the principal Plaza de Santa María entrance, but a trio of other doors.

Within, the choir, as is generally the case in Spanish cathedrals, blocks the aisle between entrance and transept; its stalls—more than 100 on two levels—are sixteenth century. The Renaissance-era transept, supported by immense and solid columns, is the site of the tomb of El Cid and his wife Jimena, a brave soldier in her own right.

There are a baker's dozen chapels. Indeed, no other Spanish church with which I am familiar has so opulent a chapel-cluster as Burgos Cathedral. Of the lot, allot priority to the one called *Capilla del Condestable*. Named for its founder, a constable of Castile, this church within a church is full of treasures, not the least of which is a triptych from the school of the Flemish master Gerard David. And more: a tomb of a local noble couple, an altarpiece by a Spanish master, de Siloé and French sculptor de Bigarny; a Ricci oil of *Santa María Magdalena*. Take time for the other chapels ringing the cathedral's inner walls; *Santa Ana, San Gregorio, Santísimo Cristo* are standouts. So, for that matter, are other parts of the Cathedral: the chapter house with works by Flemish master-painters like Memling and van Eyck; a smashing double staircase—*Escalera Dorada*—so named because of its exquisitely gilded wrought-iron bannisters. To be saved for tour's end, so that you may rest and contemplate what you've experienced: the cathedral's cloister, utterly serene.

The Cathedral's neighbor-church trio: San Nicolás (Calle Fernán González) contains a floor-to-ceiling altarpiece that is one of the sublime works of the Plateresque (elaborately detailed) style: nearly half a thousand delicately carved biblical scenes, centering around the life of the saint for which the church is named. *San Esteban* (Calle Saladaña) is a storehouse of Gothic art, especially tapestries. *Santa Águeda* (Calle de Santa Águeda), dear to the hearts of Spanish history buffs, is where El Cid confronted King Alfonso VI.

Casa de Miranda (Calle de Miranda) is a dazzler of a palace dating to the sixteenth century that is as noteworthy for its Renaissance look as for its contemporary function. This is Burgos's *Museo Arqueológico*. Two floors of galleries encircle an elegant patio, and they house exhibits dating to prehistoric Burgos, with finds from somewhat more recent centuries—medieval onwards—the real beauties. There are Moorish swords, Romanesque enamels, civil sculpture, church altars, coins from an assortment of eras, along with local documents—maps, architectural drawings, proclamations that tell the town's story. And as a bonus, a cache of fine, mostly Renaissance paintings.

Casa del Cordón (Plaza de Calvo Sotelo) goes back half a millennium to when it was built as headquarters for the constables of Castile. Façade and patio are handsome to this day, and any number of historic events occurred within. One such was an audience granted Christopher Columbus by Queen Isabella; occasion was the explorer's return to Spain from his second voyage. It was in this house that King Philip the Handsome died, an event which would not have been all that noteworthy, had not the king's widow been Queen Juana the Mad. As a consequence of Philip's death, Juana's mental condition worsened to the point where her father—Ferdinand II, widower of Queen Isabella—resumed the throne he had shared with his wife, reigning until his death, when the crown passed to Juana's offspring, Emperor Charles V.

Cartuja de Miraflores is one of the quartet of remarkable monuments in the environs of Burgos. Only a couple of miles east of town, this *Cartuja*, or charterhouse, of Carthusian monks goes back 500 years to the time when Juan II, the Castilian monarch who was the father of Queen Isabella the Catholic, established it in part as a burial place for himself and his Portuguese-born wife. He died before it was finished, but his art- and architecture-savvy daughter supervised its completion. Still a monastery, its principal treasure is its chapel, unadorned Gothic without, incredibly decorated within, with an immense gilded altarpiece—a major work, the crucifixion its central theme—by the sculptor Gil de Siloé, whose son Diego's gilded stairway can be seen in Burgos Cathedral. To be admired, too, are the elder de Siloé's sculpted alabaster tombs of Isabella's parents and of an older brother whose early death assured her the throne.

Monasterio de San Pedro de Cardeña is a near-neighbor to the *Cartuja*. You visit here if you're an El Cid buff, for this is where the warrior went first, when he was exiled by a jealous sovereign. After El Cid died in Valencia, his remains were sent first to the monastery, later to Burgos Cathedral. Deserted by the Cistercian monks, the long-empty monastery became a concentration camp during the Spanish Civil War of the 1930s. The following decade, a band of Trappist monks took possession and still are resident, subsisting partly on the sale of a liqueur of their own manufacture.

Monasterio de Santo Domingo de Silos: You've got to be game for a 40-mile drive southeast, and you've got to be enough of an architecture buff to want to see one of the ranking Romanesque cloisters of Spain, if not, for that matter, of Europe: a 1,000-year-old Benedictine masterwork. Capitals of the two levels of arches surrounding its patio from the walkways are no two alike. Proportions are splendid, the sculpture of the corner posts memorable. Much of the rest of the monastery is newer—Renaissance towers to a baroque pharmacy.

Monasterio de las Huelgas, closest to town of our out-of-Burgos foursome, is but a mile west. It was founded by the royal house of Castile in the twelfth century as a Cistercian nunnery. Royals have long since been absent, but Cistercian monks are resident, playing host to visitors intent on seeing a basically Gothic complex at once architecturally striking and art-rich. The sleeper of Las Huelgas is its Cloth Museum, a repository of still-intact, still-beautiful vestments worn by privileged Castilians seven centuries ago. The monks' capacious chapel is handsomely vaulted, with an unusual revolving pulpit and rich tapestries. Flemish Primitives dazzle in the *Chapter House*, and there are a pair of cloisters, one Romanesque, the other Gothic.

SETTLING IN
Hotel Condestable (Calle Vitoria 8) is enviably well-situated, only steps from the Plaza Mayor and the Arlanzón River. Full-facility (restaurant, bar); 85 comfortable rooms with baths. *First Class.*

Hotel Almirante Bonifaz (Calle Vitoria 22) is on the same street as the Condestable, more to the east of the center of town. Not quite as big as its neighbor, but well equipped; restaurant, bar, agreeable rooms with baths. *First Class.*

Hotel Rice (Avenida Reyes Catolicos 30) is an early 1970s house that was thoroughly renovated in the mid-1980s and boasts half a hundred full-facility rooms, a pair of attractive restaurants and a cheery bar-lounge that management likes to think of as English Pub–like; you decide. Location is nice and central. Good value. *Moderate.*

Hotel Fernán González (Calle Calera 17) is on the south bank of the Arlanzón, midway between two bridges. There are just three dozen rooms, a good number with private facilities; restaurant, too. *Moderate.*

Hotel Landa Palace is at the bottom of my selected group of hotels only because it's out of town, two miles south on the road to Madrid. This is a historic palace deftly and charmingly transformed into its contemporary form. There are just under 40 stylishly furnished rooms and suites, excellent restaurant, handsome bar-lounge, professional management. If you've a car and don't mind not being central: by all means. Member, Relais et Châteaux. *Luxury.*

DAILY BREAD

Casa Ojeda (Calle Vitoria 5) is a near-neighbor of Hotel Condestable (above), in the heart of town. This is an up-a-flight place worth the climb. Served in attractive traditional-style setting is some of the best food in town. A beans-and-sausage casserole and roast lamb, especially. *First Class.*

Arriaga (Calle Lain Calvo 4), east of the Cathedral, is an old-reliable for favorites; grilled trout, for example. *First Class.*

Mesón del Cid (Plaza Santa María 8), as a hotel and as a restaurant, could not be more convenient; it shares a square with the Cathedral, and is a good bet for lunch. Given its name, it had better be traditional in decor—and is. Order the *menú del día*, and the house wine. *Moderate.*

INCIDENTAL INTELLIGENCE ═══════════════

It's possible to make an on-your-own, day-long excursion by train from Madrid to Burgos. That's better than not going at all, but do try to stay at least overnight. *Further information:* Oficina de Turismo de Burgos, Plaza Alonso Martinez 7.

6

Canary Islands
Offshore
Spain-in-the-Atlantic

BACKGROUND BRIEFING
More African than European—geographically, at least—the
seven component parts of the Canaries archipelago constitute a
pair of Spanish provinces, are continuously inundated by
masses of sun-starved northern European air-charter tourists
(who do not, alas, always find what they're seeking), and are because of, rather than despite, their Atlantic Ocean isolation of interest as a kind of first-on-one's-block experience. At least to the
transatlantic traveler who collects such destinations.

The trick, for those of us from a hemisphere in which tropical
holiday locales are commonplace and easy of access, is not to be
lured by the Canarians' "Eternal Springtime" propaganda motif
and expect that February in Las Palmas is going to be as reliably
hot, sunny, and swimmable as, say, February in San Juan,
Puerto Rico; Montego Bay, Jamaica; Acapulco, Mexico; or
Waikiki Beach, in Hawaii. T'ain't necessarily so. Not, at least, in
my experience.

To the Stockholmer or the resident of Helsinki or Glasgow or
Amsterdam, a Canarian winter—even when it might turn cold
and wet and gray—could be an improvement over the frigid
home scene. For a New Yorker or a Torontonian or Chicagoan or
an Angeleno with a wide and easy choice of sunscapes, the Canaries in winter are a risk, much more so, it should be noted, than
mainland Spain or Continental Europe, because Canarians tend

not to heat the interiors of either public places (like restaurants) or hotels (including your room), no matter how low the temperature. And I am here to tell you: If you're unlucky enough to hit a cold snap, it can be chilly!

The rest of the year—spring through autumn—why not? Weather is milder and warmer, with no need for interior heating, and the peculiarly insular, Spain-Once-Removed kind of lifestyle can be interesting. Given these volcanic-origin islands' extraordinary background, this is not surprising, for seafarers in their neighborhood have long been attracted to them. Ancient Romans such as Pliny wrote of the Canaries, as did other classical scribes who, residents are not averse to recounting, termed them the Fortunate Isles.

Arabs from the nearby—and arid—North African coast (as close as 70 miles) have long been attracted to the terrain of the islands—at times mountainous and verdant, at others flat and lunar-like. And so have Europeans. Indeed, it was a Frenchman—Jean de Béthencourt—in the service of Castile, who established residence on the Canarian island of Lanzarote in 1404, declaring himself its king, albeit with the backing of the Castilians.

The Spanish-backed mini-monarchy of Béthencourt paved the way for Spanish hegemony over the entire archipelago later in the fifteenth century. In 1479, by which time the Portuguese had begun to evidence interest in the islands, the Spaniards and their Iberian Peninsula neighbors agreed, by treaty, to Spanish sovereignty over the Canaries.

The timing was propitious. Within decades, the islands became important as layover points for Columbus and other New World mariners. Later, their strategic location made them attractive to European powers like the English (Sir Francis Drake was bested in a battle off Las Palmas harbor) and the Dutch (who were victors in a 1599 battle).

It was during this relatively brief period that the Canaries' curious indigenous people—the fair-skinned Stone Age Guanches—were subdued, and ere long, became extinct. (A Las Palmas museum devotes a section to their culture.) And since it was incorporated into the pan-Spanish kingdom of Ferdinand

and Isabella, the archipelago has been an intrinsic part of Spain—linguistically, culturally, spiritually, economically.

Its two major cities—Las Palmas, capital of the three-island Province of Las Palmas and situated on the island of Gran Canaria; and Santa Cruz, capital of the four-island Province of Tenerife and situated on the island of Tenerife—could hold their own as provincial capitals on the mainland, or, as the Spaniards term it, *la Península*. There are a distinctive folklore, a regional cuisine, and other local variations on Spanish themes, not the least of which are a highly visible East Indian merchant class in the towns, and the immense northern-European tourist population, especially evident during the nonsummer months, and dominantly Scandinavian, with substantial British, Dutch, and German infusions. Americans? We are curiosities in the Canaries, which is possibly as good a reason as any for wanting to make a visit, especially to the two major islands, Gran Canaria and Tenerife, and Lanzarote, most spectacularly oddball of the smaller islands.

ON SCENE

Gran Canaria Island

LAS PALMAS: Gran Canaria Island, while not the largest of the archipelago (that honor is Tenerife's), is, at least to this visitor, the most interesting island if only because of its metropolis, Las Palmas—the largest, oldest, and most populous (more than a quarter million) city of the Canaries. It extends over an elongated stretch of Atlantic shore. Two of its quarters, or barrios, beckon the visitor. First, the more northern, actually a peninsula with the ocean on the east, and Confital Bay on the west, is tourist headquarters, with two principal beach areas: older *Playa Alcaravaneras* on the Atlantic, and more recently developed *Playa de las Canteras* on Confital Bay. These are districts dotted with hotels ranging from luxury five-star houses to apartment buildings (some with hotel amenities) and modest places, some little more than pensions. Add to these cafés, bars, and restaurants that cater to European visitors, frequently by nationality: a Finnish pub, a Swedish café, a British tearoom, a Dutch tavern, a Belgian bistro.

The second area of interest is historic Las Palmas, in the central Vegueta area. *Casa de Colón* (Calle Colón 1) invariably takes priority with New World visitors. This is a fifteenth-century palace wherein early governors headquartered. An English-language leaflet, after insisting that "without the help of the Canaries, Columbus could not have fulfilled his great enterprise," explains that he lived on the premises in the course of his first (1492), second (1493), and fourth (1502) voyages. Other exhibits include historical objects in the Archives and lovely old paintings in the Bellas Artes section.

Las Palmas's *Cathedral* (Plaza de Santa Ana) is sufficiently ancient—with a fifteenth-century Gothic interior and a later, neoclassic façade—to warrant inspection, even if it is not among Spain's most beautiful. Do visit its treasury. *Museo Canario* (Calle Doctor Verneau 2) makes a stab at explaining what the Guanches—the islands' pre-European, Stone Age residents—were all about, with exhibits of their ceramics: household vessels through religious figures. *Museo Diocesano de Arte Sacro* (Calle Doctor Chil 21) embraces half a dozen galleries of beautiful objects, most of them paintings and sculptures with religious themes, Canarian-created, fifteenth through the eighteenth century.

TEROR is as good a destination as any at which to get an idea of what life is like—in the villages and in the countryside—of the ruggedly mountainous interior of Gran Canaria. Big surprise of this pretty little town is a baroque church, with a façade as grand as its interior is gorgeous—and, to islanders, important. For this is the *Basílica of Nuestra Señora del Pino*. The statue of the *Virgin of the Pines*, nestled in its golden altar, was—according to legend—found in the branches of a village evergreen five centuries back, and is much venerated. Give a day to your Teror outing, combining with it beauty spots of this mountainous area, including *Pozo de las Nieves* and *Cruz de Tejeda*, site of a welcome link in the national chain of *paradores*, and the ideal locale for a lunch break.

MASPALOMAS is the focal point, on the south coast, of a cluster of resorts flanking dune-like beaches, its own as well as others such as *Playa de San Agustín* and *Playa del Inglés.* The key words here, even in winter—when it can be gray and cold and dreary in Las Palmas—are warmth and sunshine. Maspalomas is where you want to head in the cool-weather months. Unless you're a polar bear.

TENERIFE ISLAND

SANTA CRUZ DE TENERIFE, smaller and more compact than Las Palmas, revolves around a waterfront corniche variously called Avenida Tres de Mayo and Avenida de Anaga. A handsome circle of a square, Plaza de España, is its focal point.

Santa Cruz is not without visitor requisites. Its variations on the theme of the original Canarians—the early Guanche people, and their culture—are the principal subject of *Museo Arqueológico* (Plaza de España). Look at the paintings—the ones by islanders are of special interest—in the *Museo de Bellas Artes* (Calle del Castillo). By all means enter the history-rich church called *Matriz de la Concepción* (Barranco de Santos). And have a look at the stalls—housing live canaries (the bird was named for the islands, not vice versa) through live chickens (with voices not nearly as melodious)—of the city's market, *Mercado de Nuestra Señora de África,* named for the continent whose coast is not far distant.

PUERTO DE LA CRUZ—called simply Puerto, to distinguish it from larger, older Santa Cruz—is a long-dormant fishing port on the northwest coast of Tenerife Island (Santa Cruz is on the northeast coast). In recent decades, Puerto has evolved into a booming resort, its mild climate a lure to unending hordes of northern Europeans who seem not to mind that it is nearly devoid of swimmable beaches. (Hotel pools take their place.) The whole town fronts the sea, but Avenida de Colón is the center of the action, with cafés, shops, markets—and strollers unlimited. Beyond are the pretty baroque *Church of Peña de Francia,* the animated principal square, and the maze of houses lining old streets that lead to the waterfront, fringed with fishing vessels. Not far from town—and worth the taxi fare if you've no transport of your own—is *Jardín de Aclimatación,* an enchanting botanical garden with eminently respectable eighteenth-century origins that is unsurpassed anywhere in Spain.

LA OROTAVA AND PICO DE TEIDE are the classic Tenerife Island excursions best undertaken from Puerto, to which they're closer, than Santa Cruz. La Orotava is a looker of a town. If you have time for nothing else, visit the eighteenth-century *Church of Nuestra Señora de la Concepción* and the mansions of *Calle de San Francisco.* Move along then—via any of a quartet of scenic routes—to Pico de Teide, at 12,162 feet Spain's highest mountain, and nucleus of a jagged region chockablock with observation points on its promontories, constituting *Parque Nacional Las Cañadas.* If you're lucky with weather, the view will be not only of all Tenerife Island spread out below, but of the entire Canaries group. Hungry? The national chain of *paradores* has thoughtfully placed an inn at nearby Las Cañadas del Teide, at which lunch is indicated.

LAS AMÉRICAS AND LOS CRISTIANOS are to Tenerife Island what Maspalomas is to Gran Canaria: an almost guaranteed warm and sunny locale for winter holiday-makers, on the south coast, astride splendid beaches of which much more popular Puerto de la Cruz has precious few.

LANZAROTE ISLAND

Urban Lanzarote takes the form of the neat little town of Arrecife. But one concentrates, rather, on the terrain of the island beyond the city, ideally in sunny weather; when the atmosphere is gray, Lanzarote with its eerily lunar landscape—embracing some 300 volcanoes, whose black deposits are all about—can be positively depressing.

Plot excursions both north and south of Arrecife. Upper reaches of the island are ideally surveyed from an observation point, *Mirador del Río,* that bares the formidable landscape of Lanzarote and the horizons of distant, smaller Canaries. At *Jaime del Agua,* a lagoon on the coast, one finds colonies not only of an unusual species of tiny crabs, born blind, but of entertainers come to amuse increasingly substantial numbers of outlanders; their fare is the island's own dances and songs of yore, performed in traditional costume, according to regular schedules.

Still other entertainments—concerts in this case—take place upon occasion in *Cuevas de Los Verdes*, a succession of vast caves, at least as significant as those on the east coast of Majorca (see the chapter on that island).

Head south of Arrecife then, to *Montañas del Fuego*, volcanoes whose craters continue to flame. Camels—used as beasts of burden on Lanzarote—are at hand, the better to transport you through the area; and so are buses, which take the curious through fields of molten lava. Most exciting: a look from the crater rims into the fiery depths.

SETTLING IN

GRAN CANARIA ISLAND

Hotel Maspalomas Oasis (Playa de Maspalomas) is a longtime leader on the south shore: clean-lined and understated in design, with its own garden leading onto the beach; 340 rooms and suites; restaurant, bar-lounge, pool. *Luxury.*

Hotel Tamarindos Sol (Playa de San Agustín, Maspalomas) is conveniently beachfront, relatively recent, with nice-size rooms, a diverting mix of restaurants (the casual red-check tableclothed cafe is fun) and bars, wee-hours disco, swimming pool, sauna–fitness center and, if you please, the island's sole casino, with roulette and 21 among the gaming options. *Luxury.*

Hotel Parque Tropical (Avenida Italia) is not directly on, but just a couple of hundred yards from Playa del Inglés, with a striking—and enormous—butterfly-shaped pool in its garden (where the super buffet lunch is served), high-ceilinged traditional-decor restaurant, and 235 rooms. *First Class.*

Hotel Waikiki (Playa del Inglés), strikingly circular, embraces some 500 terraced rooms, with public spaces—the bar, for example, and the gardens—not without touches of the Polynesian islands whence comes the hotel's name; a bit corny, but still unusual in Spain, and not unwelcome to Hawaii buffs, of which I am one. Lunch at the pool is a pleasure, the beach is a nice walk away. Good value. *Moderate.*

Hotel Cristina (Calle Gomera 6, Las Palmas), is at once good-looking, beachfront (in the Puerto de La Luz quarter), with 300-plus rooms and suites, swimming pool, and El Galeón Restaurant, with good grilled specialties. *Luxury.*

Hotel Reina Isabel (Calle Alfredo L. Jones 40—Jones is pronounced *"hoh-ness"*—in Las Palmas) has the advantage of being on the edge of Playa de las Canteras closest to town, so that you have the best of both Las Palmas's worlds, assuming that the weather is with you. This is a cheery, full-facility, 240-room house, with a convenient coffee shop among its eateries. *Luxury.*

Hotel Santa Catalina (Parque Doramas, Las Palmas), most beloved of the older hotels in the islands, is a mock-Moorish palace situated in a verdant park. You are not, please note, on a beach, but there's a pool, adjacent tennis club, and mini-golf to compensate, not to mention pretty places to dine and drink, and some 200 winning rooms. *Luxury.*

Hotel Iberia Sol (Avenida Marítima del Norte, Las Palmas): Not for nothing does this hotel take the name of Spain's international airline; it's in the Iberia town terminal, sleek-mod in look with 300 balconied rooms, *cafetería,* bar-lounge, swimming pool, and the beach adjacent. *First Class.*

Hotel Imperial Playa (Calle Ferraras 1, Las Palmas) is smack on Playa de las Canteras. All 175 rooms have terraces. Back ones are beach-view. *Cafetería,* bar. *First Class.*

Hotel Gran Canaria (Paseo de las Canteras 38, Las Palmas) is well-located—on the beach's main street—with restaurant, bar, and fine views from its upper front rooms. *Moderate.*

TENERIFE ISLAND

Hotel Mencey (Calle José Naveiras 38, Santa Cruz) a lovely, long-on-scene, traditional-style hostelry in the grand manner, has a meticulously tended mini-park as its front lawn. There are 300 delightful rooms, suites, and junior suites; a pool in the garden, inviting restaurant, intimate bar. Your host is Italy-based Ciga Hotels. *Luxury.*

Hotel Gran Tenerife (Playa de las Américas) fills the bill for a beach home-away-from-home, with 300 terraced rooms, some detached *casitas,* or bungalows, if it's privacy you hanker after, and attractive spots for dining and drinks, along with a big pool as well as the beach. *Luxury.*

Park Hotel Troya (Playa de las Américas) is a full-facility house with more than 300 neat rooms, restaurant, pool, tennis court. And the price is right. *First Class.*

Hotel Tamaide (Rambla Franco 118, Santa Cruz), is an agreeable 65-room (many with bath) house on the town's spiffiest street. A *cafetería* takes the place of a restaurant. Swimming pool. *Moderate.*

Hotel Taburiente (Calle Doctor Guigou 25, Santa Cruz) offers 90 functional rooms—many with baths—as well as a pool and bar-lounge. *Moderate.*

Hotel Botánico Sol (Puerto de la Cruz) takes its name from the nearby Botanical Gardens. This is a looker of a modern house with smart public spaces, generous-size terraced rooms, (including a separate floor given over exclusively to suites), a pair of restaurants (with buffet-lunch served poolside) and bars, dark and dense disco. *Luxury.*

Hotel San Felipe (Playa de Martianez, Puerto de la Cruz) is at once central and on the town's main beach. This is a modern skyscraper, with 260 rooms, all with terraces, big pool (try the buffet lunch served around it), and a grill as well as a main restaurant. *Luxury.*

Hotel Ybarra Semiramis (Calle Leopoldo Cologan, Puerto de la Cruz) straddles a seaside cliff so that there are breathtaking views of sea and shore from its balconied rooms, and its broad sun terrace on which drinks are served. There are a trio of pools, one salt-water. *Luxury.*

Hotel Monnalisa (Calle Perez Zamora 2, Puerto de la Cruz) is a modern house, near the center of town, with restaurant and bar, pool and solarium. *First Class.*

Hotel Monopol (Calle Quintana 15, Puerto de la Cruz) is a find: 90 perky rooms with private facilities, in a hotel that encircles a patio; plus restaurant and pool. *Moderate.*

Hotel Tryp Puerto Playa (José del Campo Llarena, Puerto de la Cruz) is at once full-facility (all 191 rooms and suites are good-sized and terraced), with restaurant, bar-lounge, big pool, and beachfront situation. *First Class.*

Hotel Tryp Princesa Dacil (Playa de Los Cristianos) is big (330 terraced rooms, most of which are living-room-attached suites), busy (the paneled cocktail lounge is amusing, the restaurant buzzy) with swimming pool, tennis and a location not far from the beach. *Moderate.*

LANZAROTE ISLAND

Hotel Las Salinas (Teguise) is a futuristic Y-shaped complex built around a jungle-like atrium. There are 310 rooms with sea-view terraces, a pair of restaurants (along with a gargantuan poolside lunch buffet), a quartet of bars, cinema, disco. *Luxury.*

Hotel Los Fariones (Tias) is agreeably low-slung, fronting a beach, with stunning views from its picture-window lounges and restaurant, not to mention its 240 attractive terraced rooms. Garden, pool, tennis. *First Class.*

Hotel Lancelot Playa (Avenida Mancomunidad, Arrecife) is the capital's showplace hotel. It's beachfront, with a big lobby-lounge, good restaurant, two bars, and 120 rooms, all terraced, many with fine views. *First Class.*

DAILY BREAD

GRAN CANARIA ISLAND

San Agustín Beach Club (Calle San Agustín, near Maspalomas) is for a splashy lunch or dinner on the terrace. Spanish as well as international fare. Smartly contemporary. *Luxury.*

Lord Nelson (Paseo de las Canteras 8, Las Palmas): Nicely located on the beach, with a range of specialties, to please a mixed-bag clientele. *First Class.*

Novilo Precoz (Calle Portugal 9, Las Palmas) is an old reliable for steaks and roast chicken. *Moderate.*

La Terraza (Calle Luis Morote 46, Las Palmas) serves up a bountiful buffet at lunch. *First Class.*

Julio (Calle Naval 132, Las Palmas): Seafood, seafood, seafood— fresh, deliciously prepared. With the white house wine. Not far from Playa de las Canteras. *First Class.*

Mesón La Paella (Calle José María Durán 47, Las Palmas): You don't need to be told what to order here. *Moderate.*

Parador Nacional Cruz de Tejeda (Cruz de Tejeda): Detour here in the course of a day's outing in the mountains. This 20-room inn in the government *parador* chain serves copious meals, often with Canary Islands specialties; at lunch you skip the first course of *entremeses variados* at your own peril. *First Class.*

TENERIFE ISLAND

La Riviera (Rambla Generalísimo Franco 155, Santa Cruz) has ambience—the look is low-key modern—and delicious fare, Spanish, Canary Islands, international. *Luxury.*

Hotel Mencey Restaurante (Calle José Naveiras 38, Santa Cruz): A light, bright environment for a trout, a towering paella, a lamb roast. *First Class.*

La Estancia (Calle Méndez Núñez 116, Santa Cruz): Locally popular, with well-priced *menús del día,* and sound house wine. *Moderate.*

Tres Coronas (Plaza Concejil, Puerto de la Cruz): Daily specials are invariably delicious; mainland Spaniards congregate here. *Moderate.*

El Pescado (Avenida Venezuela 3, Santa Cruz) is indicated, when it's straightforward seafood you hunger for. *Moderate.*

Parador Nacional Cañadas del Teide (Las Cañadas del Teide): On the day you earmark for an ascent of Pico de Teide, make a reservation at this *parador* in the neighborhood for lunch, beginning—as you do at all outposts of this kingdom-wide group of inns—with the diverse and enormous selection of *entremeses variados* and going on from there with the hearty *menú del día.* Canary Islands specialties and wines. *First Class.*

INCIDENTAL INTELLIGENCE

At the risk of angering the Canarians, and of boring you, I repeat: winter, except on the *south coasts* of Gran Canaria and Tenerife, can be chilly, gray, damp, and nasty. On the other hand, you may be lucky, with brilliant sunshine; many visitors are. Spring through autumn is warm and delightful. Iberia flies to Gran Canaria and Tenerife non-stop from New York, as well as from Madrid and other points on *la península.* There is passenger-ship service as well; sailing time from Cádiz is two days, whereas flying time from Madrid is two hours. There is inter-island air and sea service; you may, for example, fly from Gran Canaria to Lanzarote. *Special note for shoppers:* The Canaries are duty-free, and have been well into the last century, not in selected shops, but in all shops; appliances, watches, cameras can be good buys. *Further information:* Oficina de Turismo de Gran Canaria, Casa del Turismo, Parque Santa Catalina, Las Palmas; Oficina de Turismo de Santa Cruz, Calle de la Marina 57; Oficina de Turismo de Puerto de la Cruz, Plaza de la Inglesa 3.

7

Córdoba

*Legacy
of a Caliphate*

BACKGROUND BRIEFING

Córdoba's near-neighbor, Seville, is twice as large and with twice the touristic clout. First-timers from abroad, touring Spain, frequently miss Córdoba. Even Spaniards from elsewhere in the kingdom accord it relatively low priority on a scale of contemporary major cities.

And yet, centuries before Madrid—to cite the case of today's No. 1 city—was more than an isolated trading post, Córdoba had become one of Europe's preeminent centers of intellect, political power and tangible grandeur.

Prehistoric Iberians were known to have settled Córdoba, but it was the Romans who made it one of their proudest overseas colonies, easily on a par with Germany's Trier and northern Spain's Tarragona. The great Roman father-son philosophers, Seneca the Elder and his son the junior Seneca (who was even more prominent), were Córdoba-born; it is interesting to observe that even in those days of snail-slow transport, the father was a virtual commuter between capital and colony, the son less so only because he became involved in the empire's politics. The point I make is that as long as 2,000 years back there was intercourse—intellectual and well as actual—between this Andalusian outpost and Rome, which was at that time the nerve-center of the planet.

In the sixth century, Visigoths out of Germany routed the Romans, in the course of their pan-Spanish takeover. Christians, they made Córdoba the principal seat of their Andalusian territory. And so it was, for a good two centuries, till the coming of the Moors. No city in Spain was more utterly transformed by the arrival of the North Africans. Córdoba became center of the action. For the eighth through early eleventh centuries it was an emirate, under the control of an aggressive, creative dynasty, Umayyad by name. Later, the emirate moved up the ladder of Moorish nomenclature and became a caliphate whose realm included most of Spain.

With this political control came cultural wealth. The court of the caliphate was known as much for its opulence as its power, for its scholars as well as its soldiers, for its myriad mosques, as for its money. University and libraries attracted foreign scholars. The court built cavernous public baths, and its town houses wrapped themselves around fountain-centered patios. Massive walls and ceremonial gates surrounded what historians recorded as one of the greatest medieval cities, a center of art and science, and like the other big Moorish cities, with cultural stimulation that resulted from cross-currents of Moslem, Christian, and Jewish communities. (The Jewish philosopher-writer-physician Maimónides, for whom a Córdoba square is named, was the leading Córdoban intellectual of the city's golden twelfth century, an era in which artisanship—work in gold, silver, leather—flourished, along with the intellectual disciplines.)

In the thirteenth century, Castile's Ferdinand III, as pious (he was later sainted) as he was war-like, conquered Córdoba for the Christians, and in the united Spain that resulted, monarchs came with courtiers for Córdoba visits. During two such visits, Queen Isabella conferred with Columbus; it was in Córdoba that she determined to sponsor the Genoan's New World voyages.

ON SCENE
Lay of the Land: The railway station is on its northern flank. But Córdoba is one of several Spanish cities—Salamanca is another—wherein I suggest that the visitor gain perspective on what lies ahead by crossing a bridge of a bordering river. Which means going south. In Córdoba's case—again as in Salamanca's—the bridge dates to Roman times, is still in use, and—

from its far side on the fringe of town, across the Guadalquivir River, allows one to perceive the low-slung city dominated now as for many centuries by the silhouette of a brilliant complex that began life as a mosque, and has weathered its old age in great style as a cathedral. Calle Torrijos leads from the bridge to *La Mezquita*—the mosque/cathedral. Amble east along the river and you pass what remains of the *Alcázar*, the old royal palace-fortress. Walk west, via Calle Manríquez, and ere long you have reached Plaza de Maimónides, core of the old *Barrio de la Judería*, or Jewish Quarter. It continues north to the ancient gate, Puerta de Almodóvar, along Calle de los Judíos, with lovely lanes leading from it; the area brims with houses whose patios constitute major Córdoba treats. Equally requisite—and eye-filling—is the quarter immediately north of the Mezquita, beyond Calle Cárdenas Herrero, in and about Calle de Las Flores, where whitewashed walls are a foil for climbing, blossoming plants.

Continue, from the Calle de Las Flores area, along the commercial thoroughfare called Calle Blanco Belmonte, and you arrive at the modern city's main square, Plaza de las Tendillas. Gran Vía—the main shopping street—lies beyond.

Contrast? From Plaza de las Tendillas take Calle Claudio Marcelo due east and you're soon at Plaza de la Corredera: a fully enclosed, Renaissance-era masterwork, with cafés, shops in its arcades, and vendors of pottery on its broad pavement.

La Mezquita (Calle Cardenal Herrero) is how Córdobans identify the remarkable pile that ranks with Granada's Alhambra as the greatest work of Moorish architecture in Spain. It is at once a Roman Catholic cathedral and a mosque that dates to the eighth century. It is a maze—at times seemingly interminable—of marble, granite, and jasper columns topped mostly with Corinthian capitals, then surmounted by a double level of red-and-white striped arches. Statistics stagger. There are some 850 columns supporting nearly a score of naves, with a kind of sanctuary—the *Third Mihráb*, it is called—the focal point. A mosaic-floored shrine, facing east toward Mecca, it contained holy relics, so revered during the period of the caliphate that a pilgrimage to Córdoba was second only to a trek to Mecca.

The Cathedral came about in several stages, following the

Christian reconquest, and its transformation was just the reverse of what happened in Istanbul in the fifteenth century when Moslems converted the original Church of Santa Sophia into a mosque. But there was a major difference between how the Turkish Moslems handled their transformation and how the Christians in Córdoba handled theirs. In the case of Hagia Sofía, the architectural fabric of the great church remained unchanged. The Turks simply removed the pews, redecorated some wall surfaces, and set about worshipping Allah. In the case of the Mezquita, the Christians tore out a great chunk of the mosque to replace it with a Western-motif church, destroying some 150 of the original pillars, and much else as well. Their handiwork did not go uncriticized. Critics ranged from city fathers through to Emperor Charles V. Saddened though one may be at the thought of such consequential destruction, the resultant cathedral— though an oddball mix of styles, Gothic transept through sumptuous baroque choir—is not to be despised. And even though we may dislike its being plopped into so splendid and incongruous an environment, the manner in which it was accomplished has to be admired, technologically if not aesthetically.

El Alcázar (Avenida del Alcázar) is nothing like as sumptuous as that of Seville, but on the other hand, far more evocative of its heyday than the reconstructed Alcázar of Toledo. Prides of the Córdoba Alcázar are its terraced gardens, accented with reflecting pools, embellished with flower beds, cooled by fountains, with walls and towers of the ancient palace-fortress as a backdrop. The gardens are illuminated at night—a lovely time for a stroll. Within, precious little remains of a residence where Isabella received Columbus, and from where the dreaded Spanish Inquisition was conducted for a long stretch, beginning in the late fifteenth century.

La Sinagoga (Calle de los Judíos) can't compare with either the del Tránsito or Santa María la Blanca synagogues in Toledo. But it is, with that pair, one of only three remaining structures in Spain that served as ancient houses of Jewish worship. Like its Toledo counterparts, it became a church (as well as a hospital) after the expulsion of the Jews in the fifteenth century and is now a national monument.

Museo Municipal de Arte Cordobés y Taurino (Plaza de Maimónides) is a near-neighbor of the synagogue (above) and easily visited in tandem with it. This is a charming house, typical of the quarter, with exhibits in two floors of galleries surrounding a sun-dappled, plant-jammed patio. Principal subject matter is the art and lore of the bullfight, of which Córdoba is a leading center. There are antique posters advertising fights of the last century, impedimenta of the famous *torero* Manolete (a Cordobés), including his scarlet cape and a portrait of him by an expatriate Virginian. There are, as well, displays of traditional crafts of the city, especially beautifully worked leather and delicately chiseled silver.

Museo Provincial de Bellas Artes (Plaza del Potro) occupies the better part of a patio-centered hospital almost six centuries old. Its problem in recent seasons has been remaining open. More often than not, visitors eager to see its outstanding collection have been disappointed to find it closed, and—for some reason or other—have had to settle for third-rate portrayals of gypsies by an early twentieth-century painter named Julio Romero de Torres in an across-the-patio gallery devoted entirely to his works. The Bellas Artes is something else again, much smaller than Seville's to be sure, but with Spain's great painters represented in a collection including Goya and Zurbarán, Bartolomé Murillo and Ribera. I hope you get in.

Museo Arqueológico (Plaza de Jerónimo Páez): Water lilies float in the pool of the patio of the onetime palace this museum occupies. Exhibits run a wide gamut, and are first-rate: ravishing mosaics dating to Roman Córdoba, a graceful and fanciful stag sculpted of bronze by early local Arabs, Christian remnants—rare because the Christians left so little—from the Visigothic period, pottery and jewelry, coins and crosses. And the lot is beautifully exhibited.

Museo Histórico de Córdoba (Castillo de Calahorra) occupies a tower out of the Middle Ages, crenellated atop, its stark façade dotted with peephole windows, irregularly placed. Contents are minimal—a tapestry-hung brick-walled hall, some ancient documents, and objects of municipal importance. Go for the view from on high, and the building's architecture.

Church of San Pedro (Plaza de San Pedro) is a near-neighbor of atmospheric Plaza de la Corredera (above), and representative of a number of visit-worthy Córdoba churches. San Pedro blends Romanesque with much later Gothic.

Churches of San Lorenzo and San Rafael (Calle de San Rafael) are a neighboring pair that constitute a good reason for a walk to the east side of town. Both have tall, landmark bell towers, but San Lorenzo is perhaps the more remarkable of the two, with stone tracery over its rose window, and a vast triple-arched Gothic porch.

SETTLING IN

Hotel Meliá Córdoba (Jardines de la Vitoria) is a leader among the Spain-wide Meliá group, and Número Uno in Córdoba. There's an agreeably intimate quality to this 125-room house: capacious, to be sure, but neither too bustling nor impersonal. Public spaces—including a pool that's a winner in summer—are attractive, rooms likewise. An easy walk to the historic core. Restaurant, bar-lounge. *Luxury.*

Hotel Maimónides (Calle Torrijos 4) is at once central, contemporary, and cozy, with some 60 attractive rooms and a bar-café (where you may breakfast), but no proper restaurant. Very nice indeed. *First Class.*

Hotel Marisa (Calle Cardenal Herrero 6) is a find: a charming antique of a house, with traditional-style rooms (many with baths), a convenient bar-café, and an inspired location just opposite La Mezquita. *Moderate.*

Hotel El Triunfo (Calle Cardenal González 87) is perfectly situated, across from the Cathedral. There are a score-plus okay rooms, a number with private bathrooms. And a restaurant, of which I write more later. *Moderate.*

Hotel Riviera (Plaza de Aladeros 5) compensates with location (it's central) and modernity (many rooms have private baths) for what it lacks in ambience. Breakfast only. *Moderate.*

Hotel Selu (Calle Eduardo Dato 7) is midway between the business district and the historic area. Its 105 rooms all have baths and are good buys. Big contemporary lobby-lounge. Breakfast only. *Moderate.*

Hotel Los Gallos (Avenida Medina Azahara 7) is neither central nor especially cordial. But its 100-plus rooms—all with baths—are comfortable and reasonable. And facilities include both restaurant and pool. *First Class.*

Hotel Gran Capitán (Avenida de América 3) is near the bottom of my selected group only because it's a good 20-minute walk from the old part of town, which is, after all, what pleasure-visitors come to experience. Otherwise, I couldn't be more enthusiastic. There are 100 handsome rooms and suites, a lobby deftly combining contemporary and period styles, and a honey of a restaurant-bar-lounge. A link of the nationwide Husa chain. *Luxury.*

Parador Nacional de la Arruzafa is a couple of miles north of town, on the El Brillante road. This modern unit of the national chain of *paradores* is a boon to motorists, who in the course of a summer visit may enjoy combining swims with fine accommodations. *First Class.*

DAILY BREAD
El Churrasco (Plazuela del Cardenal Salazar): You'll be peeking into patios of old Córdoba houses in the course of your exploration of the city. Here's a chance to lunch or dine in such a house. The specialty is beef. *First Class.*

El Caballo Rojo (Calle Cardenal Herrero 28) is a rambling house, heart of town, with a menu at once local (try the *cola a la Andaluza*, a delicious oxtail stew) and international. In summer, avoid tour-groups on the main floor by proceeding to the quiet upstairs dining room. *First Class.*

Califa (Calle Deanes 9) is ideal for a lunch pause in the course of sightseeing. Look is traditional. Order the well-priced *menú del día.* Central. *Moderate.*

El Triunfo (Calle Cardenal González 87) is earlier called to your attention as a *Moderate*-category hotel. It is, as well, a restaurant—brick-walled, wrought-iron-grilled. Central. *Moderate.*

El Zoco (Museo Municipal de Arte Cordobés y Taurino, Plaza de Maimónides) is still another lunch spot worth considering, if your travels bring you to this popular part of town at midday. Traditional specialties, including a deliciously cooling gazpacho, the Andalusian cold soup. *First Class.*

INCIDENTAL INTELLIGENCE

Córdoba is favored by Aviaco, which flies to it from Madrid. You may visit Córdoba on day-long bus tours from the Costa del Sol, or via train out of Seville, on an excursion of your own making. *Further information:* Oficina de Turismo de Córdoba, Avenida Gran Capitán 13.

8

Costa Brava and Gerona

Rugged Shore,
Inland Treasure

BACKGROUND BRIEFING

The pattern in resort areas the world over appears unchangeable. First, nature creates spectacular natural beauty. Man follows, building and creating, sometimes over a course of centuries, the better to attract attention from writers and artists. They settle in as relatively modern pioneers and carry on with their crafts, using their new home ground as subject matter. And poof! As the night follows the day, tourists arrive—in a trickle at first, ere long, en masse.

Spain's Costa Brava is a classic case (*brava* means wild, but read it here as rugged, rock-coved, and magnificent). This 125-mile stretch extends from a little town on the French frontier called Port-Bou south to Blanes, which is but 35 miles north of giant Barcelona. The location, as regards tourism, could not be more strategic. Barcelonans and fellow Spaniards invade from the south by the scores upon scores of thousands, while simultaneously, French sun-seekers do likewise—in similarly massive doses—from the north.

These swellers of the summertime population are relative upstarts on the Costa Brava. Even the region's evocative name was coined in the twentieth century. But there were earlier invaders. The white-sand beaches—lining horseshoe-like coves, with rocky cliffs providing natural cover—that attract today's vacationers attracted prehistoric seamen, starting with the dawn-of-history Iberians and somewhat later Phoenicians, who saw the beaches as ideal harbors for their vessels. The colonists of the then great powers followed: Greeks first, in the sixth century B.C.; Romans three centuries later, and in force; Germanic Visigoths in the early centuries after Christ. As elsewhere on the Iberian peninsula, Moors came in the eighth century, but their contributions were minimal and their stay brief. Franks from the north began routing them within decades of their arrival, so that from the early Middle Ages onward the region developed as Christian, culturally as well as spiritually. (Its inland metropolis, Gerona, splendidly attests to this pattern.)

Today's Costa Brava is an extraordinarily complex amalgam of the centuries and of the elements and of a contemporary lifestyle that dictates sun-in-summer-or-bust. It comprises some two score communities—still-relaxed hamlets through overbuilt high-rise towns—whose visitor populaces lack the cosmopolitan diversity of, say, Majorca and the Costa del Sol. Costa Brava visitors are essentially Spanish and French, who arrive in their own cars, mostly staying in apartments that they either own or rent for the season, or in campgrounds. Hotel guests are a minority, and so, for that matter, are visitors from countries other than France and Spain. The extraordinary mix encountered at, say, Torremolinos—Germans and Dutch and Finns and Scots and Americans and Canadians, not to mention native Spaniards—is not duplicated on the Costa Brava.

Nor, to the uninitiated newcomer, is the geography easily mastered. You don't just fly in and taxi to your hotel. You must decide in advance which of a maze of resorts you want to headquarter in, aware that you'll need your own or a rented car to provide the necessary mobility to get about, exploring, dining, disco-dancing, or whatever. It's a scene that visitors from nearby Spanish and French points—many of whom return season in and season out—adore. But it is not necessarily the transatlantic vacationer's cup of tea. That said, I should also emphasize the extraordinary physical beauty of the coastline, and the extraordinary man-made beauty of the sole metropolis, Gerona, in the interior.

ON SCENE

Lay of the Land: Chances are you'll take in the Costa Brava as an extension of a Barcelona visit, or as a consequence of arrival by air at Gerona, site of the region's only airport with scheduled service. The jumble of towns along the 125-mile coast—some are tucked just inland as well—is linked by highway and rail, and there is also bus service. If your destination is Barcelona, concentrate on Gerona and Costa Brava resorts from, say, Bagur, southward. If you're more curious, and have more time, there are visit-worthy northern points.

GERONA

The Gothic-origin *Cathedral* is like no other—anywhere. Look up, at what must be one of all Europe's broadest and highest outer stairways. Way, way, *way* at the top (I'm not going to tell you how many steps there are since I don't want to discourage you) a baroque overlay—three levels of Corinthian columns with saints' statues between them—has been superimposed on a broad medieval façade topped by a squat bell tower on its right flank. The sense of drama does not lessen within, what with the Cathedral's single nave—high, wide, handsome, and inventively vaulted. But there is more: a stunningly arched cloister even older than the church proper, with double rows of capitals supporting the arches of its arcade.

Then there are the treasures of the Cathedral's museum, constituting one of the finest such in the kingdom. Four galleries shelter goodies—Renaissance altarpieces in the first; French King Charles V's Italian-made Bible along with Gothic processional crosses and choir stalls in the second; exquisite altar cloths, prayer rails, candelabra, even a thousand-year-old papal bull on papyrus in the third; and best for the last: a massive eleventh-century tapestry whose fine multi-hued embroidery has as its theme *The Creation.*

Beyond, a walk through the core of the ancient area—*Paseo Arqueológico* it is called—leads to other destinations. *Baños Árabes*—Arab baths—is a three-pavilion complex, one each for hot, steamy, and tepid dunks, its origin twelfth century and the style more Romanesque than Moorish. The *Church of San Félix* is a Romanesque-Gothic meld, with its lure a cluster of brilliantly carved tombs in the apse. *Museo Arqueológico* occupies a somber desanctified church—it had been called San Pedro de Galligans—that is visitable for its high central nave alone. But there are exhibits—Roman remnants, medieval crucifixes, Renaissance sculptures—as well. And it is worth strolling through the *medieval Jewish Quarter*, recently re-created, as a consequence of archeologists' discoveries.

ALONG THE COAST

Costa Brava towns appear innumerable: Some are big, vertical, and with no special grace; others are smaller and barefoot; and even upon occasion, with vestiges of pretouristic pasts. In between, beaches are wedged into coves made to order for picnics-cum-sun and surf, and promenade points straddle craggy bluffs where you'll want to stop and seep in the scenery. Hope for sunshine. No area of Spain is more eye-filling when the atmosphere is clear and the light sharp. Still, this is northern Spain, and weather is not as reliable as on the Costa del Sol or Majorca, to the south.

BLANES, closest of the Costa Brava towns to Barcelona, tends in summer to be packed with vacationing city slickers, and is a case more of quantity than quality, with crowded beaches and, literally, slews of hotels in all categories. Still, there are touches of old—parts of castles, and charming churches like Esperanza and Santa María Antigua.

LLORET DE MAR is a case of Blanes multiplied, with several times as many hotels and correspondingly immense crowds. Stop, though, for a walk on the seaside promenade. Or try your luck in the casino at the edge of town.

TOSSA DE MAR: Another biggie. But pretty, especially when seen from its environs as one approaches. There are hotels—and hotel guests—unlimited, but there are charm spots in and about the worthy medieval quarter called *Villa Vella,* including a museum of historic artifacts and an adjacent gallery of contemporary artists' work.

SANT FELIÚ DE GUIXOLS—that is the Catalán-language spelling it prefers—likes to think of itself as the coast's "capital." It's a still-busy port, with the biggest permanent population, an agreeable setting easily appreciated from its coastal promenade, a superb Benedictine monastery-church complex, a respectably venerable core, in and about Plaza del Ayuntamiento, and a museum of local lore that's among the best on the coast.

S'AGARÓ is a quiet contemporary village, whose treats are a hotel than which none is more luxurious on the Costa Brava (see *Settling In*), and a nifty crescent of a beach.

PALAMÓS compensates with good shops and kicky discos for what it lacks in beauty, natural or otherwise.

CALELLA DE PALAFRUGELL—Calella to its friends—is smallish, with rocky walls enclosing a succession of intimately scaled beaches, and a nicely barefoot ambience, with a limited albeit choice range of hotels.

BAGUR, a bit inland, is perched atop a mini-mountain, surmounted by a picture-book castle. In ruins, to be sure, but worth one's acquaintance, if only for the coastal panoramas from its walls. The only link of the national chain of *paradores* on the Costa Brava (see *Settling In*) can be found nearby.

AMPURIAS: One pauses here to pay respects to its remarkable museum with exhibits, alfrésco and under shelter, of Greek and later Roman settlements. Range is original Doric columns to decorated pottery, with some exceptional sculpture.

CASTELLÓ DE AMPURIAS is inland from the unexceptional coastal town of Rosas. Do detour, if you would experience a small but sumptuous Gothic cathedral with a Romanesque tower, a richly detailed central portal, and a gorgeous central altar. The neighboring mercantile exchange, *La Lonja*, is still another Gothic reason for a visit.

FIGUERAS, also inland (and easily taken in as an extension of a Gerona visit) is principally for Salvador Dalí buffs. Which is not all of us. Still, this is where the painter was born, and its onetime theater has been transformed into a *Museo de Dalí*, with his works—very large to very small—hanging from its brick walls.

CADAQUÉS: I've saved my favorite Costa Brava town for last. It's an enchanting cluster of white-walled houses surmounted by the towering bulk of its parish church, the lot fronting a pretty bay. Bed down here, if you can.

SETTLING IN

Hotel Ultonia (Avenida Jaime 1, Gerona): Not many people stay overnight in Gerona. Still, there are worse places than this mellow old city. The Ultonia is No. 1 in town: a welcoming house with 45 pleasant rooms, most with private baths, and a central location. Breakfast only. I like. *First Class.*

Hotel Ruiz (Calle Flechas Azules 45, Blanes) is an unpretentious but acceptable setting for a halt in this teeming town, closest to Barcelona of the Costa Brava communities. Some 50 rooms, many with baths. *Cafetería,* bar. *Moderate.*

Hotel Cluamarsol (Paseo Mosen J. Verdaguer 2, Lloret de Mar) is my No. 1 choice in this busy resort. Location is the seafront promenade, within walking distance of everything. Nearly 90 nice rooms, convenient restaurant, bar. *Moderate.*

Hotel Metropol (Plaza de la Torre 2, Lloret de Mar) is another central Lloret house, on a square parallel with the seafront *paseo.* All 86 rooms have baths; restaurant. *Moderate.*

Hotel Reymar (Playa de Mar Menuda, Tossa de Mar) is a stunner of a mod-look pavilion on an idyllic beach at the edge of Tossa.

There are 130 attractive rooms, restaurant, bar-lounges, pool. *Luxury.*

Hotel Mar Menuda (Playa de Mar Menuda, Tossa de Mar) is a smaller, simpler neighbor to the Reymar (above), for the traveler who wants the beach on a budget. Restaurant. Forty rooms with bath. *Moderate.*

Hotel Reina Elisenda (Paseo del Guixols 8, Sant Feliú de Guixols) is a full-facility modern house smack on the seafront promenade, with 100 smart rooms, restaurant, bar-lounge, pool, and the beach across the street. *First Class.*

Hotel Les Noies (Rambla Portalet 10, Sant Feliú de Guixols) has nearly 50 rooms, many with baths, a restaurant, and a location that's central, just a bit inland from the seafront. *Moderate.*

Hostal de la Gavina (on the beach at S'Agaró) is the Costa Brava's homage to opulence. The marble lobbies are coolly elegant. The 75 suites and rooms are at once capacious, antiques-accented, and with knock-'em-dead baths. Top-floor rooms are the most charming. And the public spaces are lovely—lounges with coffered ceilings, lounges with paneled walls, a pair of top-class restaurants within (of which more later), buffet lunch at the pool-café, with the village's crescent-shaped beach just below. There are yachts for hire, tennis, and 18 holes of golf, to boot. Bring your classiest duds, and gents, remember: jacket and tie for dinner (the moneybags Spaniards, French, and Germans who mostly populate La Gavina like to dress up). Member Relais et Châteaux. *Luxury.*

Hotel Santa Marta (Playa de Santa Cristina, near Lloret de Mar) is a secluded, low-slung complex backed by green hills, fronted by a crescent of white sand, with 80 smart rooms and suites, an oblong of pool adjacent to the beach, and a top-class restaurant. Member Relais et Châteaux. *Luxury.*

Hotel Trias (Paseo del Mar, Palamós) is center-of-the-action in this lively town. There are a wide main beach, trendy boutiques, and a range of after-dark diversions. Eighty rooms, restaurant, bar, pool. *First Class.*

Parador Nacional de la Costa Brava (Aiguablava, near Bagur) is the sole link of the government-run Spain-wide chain of *paradores* on the Costa Brava. It's spectacularly situated on a cliff overlooking the rocky coves enclosing beaches way, way below. And it's spectacular-looking, as well: Spanish contemporary design in bold, broad strokes. There are 88 fine rooms, handsome lounges, excellent restaurant (of which more later), bar, pool, and access, of course, to the beaches below. *First Class.*

Hotel Aiguablava (on the beach at Aiguablava, near Bagur) offers a beachfront location to compensate for the views from the *parador*, almost overhead, that it lacks. There are 85 pleasant rooms, swimming pool, tennis, and a good restaurant. *First Class.*

Hotel Hostalillo (on the beach at Tamaríu, near Bagur) is in hilly terrain alongside the quiet waters of a pretty beach. There are 72 classy rooms-cum-views (of either the beach or the piney woods out front), nice restaurant, bar, and delightful owner-management. *First Class.*

Hotel Playa Sol (Playa Pianch, Cadaqués) is a wise choice, compensating with coziness for what it misses in elegance. There are 50 neat rooms, most with private facilities, restaurant, bar, pool, and a beach location. *First Class.*

DAILY BREAD

Jim's (Plaza Independencia, Gerona) is my favorite of the restaurants that line this busy downtown square. As good a place as any in town for fresh seafood, simply grilled. If you order the *menú del día, Moderate;* otherwise, *First Class.*

Casa Patacano (Paseo del Mar, Blanes) is a nicely central, up-a-flight spot for the freshest of the coast's fish. Order the white house wine with your meal. *Moderate.*

Hotel Cluamarsol Restaurante (Paseo Mosen J. Verdaguer 2, Lloret de Mar): The dining room of this seafront hotel is as agreeable a locale as any for a tasty meal, with the roasts and grills as good as the seafood. *First Class.*

Castell Vell (Plaza Roig y Soler 1, Tossa de Mar): Earlier on, I counsel a stroll through Tossa's ancient Villa Vella quarter. I hereby suggest staying on for lunch, or returning for dinner, at Castell Vell, which is quite as atmospheric as the quarter, with well-priced *menús del día. Moderate/First Class.*

Bahia (Paseo del Mar 18, San Feliu de Guixols) is center-of-the-action, with seafood its specialty. *First Class.*

La Cuineta (Calle Adriá Alvarez 111, Palamós) occupies a venerable house, antique-accented, with brass chandeliers hanging from a beamed ceiling. Fare is similar to the same management's restaurant in Barcelona (Chapter 4), albeit perhaps with more seafood emphasis. You want to try cod specialties, *bacalao con ali i oli* (with garlic and oil) especially. House pâtés are likewise good; ditto grilled steaks. *First Class.*

Hostal de la Gavina— the showplace hotel of the coast (above), overlooking the beach in S'Agaró—has two extraordinary restaurants, Villa d'Este for lunch (my favorite, with a buzzy crowd of locals as well as tourists), and Candlelight, more formal, for dinner. Go at either meal for seafood perfectly grilled and delicately sauced, excellent beef, and roast duck among the entrées, a lavish dessert trolley, a wine list unsurpassed in the area. Jacket and tie for dinner. Book in advance or take your chances. *Luxury.*

L'Art (Paseo del Mar 7, Palamós) offers an agreeable view while you lunch or dine, maritime specialties and others, and easy-to-take tabs. *Moderate.*

Don Quijote (Avenida Caridad Seriñana, Cadaqués): A restaurant so named has to have something going for it. Don Q's is its bright garden of a terrace, with tasty *menús del día*, and an agreeable house wine. *Moderate.*

INCIDENTAL INTELLIGENCE ════════════

Aeropuerto Gerona-Costa Brava is six miles from Gerona, and the region's only scheduled-service airport; the carrier is Iberia, domestically; although there are flights from the Continent, too. There are extensive rail connections between Costa Brava towns to others in Spain, and, via Port-Bou, with France and the Continent. Most visitors, though, are motorists come from Barcelona and other Spanish points, and, again via Port-Bou, from France and other European lands. *Further information:* Oficina de Turismo de Gerona, Calle Diudadanos 12; in the smaller Costa Brava towns, municipal tourist offices are invariably in the *Ayuntamiento*, or town hall. Inquire and you will be directed.

9

Costa de la Luz

Huelva
Cádiz
Jerez de la Frontera
Arcos de la Frontera
Algeciras and the Rock

BACKGROUND BRIEFING

Of course one can tarry longer. But this chunk of southwest Spain, from the Portuguese frontier eastwards along the short Spanish stretch of Atlantic to the Rock of Gibraltar, with incursions north into the hills, is comfortably navigated in the course of a few leisurely albeit well-planned days. Which is just the way I'll deal with it, beginning at its most westerly point.

ON SCENE

HUELVA

Not unlike similarly obscure Cáceres to the north (see the chapter on Extremadura), Huelva is small, venerable, and with remarkable New World associations. Unlike Cáceres, it is at once a sea and river port: on the Atlantic, and constituting the delta of not one but a pair of rivers—the Tinto and Odiel. A visit of Columbus to an influential Huelva monk paid off. The Genoan convinced Fray Juan Pérez of the potential in a westbound journey to the elusive Indies. The monk's aid opened doors to Columbus that resulted in audiences with Queen Isabella—and the fateful New World voyages. Columbus first set off from the up-river port of Palos de la Frontera. That town's *Church of San Jorge* is about all that remains from his time. A more worthwhile pilgrimage for New Worlders would be to the *Monastery of La Rábida*, just south of Huelva, where a monk will open up the modest *Museo de Colón*, with ancient documents relating to the travels of that trio of ships—therein reproduced in miniature—the *Niña, Pinta,* and *Santa María.* In Huelva proper, the principal Columbus-related monuments are an American-sculpted statue of the explorer and the *Monastery of the Virgin de la Cinta* (Paseo del Conquero), where Columbus is believed to have stayed. The square called La Placeta is lively, as are the cafés and restaurants of adjacent Gran Vía.

Huelva has still another claim to celebrity: beaches flanking it, both west (Portugal is but 30 miles distant) and going east. Indeed, these wide stretches of white sand give the Costa de la Luz—Coast of Light—its name. See what I mean by taking a swim and a sunbath at *Las Antillas,* just west of town, or if you're going on to Portugal, at the more westerly port of *Ayamonte,* preparatory to the ferry-crossing over the Guadiana River, to the neighboring country.

CÁDIZ

Cádiz, which in Spain is reputed to be the oldest city in the Western world, and as history-rich as any half-dozen others of the kingdom, comes through to today's visitors as Spain's Urban Disaster Area. Though with pockets of aesthetic worth and extraordinary beauty, it appears to be falling apart. For an ancient city to exude an ambience of mellowed age is highly desirable. To emerge as tacky—with care and maintenance at a minimum, if at all discernible in some areas—is something else again.

One wonders why. This is, after all, Spain's major Atlantic port. If it did nothing more than serve as point of departure for millions of bottles of sherry from nearby Jerez, one would believe it to be solvent enough to take better care of itself than appears to be the case.

And surely its economy does not suffer from the presence of the American naval base at neighboring Rota. Withal, its beachfront is the most appalling of any such in Spain (I recommend but one Cádiz hotel) and its historic core—possibly for want of the visitors it makes no attempt to lure—has seen far, far better days.

How very sad. If it is not a Seville or a Granada, Cádiz is at least as linked with Spain's greatness as, say, Valencia or Valladolid. The world coveted the promontory it occupies—extending finger-like into the Atlantic—as long ago as eleven hundred years before Christ, when Phoenicians settled in. Half a millennium later, Carthaginians, coming through the Strait of Gibraltar, took over only to yield to Romans after two centuries, with Barbarians, Visigoths, and Moors following in succession.

Castile's Alfonso X reconquered Cádiz for the Christians in the thirteenth century. But it was in the fifteenth, during the event-packed reign of Ferdinand and Isabella, that Cádiz came into its own. Columbus set sail from its harbor on his second voyage, and Cádiz became the principal Spanish port for the fabulous trade with the colonies of Spanish America.

History books are filled with Cádiz battles—Sir Francis Drake's 1587 burning of the fleet in its harbor, and the Earl of Essex's 1596 attack are but two. Decline set in after Spain bowed out of the New World, but not, one would have hoped, to the present extent. Withal, a full day in Cádiz is not overlong for the curious explorer. Swimming is skippable. Forget the grim sands and even grimmer hotels of Playa Victoria. Concentrate on a bit of exploration.

Cathedral (Plaza Pius XII): Spain's only all-baroque cathedral is a massive and magnificent pile, with a twin-towered façade that's the city's trademark, and a dazzling interior, with towering Corinthian columns supporting a long, high nave. An attendant will open the Cathedral's usually dark museum, to show off its treasures; monstrances of gold and silver, uncelebrated albeit lovely paintings, crosses of ivory, sculptures in marble, vestments of centuries-old silk. Neighboring *Church of Santa Cruz* is a onetime mosque; pop in to see its magnificent vaulting.

Museo de Bellas Artes (Plaza Generalísimo Franco) occupies a handsome, if crumbling, mansion out of the last century, keeps minimal hours, and has a dozen galleries of paintings. The ones you want most to see are the score by Zurbarán, about half of which are striking elongated portraits of saints. Next-door *Museo Arqueológico*, with souvenirs of Phoenician, Carthaginian, and Roman Cádiz, though not uninteresting, is skippable, if your schedule is tight.

Hospital de Nuestra Señora del Carmen (Calle Rosana Cepeda) is a gracious baroque complex, no longer serving its original function, but often open to visitors, the better to see its pretty patio and a chapel filled with good art, not the least of which is El Greco's *Ecstasy of St. Francis*.

Church of Santa Catalina (Avenida Primo de Rivera), more properly the chapel of a onetime baroque monastery now serving as a mental hospital, is art-rich and pilgrimage-worthy. The high-altar portrait of Santa Catalina, painted by the seventeenth-century Sevillian Murillo, proved to be his last. He died after falling from a scaffolding over this church's altar while completing it.

Church of Santa Cueva (Calle del Rosario) is actually a pair of churches, more properly chapels, in the elegant neoclassic style of the eighteenth century. Head for the elliptical upper chapel, framed by Ionic columns, its surprise a trio of paintings, including an extraordinary *Last Supper* with the diners taking their meal in a reclining position. The painter: Goya.

JEREZ DE LA FRONTERA

The mileage difference is under twenty miles. But, while Cádiz bespeaks hard times, Jerez de la Frontera—with its lavish mansions, treasure-filled churches, garden-centered plazas—reflects the wealth that has come to it from sherry. Thank the English. Their peaceful albeit aggressively commercial invasion of this area in the eighteenth century saw the start of substantial production of grapes, and the distinctive wine made from them. Sherry—the English bastardization of what Spaniards pronounce as *hereth*—is copied (most notably in California), but the genuine article remains prized the world over and inimitable anywhere.

What one first notices in Jerez—aside from its good looks and good housekeeping—is the prevalence of whitewashed, warehouse-like repositories of aging wine called *bodegas*. They fly the colors of a score-plus producers, many still with the names of the British founders: Harvey, Garvey, Osborne, Sandeman, and William & Humbert among them: others distinctively Spanish, like González Byass, Diez Hermanos, Zoilo, Ruiz-Mateos, and—last but hardly least—Pedro Domecq. This last name—Domecq—is one you will have heard about (its La Ina sherry is popular in North America). And one you will notice all over Jerez. The firm maintains more than 150 *bodegas* in and around town, grows grapes on some 7,000 surrounding acres, raises Arabian horses, cattle, and bulls for fighting on nine ranches, with additional vineyards for table wine in the Rioja country of the north, not to mention subsidiaries in Latin America. There are estimated to be well over 400 members of the family locally, with a small nucleus in command of the business.

VIPs—society-page personalities, wine press, the liquor fraternity—are frequent guests in Domecq family residences or palatial guest houses, especially during the two annual Jerez fairs, one devoted to the region's celebrated horses (in April), the other to harvest its wine (in September). Ordinary souls like ourselves do well to avoid Jerez at those crowded times. During the rest of the year, though, this is a pleasant town for a brief visit.

All of the wine houses regularly open their *bodegas* to visitors, but of the lot it's the Domecq operation, which has the lion's share of the business and is the most star-studded, that is perhaps the most fun to inspect. Domecq's historic El Molina *bodega* is the most noteworthy, with casks on view signed by visitors ranging from the Duke of Wellington to Caroline Kennedy. Address: Calle San Ildefonso 3. All of the other houses welcome visitors, too. Still other interesting *bodegas*: Sandeman (Calle Pizarro 10) and González Byass (Calle José Luis Diez 250). And you'll be given tastes. (Worth remembering, if you aren't a sherry buff already: the four major species are *fino*—pale, crisp, dry, in Spain drunk chilled; fuller-bodied albeit still dry *amontillado*; *oloroso*, medium-sweet; and *dulce*, no-nonsense dessert-sweet.)

Your *bodega* visit behind you, consider other aspects of Jerez. Its Collegiate Church—*Iglesia Colegiata* (Plaza Encarnación)—is a baroque refurbishing of a much older mosque, with an unusual painting of the Virgin as a red-robed child by Zurbarán. *Museo Arqueológico* and *Museo Municipal* share a Renaissance-era palace with the town library on pretty Plaza Asunción, also the site of the fifteenth-century *Church of San Dionisio*, where the lures are Mudéjar architecture and a dazzler of a baroque altar. The *Church of San Miguel* (Calle León XIII) is one of Isabelline-Gothic splendor, with masterful altarpieces of later eras. The twisted columns forming the massive and gilded baroque altar of the Gothic-origin *Church of Santo Domingo* (Alameda Marqués de Domecq) create a spectacular effect. And outside of town, en route to Cádiz, is the *Cartuja de Santa María de la Defensión*, a onetime monastery with an intricate Plateresque façade and a serene Gothic cloister.

ARCOS DE LA FRONTERA

Arcos de la Frontera is a town, perched like an eagle's nest atop a craggy mountain, some 20 miles inland from Jerez. One goes to Arcos principally to lunch, dine, and/or bed down in its *parador* (about which more later), to stroll its narrow streets, peeking into the multi-epoch handsomeness of its *Church of Santa María de la Asunción*, to admire the Mudéjar ceiling of its *Ayuntamiento*, or town hall, to photograph the crenellated walls of its medieval castle, or, most of all, to take in the panorama of the vast and verdant valley, way, way below.

ALGECIRAS

The point of Algeciras—and its bay—is Gibraltar: the classic silhouette of its Rock, and its strategic Strait, a deceptively innocuous-appearing eight-mile-wide channel that links the Mediterranean with the Atlantic and has, as a consequence, been battled over these many centuries by Europeans from its north shore and Arabs from its close-by southern flank.

Indeed, it was Arabs who gave Algeciras its name. Like the rest of Spain, it became Christian and Spanish with the medieval reconquest. And from the time the British gained control of

Gibraltar in the eighteenth century, operating it as a crown colony, Algeciras became a mainland appurtenance of the Rock, with a peculiarly Spanish-British flavor, and close Algeciras-Gibraltar contacts, as exemplified by both a causeway and a ferry connecting the two points. Long-smoldering Spanish resentment of the British presence on Gibraltar resulted in cessation of ferry service and closure of the land frontier from the late 1960s through the mid-1980s, when Gibraltar once again became accessible from Spain.

A brief layover in Algeciras to view the splendid Rock is not wasted time. Any American of a certain age who has grown up looking at Prudential Life Insurance Company ads—"Strong as the Rock of Gibraltar"—knows its profile: almost 1,400 feet at its highest point, with an area of but two square miles, and a situation smack in the center of the channel of the strait bearing its name, through which all shipping between the Mediterranean and the Atlantic must pass.

Hop over to Gibraltar—from *La Línea de la Concepción*, point of entry to the road connecting The Rock with the mainland—for lunch at the colonial-style *Rock Hotel, Holiday Inn,* or *Da Paolo* at Marina Bay; a beer in one of the many British-style pubs; a visit with the long-on-the-scene Barbary apes in their rocky zoo-like home; a stroll along shop-lined Main Street, and to destinations—a Catholic church, especially, converted from an ancient mosque—that reflect Gibraltar's Spanish and Moorish centuries. And don't forget your passport; you're leaving Spain for a British colony.

SETTLING IN

Hotel Luz Huelva (Avenida Sundheim 26, Huelva) is Huelva's Número Uno: a 100-room house that would be even nicer if it had a restaurant. Breakfast only. *First Class.*

Hotel Tartessos (Avenida Martín Alonso Pinzón 13, Huelva) is neither as big nor as glossy as the Luz Huelva (above), nor does it have a dining room. But all 119 rooms have baths. *Moderate.*

Hotel Atlántico (Calle Duque de Najerava 22, Cádiz) is the only Cádiz hotel I recommend. It's pleasantly situated at the edge of

Parque Genovés, near the sea, albeit a good distance from the historic center. There are 170 rooms with bath, lounge, restaurant and bar. Affiliated with the Paradores de España chain. *First Class.*

Hotel Jerez (Avenida Alcalde Alvaro Domecq 41, Jerez de la Frontera) is Jerez putting its poshest foot forward: a contemporary house of considerable panache, with 120 sleekly handsome rooms and suites, a restaurant whose staff knows what food, service—and, it should go without saying, wines—are all about, a snug bar-lounge, and a palm-dotted garden in which is situated a king-size swimming pool. This is where the sherry barons put up their guests when there's no room at the family *palacio*. A link of Italy's crack Ciga Hotels chain, whose hotels include Venice's legendary Gritti Palace and Seville's Alfonso XIII. *Luxury.*

Hotel Capele (Calle Corredera 58, Jerez de la Frontera) is No. 2 in Jerez. Tiny lobby with bar-lounge, 30 adequate rooms, many with baths and shower. Central. *Moderate.*

Parador Nacional Casa del Corregidor (Plaza de España, Arcos de la Frontera): A score of rooms-cum-white tile baths in handsome Renaissance style and balconies overlooking the farms and hamlets of a vast valley are the pluses of this gorgeously situated contemporary link of the nationwide *parador* chain. The restaurant (about which more later) and bar, like the rooms, are in traditional style, although the inn is modern. *First Class.*

Hotel Reina Cristina (Paseo de la Conferencia, Algeciras)—set in its own lush garden-cum-pool, at water's edge, in full view of the Rock—remains impeccably old-school in all 135 rooms and suites and public spaces, too; these include both restaurant and cocktail lounge. Attractive. A Trusthouse Forte hotel. *Luxury.*

Hotel Octavio (Calle San Bernardo 1, Algeciras) has the appearance from without of an unprepossessing modern house. Within, there are 80 good-looking rooms and suites, an inviting lobby with bar, one of the best in-town restaurants, and an enviable location a step or two from the boat terminal and train station. *First Class.*

Hotel Alarde (Calle Alfonso XI, Algeciras) is a modest house worth knowing about if you would overnight in Algeciras, perhaps to make a boat connection to North Africa. Close to 70 rooms with bath. Breakfast only. *Moderate.*

DAILY BREAD
Otra Doñana (Avenida Martín Alonso Pinzón 613, Huelva) is a down-the-street neighbor of Hotel Tartessos (above), which operates it. Order fish fresh from the sea, prepared as you like it. *First Class.*

Mariama (Calle Pedro Laraña 2, Huelva) is a satisfactory spot for a seafood lunch or dinner. *Moderate.*

El Faro (Calle San Felix 15, at Avenida Venezuela, Cádiz) is but a block from the sea, within walking distance of Hotel Atlántico (above). Ask for a just-caught fish and specify *pescaito frito*—fried, Cádiz-style. *First Class.*

El Anteojo (Alameda de Apodaca 22, Cádiz) is heart-of-town and thus convenient for a lunch pause in the course of a day's poking about. Caveat: no credit cards. *First Class.*

El Bosque (Avenida Alcalde Alvaro Domecq 26, Jerez de la Frontera) is a near-neighbor (you can walk it) of Hotel Jerez, in a handsome house of its own, garden-encircled. The range is paella to *pesce*. And served with style. Extensive wine card. *Luxury.*

Gaitán (Calle Gaitán 3, Jerez de la Frontera) is away from the center, but exemplary, nonetheless, for its seafood: crab soup and braised squid, to name two dishes. Grills and roasts, as well. You had better start with a *fino* sherry, and end, here in this city of sherry, with a *dulce*, post-dessert. *First Class.*

Hotel Jerez Restaurante (Avenida Alcalde Alvaro Domecq 41, Jerez de la Frontera) is coolly contemporary, continental, albeit

Spanish-accented. And with an extraordinary selection of sherries. *Luxury.*

San Francisco (Plaza Esteve 2, Jerez de la Frontera) is at once central—convenient in the course of sightseeing—and inexpensive, with both *cafetería* and *comedor. Moderate.*

Parador Nacional Casa del Corregidor Restaurante (Plaza de España, Arcos de la Frontera) is for lunch with a panoramic view (see above). As in every *parador,* you do well to start your midday meal with the score-plus varieties of *entremeses;* the rest of the meal will be anticlimactic, but not at all bad. Well-priced wines. *First Class.*

Mesón de la Molinera is a combination restaurant-motel (there are a score of bungalows and a pool on the grounds) at the edge of the artificial lake some four miles east of Arcos de la Frontera. *Moderate.*

Cazuela (Calle Castelar 59, Algeciras) is a find: Seafood, Basque-style, is the specialty. Traditional decor. *Moderate.*

Iris (Hotel Octavio, Calle San Bernardo 1, Algeciras) is up a flight, with its own entrance. Substantial fare, fair tabs. *Moderate/First Class.*

INCIDENTAL INTELLIGENCE

Further information: Oficina de Turismo de Huelva, Calle Plus Ultra 10; Oficina de Turismo de Jerez de la Frontera, Alameda Cristina; Oficina de Turismo de Cádiz, Calle Calderón de la Barca 1; Oficina de Turismo de Algeciras, Avenida de la Marina.

10

Costa del Sol

Málaga
Marbella
Ronda
Torremolinos

BACKGROUND BRIEFING
It lacks the spontaneous charm of Italy's Riviera. It is no match either for the Gallic insouciance of France's Côte d'Azur. It has not quite achieved the relaxed approach toward outlanders of its major Spanish competition, Majorca. And, because it has to a great extent allowed uncontrolled development along its shore, more's the pity, you could never call it beautiful. Still, its beaches are wide and white-sand, its hotels run a wide gamut of luxury, its towns are interesting, it is easy of air access from distant points, and, in contrast to the Costa Brava up north, the southern Costa del Sol is of infinitely less geographic complexity.

And when one considers that the bulk of its clients are packaged ciphers, flown in almost in one fell swoop from the beds of their Northern European homes to those of Spanish Mediterranean hotels, this region deserves more credit than it is sometimes accorded. It knows how to handle crowds.

And it had just better. For in the hundreds of hotels and guest houses—luxury to pension—that line the 240-mile Andalusian coast from the cathedral city of Almería in the west, east to the Rock of Gibraltar, there are a solid quarter-million beds. How to sort it all out for the relatively short-term transatlantic visitor? This way: Concentrate on what might be termed the Málaga Stretch, which hits the highlights in the course of less than a third of the total coastal mileage, beginning with the extraordinary caves in the cliff town of Nerja (they rival those of Majorca and the Canarian Island of Lanzarote), some 30 miles east of the metropolis of Málaga (with the region's international airport), and concluding at quiet Manilva, not quite 60 miles to its west.

MÁLAGA

Left to its own devices, this is a city that can stand by itself, touristically. And did, in the bad old days—a couple of decades back before the resorts of the Costa del Sol superseded it. Travelers of a certain age remember when Málaga was the subject of a proper visit, as one would journey today to, say, Seville or Valencia. What happens, contemporarily, is that its inspectors are pretty much day-trippers, with just enough curiosity to rouse themselves from beaches up or down the coast.

Well, half a shake is better than none. This is, after all, Spain's seventh largest urban center (population hovers at half a million), at once ancient (Phoenicians, Carthaginians, Romans, Visigoths, Arabs, conquering Christians, including Ferdinand and Isabella, followed one after the other), and beautifully sited with a rugged range—Montes de Málaga—as a backdrop, a natural Mediterranean harbor out front, and not a few destinations of consequence.

Málaga has a relatively compact, easy-to-negotiate core. Both the train and bus stations—where excursionists from coastal points arrive—are fairly central. Calle Larios is the city's lively Main Street, while the landmark spire of the Cathedral is almost adjacent to Plaza del General Queipo de Llano. Look south and the harbor spreads before you, boulevard-like Paseo Marítimo flanking it, in an eastward direction, with still other monuments, the Alcazaba and Castillo de Gibralfaro on verdant heights, due north.

Cathedral and Museo Diocesano (Plaza Obispo): If the Renaissance-baroque Cathedral is not of the top Spanish rank, along with, say, Seville and Burgos or even León, it deserves considerably more than once-over-lightly attention. Its proportions are almost startlingly generous, and you are not going to forget the magnificent rows of soaring Corinthian columns that support the central nave. Nor will you, for that matter, be unimpressed with the choir that, as is the rule in Spanish cathedrals, blocks the high altar from the entrance. Its carved-wood stalls—some two score of saints created by ranking sculptor Pedro de Mena in the sixteenth century—are all-Spain standouts. So are de Mena's statues of Ferdinand and Isabella in the chapel called *Nuestra Señora de los Reyes Católicos*. Next door, in the *Palacio Episcopal*, one passes by a fountain-centered patio through to the upstairs *Museo Diocesano*, whose lures are ecclesiastic treasures from over the centuries—altars, tapestries, paintings, prints—in a felicitous baroque setting, not unworthy of the bishops of Málaga, whose seat it has been these several centuries.

Church of the Sagrario (Calle Cistero) is a next-door neighbor to the cathedral, and—originally a mosque—much its senior in age. Ferdinand and Isabella converted it in the fifteenth century, and its façade—the elaborate Gothic style called Isabelline, after the queen—is quite as striking as the high altar within, a century newer, and with more than two dozen biblical scenes carved into its gilded panels.

Museo Provincial de Bellas Artes (Calle San Agustín 6): A sleeper, this. Shame on the Malagueños for not blowing their museum's horn. This is one of the best city art repositories in the kingdom. Setting is an elegant Renaissance palace, with two floors of galleries encircling a tiled patio, set off by masses of potted scarlet geraniums. Head first for the Picasso rooms. Though more associated with Barcelona, Picasso was Málaga-born (the year was 1881), and before he set off for the bigger city he had begun drawing and painting. Have a look at these early, early Picassos: his very first oil, of an elderly seated couple, *Los Viejos*, as well as drawings and graphics, and an American import—a catalog of a 1949 Picasso show at Princeton University, with the master's autograph. Work backward, then, to paintings by baroque Spanish masters like Murillo, Zurbarán, and Ribera, sculpture by the same de Mena whose work you'll have seen in Málaga Cathedral and elsewhere in Spain, and as a bonus, galleries—one of which is an intact chapel-cum-altar—filled with splendid furniture and art objects of the seventeenth to nineteen centuries, all Spanish.

Alcazaba/Museo Arqueológico (Calle Alcazabilla): Originally Roman, later Moorish and Christian, this complex, restored in recent decades with style and charm, is an extraordinary maze of gardened patios and exquisitely embellished pavilions, doubling as Málaga's Archeological Museum—as if the architecture and horticulture were not in themselves treats enough. Apart from a still-used Roman theater, there are souvenirs, throughout, of Roman, Islamic, and early Christian Málaga. Special.

Castillo Gibralfaro (Parque Gibralfaro) is the Alcazaba's next-door neighbor (they once were linked by a covered walkway) and is today more a jumble of partially restored Moorish ruins—battlements, walls, gates, a mosque—than a storybook castle. Views of the city and the sea below are ravishing, and a *parador* of the national inns chain (about which more later) is on the premises.

Museo Mesón de la Victoria (Pasillo de Santa Isabel 10) is a baroque mansion with a worthy contemporary mission: it is Málaga's museum of the decorative arts, its rooms authentically furnished and accessorized to convey the lifestyles of affluent Malagueños in past centuries. Very attractive.

Church of Santiago (Plaza de la Merced): See its strong square tower, and the half-millennium-old interior, in which Picasso was baptized. Not far northwest of the Cathedral.

Church of Nuestra Señora de la Victoria (Calle de San Patricio) is in the northeast corner of town, too far from the center to be walkable, but eminently visitable. Reasons are a fifteenth-century Flemish Madonna—the city's patron saint—reposing in its own baroque chapel (note the ceiling) and a pair of luminous Pedro de Mena sculptures.

MARBELLA AND PUERTO BANÚS

Lowest-key and most stylish of the coastal resort towns, Marbella is also the most expensive, a good 25 percent more, on the average, locals tell you, than, say, Torremolinos, the other Costa del Sol resort that draws Americans in quantity.

Aside from costing more than Torremolinos—which is right next door to Málaga and its international airport—Marbella is farther away from the big city, some 35 miles along the highway. Which is hardly to say it is neither appealing nor attractive. Increased costs mean a degree of exclusivity—and fewer crowds. Additionally, there is the look of the place to be considered: Marbella is handsome.

Paseo Marítimo flanks the sea, running the length of the town, with a series of wide white-sand beaches between it and the Mediterranean. The core is a mix of whitewashed houses, set off by black wrought-iron grilles on their windows, flanking narrow streets that are punctuated by fountain-centered, geranium-accented, shop-and-café-lined plazas.

The main square, Plaza de los Naranjos, is so named because of orange trees on its fringes, one of which is occupied by the rambling white stucco *Ayuntamiento*, or town hall. The slim tower of a neighboring baroque church is as much a landmark as the Ayuntamiento. It's fun to walk the main street, Calle Ramón y Cajal, deviating from it to smaller, smarter thoroughfares like Calle San Juan de Dios and Calle González-Badia, pausing in the plazas—Plaza José Palomo, say, or Plaza Coronel Borbón—for coffee or a sherry. Downtown Marbella is essentially for daytime exploration (although its cafés and restaurants attract evening clients). After dark, though, one wants to visit *Puerto Banús*, an away-from-the-center yacht harbor around which are clustered the coast's smartest casino (roulette and blackjack) and the region's kickiest discos, not to mention considerable shops (not a few of them trendy) and a host of attractive restaurants; some are later recommended.

RONDA

Villages like Coín and Mijas, each a few miles up in the hills between Marbella and Torremolinos, and Casares, a little inland, from Marbella and to the west, make for agreeable short excursions from the coast. Still—and I mean no disrespect—they are small potatoes in contrast to Ronda, a proper mini-city (there are about 30,000 Rondeños) some 60 miles from Málaga. Ronda has two principal attributes: great age and top-of-the-world setting, some 2,400 feet up in the mountains, straddling a plain, with an eighteenth-century bridge connecting its component parts. These are separated by a dramatic *tajo*, or ravine, whose edge is flanked by a group of so-called hanging houses—not unlike counterparts in Cuenca, which I call to you attention in the chapter on that city to the northeast. Puente Nuevo, the bridge over the ravine—with the Guadelevin gorge way, way below—separates new Ronda from old. The modern sector, Mercadillo, is mostly uninteresting, save for the small antique bullring, where local *matadors* of a family called Romero are credited with having created the still-observed procedures for classical bullfighting. The *Plaza de Toros* excepted (it's open all day for inspection), it's the old town that most beckons. This is a city whose sum is greater than the individual parts. Simply walking the hilly streets, lined by sturdy stone palaces and churches, pausing in the little squares or atop the hills, is tonic in and of itself. Still, there are also specific destinations, which I call to your attention.

Church of Santa María la Mayor (Plaza de la Duquesa de Parcent), often called Ronda's Cathedral, is not the seat of a bishop. It is, however, a beautiful church built over the remains of a mosque, melding Gothic and Renaissance with baroque, this last in the form of a spectacular high altar.

Palacio Mondragón (Calle Sor Angela de la Cruz) is a onetime royal residence (Ferdinand and Isabella were among its occupants) dating back six centuries, with an arresting patio and state rooms finely detailed in Mudéjar style.

Baños Árabes (Puente Árabe) is a Moorish bathhouse alongside a Moorish-built bridge over the Guadelevin, inland from the gorge. The baths are not unlike counterparts throughout Spain, with a trio of rooms, each for water at a differing temperature: cool, tepid, and hot.

Convento de San Francisco (Calle de San Francisco, on the approach to the road to Algeciras) is another gift of the Catholic
kings; Ferdinand and Isabella ordered it built. Its intricate
Isabelline-Gothic façade complements the austerity of the high-
walled fortress-like (and neighboring) *Church of Espíritu Santo,*
which King Ferdinand commissioned to rise on the ruins of the
Moorish battlement; it was completed in 1505, the year after his
wife Isabella died.

TORREMOLINOS

The point about Torremolinos is that it works. No major world
resort that I know of—and Torremolinos is indeed a world
resort—has been subjected to more derision. Honky-tonk.
Tacky. And most inaccurate epithet of all—especially by Europeans who have never been near Florida—Miami Beach. What critics decry is overbuilding. When I first visited Torremolinos a
quarter-century back, it was a fishing village whose hotels could
be counted on the fingers of one hand. I went home and reported
with enthusiasm, in the *New York Times,* and so I am probably as
much at fault as any of the early *aficionados,* who not only told
their friends but, if they were writers like me, told their readers.
Well, a couple of old mill towers from which the town takes its
name have been retained for the historians. (I have yet to meet a
vacationer who is aware of them.) But today's Torremolinos is a
giant dormitory, catering in large part to groups of northern Europeans, flown south on giant charters to Málaga International
Airport a few miles down the road, and whisked to their hotels,
the better to seep in a fortnight of sun, with interjections of disco,
golf, or tennis, and the occasional excursion—to Málaga, say, or
Ronda—for spice.

It works very well. The airport takes the wide-bodies that
come nonstop, not only from northern Europe but from the
United States and Spanish urban centers such as Madrid. The
hotels are close by, enough of them are big and well enough
equipped to accommodate groups efficiently and comfortably,
and they are operated by professionals, mostly with high standards. Smart-setters will prefer Marbella. Gourmets will want
Monte Carlo or Cannes or the Italian Riviera. (Not that one does

much better in France or Italy than in the unpretentious, simple seafood restaurants lining Torremolinos's Paseo Marítimo in the *barrio* of La Carihuela.)

Historic monuments? Cultural attractions? Forget it. Orientation in this town is on the basis of one's hotel and its relation to the shops, cafés, and discos of central, pedestrians-only Calle San Miguel, adjacent Plazas de Andalusia and Costa del Sol, and ancillary thoroughfares leading to waterfront Paseo Marítimo, and to the two-section beach. A rocky headland separates Playa de la Carihuela, with its half-a-hundred-plus fish restaurants, from Playa del Bajondillo, which has nary an eatery for its entire stretch.

Torremolinos spills over into Málaga, a few miles to its west. By the same token, it's hard to tell where it ends on the east, and where the adjacent resort town of Benalmádena begins; later on, I include descriptions of a sprinkling of better Benalmádena hotels with those of Torremolinos.

SETTLING IN

MÁLAGA

Hotel Málaga Palacio (Avenida Cotina del Muelle 1): If you're without wheels and want to explore Málaga on foot, or if your mission is business, this is your hotel. It's Número Uno, central, 15 stories high, with 225 well-equipped rooms, from many of which there are views of the core of town and the harbor. The lobby is big, dotted with red-leather chairs that you sink into, and there's a bar-lounge. There's a pool with sundeck up on the roof and a *cafetería* (that takes the place of a proper restaurant) on the second floor. *First Class.*

Parador Nacional de Gibralfaro (Parque Gibralfaro): You're away from the center if you stay here, with the disadvantage of being detached from town, but with compensations—gorgeous views of the city and the sea, accommodations in one of a dozen eminently comfortable rooms—in this contemporary but traditional-style stone house on the Castillo de Gibralfaro grounds. Of the kingdom-wide, government-operated chain of *paradores*, this is one of my favorites. It has a bar-lounge and a restaurant that's one of the best on the coast (about which more later), with an adjacent terrace. *First Class.*

Hotel Casa Curro (Calle Sancha de Lara 9) has as its chief attribute a location quite as central as the Málaga Palacio (above). There is not a great deal else to recommend this place, other than to say its 90 rooms all have baths; breakfast only. *Moderate.*

Hotel Niza (Calle Larios 2) is smack on Málaga's main shopping street. Half a hundred functional rooms, many with private baths; restaurant. *Moderate.*

MARBELLA

Marbella Club (Carretera de Cádiz) embraces a score of two-story bungalows—suites, twins, and singles—that lie between a main pavilion-cum-terrace and a brilliant garden, ending at the white sands of the Mediterranean. It's that simple. Decor is understated albeit luxurious, with lots of space in white-walled, pastel-upholstered bedrooms with chaise-longue-equipped terraces for sunning and breakfasts. One of two pools edges the beach. There are, as well, a classy disco, tennis and sauna, card room and beauty salon, a convivial bar-lounge, and an exemplary restaurant that moves outdoors for warm-weather buffet lunches, evaluated on a later page. Clientele is modishly multinational, multilingual, moneyed. Member, Leading Hotels of the World and Relais et Châteaux. *Luxury.*

Hotel Puente Romano (Carretera de Cádiz) is a veritable Spanish village, traditional-style, reproduced with all the trappings of luxury—240 rooms and suites, trio of restaurants, quartet of bars, pair of pools, beach club, disco, 11 tennis courts, and an especially skilled and cordial concierge staff. The Marbella Club (above) is a near-neighbor, and shares the same ownership, although the hotels are separately managed, each with its own personality. Member, Leading Hotels of the World. *Luxury.*

Hotel Los Monteros (Carretera de Málaga) occupies a verdant park, climbing up from the Mediterranean shore, with a flock of spindly legged, pink-feathered flamingos possibly its most endearing residents. There is a tallish main pavilion in which smartly decorated spaces cater to diners, drinkers, dancers, and loungers, with low-slung wings that extend around the pool-centered garden. There are close to 170 rooms and they range from oversized twins to duplex suites; all are terraced. An à la carte restaurant—El Corzo—is worthy of later comment. There are, as well, a vast principal dining room, the garden café, and places to eat at the beach (a short drive distant and with one of the coast's finest buffet lunches) and at the clubhouse of the sporty 18-hole golf course that Los Monteros shares with a sister-hotel; and no less than 10 tennis courts. Distinguished Hotels/Robert F. Warner. *Luxury.*

Hotel Incosol (Carretera de Málaga). Your health: That's the thrust of this 10-story tower, inland from the sea and not far from the same management's Los Monteros (above). There's an entire wing devoted to physiotherapy: saunas and baths. Go for a general check-up, for geriatric treatment, for weight loss. Or simply to unwind. There are indoor and outdoor pools, the adjacent 18-hole Los Monteros golf course, restaurant, bar-lounge, and a disco. Distinguished Hotels/Robert F. Warner. *Luxury.*

Hotel Meliá Don Pepe (Carretera de Cádiz): Meliá in Marbella is a pleasure. The Spain-wide chain's 220-room hotel here is well-located, a short walk from Marbella town, but still beachfront. This is a beautifully operated house. Bellmen wear white gloves. The tapestry-walled lobby is welcoming, the bedrooms tastefully traditional and terraced. There are a pair of restaurants, a trio of bars, as many circular pools in the garden leading to the beach. *Luxury.*

Hotel Don Carlos (Carretera de Málaga): I admit to a soft spot for this one: I covered its press opening—as the Marbella Hilton—a decade or so back. Now with its own name and management for several seasons, it remains distinguished. Public spaces—in which to dine and drink and dance—are mostly in the tall main tower, with 240 rooms there, and in auxiliary wings fronting a pool-equipped garden backing the beach. Hilton International may have departed, but a contented, heavily American clientele lingers on. *Luxury.*

Hotel El Fuerte (Castillo de San Luis) has the advantage of a location at once central and beachfront; you swim from the sands or in the hotel's own big pool. This is a modern house with 146 full-facility rooms (specify sea or mountain view), lots of lounge space, restaurant and bar. *First Class.*

Hotel Las Fuentes del Rodeo (Carretera de Cádiz) is agreeably Andalusian-style, with a hundred-plus tile-floored rooms with terraces, pair of pools in the garden, dining room, bar and—perhaps best for last—a location just next-door to Puerto Banús, so that you easily hop over to that complex's restaurants and shops. *Moderate.*

Hotel Andalucía Plaza (Urbanizacion Nueva Andalucía) is a biggie (there are 418 rooms and suites) that, not surprisingly—given its room capacity—specializes in groups. Although the suite I inspected was good-sized, those of the rooms I have seen (you want to insist on a recently refurbished one) are very small but with okay baths. The lobby, on the other hand, is ballroom-size, the main restaurant is attractive, a tunnel leads under the road to a pair of pools, one covered, the other alfresco; and the area's casino (see *Incidental Intelligence*, below) is on-premises, albeit with its own entrance. *First Class.*

Hotel El Rodeo (Calle Victor de la Serna 1) is, name notwithstanding, as far removed from Texas as Marbella can be. This is a good-value, in-town house with a rambling lobby and a rooftop pool-sundeck, where a sign in English makes this request: "We beg guests don't go down without a well-dry." Rooms, all with terrace and bath, have but one drawback: thin mattresses. Restaurant, bar-café. *Moderate.*

Hotel San Cristóbal (Calle Ramón y Cajal) is heart-of-town and a brief stroll from the sands. The lobby is unmemorable, but the rest of the hotel pleases, with 100 mostly terraced, attractively decorated rooms, all with baths, some with super views. Bar. Breakfast only. *Moderate.*

Hotel Lima (Avenida Antonio Belon 2) is a charming, smaller downtown house. The lobby-lounge could be a residential living room. The bedrooms are good-sized, good-looking, with baths and terraces. And the beach is three minutes distant. Breakfast only. *Moderate.*

Hotel Byblos Andaluz (near the village of Mijas, inland from Fuengirola, just east of Marbella) is a Costa del Sol stunner that straddles its own two, Robert Trent Jones–designed 18-hole golf courses, amidst a complex comprising a pair of oversized outdoor swimming pools, five tennis courts, and a spa—offering both weight-reduction and medical programs and with its own trio of indoor pools. French roots notwithstanding (I first met General Manager Pierre Aron when he was with Paris's lovely Bristol Hotel, and I recommend St. Tropez's Byblos Hotel in *France At Its Best*), the look of the Byblos Andaluz, especially in public spaces, is Andalusian, a delightful mix of arched patios and tiled fountains. Those of the 135 suites and rooms I have inspected (80 are exceptionally capacious mini-suites) embrace a mix of four decor schemes and feature superb baths. I evaluate Le Nailhac Restaurant on a later page; the other eatery, El Andaluz, serves a fabulous buffet lunch, as well as Andalusian specialties and a diet menu for spa guests. *Luxury.*

Hotel Mijas (Urbanización Tamisa, Mijas): You've got to be willing to sacrifice being on the beach for an absolutely idyllic setting with views, high up, in one of the region's classically handsome mountain towns. Mijas in and of itself—white-walled houses, baroque church, oddball square bullring, trendy shops—is diverting. Traditional-style Hotel Mijas is diverting. Its garden pool and terraces of many rooms overlook a broad green valley and, beyond, the sea. Restaurant, bar-lounge, and public spaces are attractive, and Marbella is a quarter-hour's drive away. *First Class.*

RONDA

Hotel Reina Victoria (Calle Jerez 25) went up at the turn of the century, near the end of Queen Victoria's reign. As one approaches, the look is of an English country house. Within, one knows the setting is Ronda: views from many of the 90 handsome updated rooms, as well as from restaurant, bar, and terrace, are of the deep-down Río Guadalevin gorge, with mountain vistas in the other direction. Swimming pool. Friendly staff. I can't imagine any Costa del Sol visitor not enjoying a restful Ronda respite. *Luxury.*

Hotel Polo (Calle Mariano Souvirón 8): You're a little closer to the core of town here than at the Reina Victoria, and this is a smaller, less luxurious house. Which is hardly to be critical, considering that there are a smartly handsome, traditional-style lobby, a bar-lounge, equally sophisticated rooms—some 30 all told—and a good restaurant, though technically not part of the hotel, in connection. Charming. *First Class.*

TORREMOLINOS

Hotel Pez Espada (Avenida de Montemar): This is where it all began. Mass-tourism in Torremolinos, that is. The Pez Espada (swordfish, translated) granddaddy of the big hotels, pioneered the scene in 1959. It remains a dignified, attractive, professionally operated house, with nearly 170 terraced rooms and suites; a glorious garden big enough to easily contain its pair of pools, two tennis courts, and a mini-golf course, with the beach flanking it; restaurants and drinking parlors within and without: a *boîte* with entertainment in summer; and the core of town a short walk away. *First Class.*

Hotel Castillo de Santa Clara (Calle Suecia 1) has the best of both worlds: a location at the rocky eminence that divides Torremolinos's two principal beaches, La Carihuela and El Bajondillo, with downtown directly to the rear. There are 225 snazzy rooms and studio-apartments, all terraced; elaborate public spaces including a dressy restaurant and busy bar; and a big pool around which a buffet lunch is served. Arrangement is upside-down; lobby and public spaces are topside, bedroom floors below. *Luxury.*

Hotel Meliá Torremolinos (Avenida de Carlota Asessandri 109) is a contemporary house, with just under 300 terraced rooms, that's set in a honey of a palm-planted garden-cum-swimming pool. Public spaces are attractive, and include a reliable restaurant and a relaxing cocktail lounge. Moreover, you're a hop and a skip from the beach. *Luxury.*

Hotel Aloha Puerto (Vía Imperial 44) first attracted me—as it does other Hawaii buffs—with its half-Hawaiian title. Which is just as well: I was to discover a handsome, two-building house, with nothing Polynesian save its name, but considerable else to recommend it, including a beachfront, pair of pools (one heated), good restaurants, big bar-lounge, and 420 rooms that are, in actuality, apartments—each has a living room and bar with refrigerator, as well as a terraced bedroom. Americans in abundance. *First Class.*

Hotel Don Pablo (Paseo Marítimo) is a modern 400-room giant that attempts to purvey the flavor of traditional Andalusia in its look, and succeeds. The beamed-ceiling, brick-arched public areas—restaurants, bars, lounges—exude atmosphere. So do the 400 balconied rooms. There's a pretty pool-centered garden leading not only to the beach but to sister-hotel Don Pedro (not quite as luxurious) just next door—around the corner. And there's tennis. *Luxury.*

Hotel Al-Andalus (Carretera de Cádiz) is attractively contemporary, with close to 200 pleasant rooms and suites, restaurant, bar-lounge, and pool, the lot accented by a luxuriant garden, with the beach a short stroll away. *First Class.*

Hotel Don Pedro (Avenida del Lida) has 100 or so fewer rooms than its partner-hotel, the Don Pablo (above). But it is full-facility, with attractive places to eat, have a drink, go dancing, be entertained, swim, and sun. *First Class.*

Hotel Cervantes (Calle Las Mercedes) is sleekly contemporary, centrally situated, with a big pool, the beach nearby (but not adjacent), 400 really big rooms, all terraced; choice of restaurants, bars, and cafés. *First Class.*

Hotel Las Palomas (Calle Carmen Montes 1): The Doves, to translate, is modern and crescent-shaped, with 300 perky rooms, all terraced, buzzy bar and lounges, smart restaurant, pool in the garden, and the beach close by. One of the Agrupados chain, all of whose properties are named for either birds or animals. Good value. *First Class.*

Hotel Miami (Calle Aladino): The Miami, architecturally, is what Floridians would call Spanish Colonial. With its own verdant garden with pool and palms, the requisite quantity of wrought-iron grilles and railings, tile-floored lounge, and 26 really nice rooms, all with baths and terraces affording seaviews. Breakfast only. The English of the Miami's brochure can perhaps be faulted—"Ideal place for a parfait relax"—but it's truthful. *Moderate.*

Hotel Camino Real (Playa de los Alamos) is a good-value house, with the advantages of 150 terraced rooms (ask for one that's seafront), the beach just outside the back door, a swimming pool as well, along with restaurant and bar-lounge. *Moderate.*

Parador Nacional del Golf (Campo de Golf) is a 10-minute ride from the center, but if you're a golfer, this unit of the Spain-wide government-operated chain of inns may well be for you. Traditional-style architecturally, although modern and with modern touches in its decor, this is a comfortable 40-room facility, edging a sporty 18-hole course—or *campo*—with a swimming pool in the garden, the beach yards distant, a convivial bar-lounge, and reliable restaurant typical of the chain. *First Class.*

Hotel Tritón (Benalmádena Costa) is the queen bee of Benalmádena Costa, Torremolinos's hotel-filled next-door neighbor. This is a honey of a beachfront, H-shaped, 200-room house. The low-slung cross-section of the H constitutes a series of public rooms, and the vertical areas are five-story pavilions. Attention to detail is commonplace: maintenance, housekeeping, quality of service, all are A+. I especially like the good-sized rooms and suites, pair of pools (around which buffet lunch is served in the warm-weather months), and indoor facilities, as well. *Luxury.*

Hotel Bali (Carretera de la Telefónica, Benalmádena Costa): The Bali is a find: 200 attractive rooms (each with bath and terrace), a giant pool, restaurant, café-bar, generous lounge, and the beach not far distant. Sound value. *Moderate.*

NERJA

Parador Nacional de Nerja (Playa de Burriana) is a rare beachfront link of the national chain of *paradores*. This is a relaxing 60-room house with a restaurant of the caliber for which the chain is celebrated, bar-lounge, and pretty gardens. With Nerja's caves and its Balcón de Europa belvedere nearby. *First Class.*

Hotel Balcón de Europa (Paseo Balcón de Europa): If you would prefer the top-of-the-world view from this stretch of elevated Nerja to the beach of the *parador* (above), well, then, book one of the 100 neat rooms here. Most have private bathrooms, and there's a restaurant. *Moderate.*

DAILY BREAD

MÁLAGA

Antonio Martín (Paseo Marítimo): You're in the midst of a fascinating—but hot and humid—day of Málaga exploration. Come lunchtime, what you want to do to cool off is hop a cab to this coastal restaurant, take a table on the breezy terrace, order a bowl of gazpacho and *fritura Malagueña*—the local mixed seafood triumph—accompany it with a bottle, say, of Rioja *blanco*, and with the *flan*, or custard, *con nata* (with whipped cream). *First Class.*

Parador Nacional de Gibralfaro (Parque Gibralfaro) is an alternative to Antonio Martín (above). Except that for being alongside the sea, you're going to be way above it—and the core of Málaga as well. As with every *parador*, lunch is the favored meal, because that's when the first course can be *entremeses variados*—a vast tray embracing a score of individual dishes containing hot and cold appetizers. The remainder of lunch may be anticlimactic, but you won't be sorry. *First Class.*

Cortijo de Pepe (Plaza de la Merced) is conveniently central, attractive, typical in its decor, with substantial *menús del día*, and sound enough house wine. *Moderate.*

Casa Pedro (Playa de El Palo) is on a Málaga beach a couple of miles from the center and easily reached by cab at midday. You go here for the fresh, delicious, unpretentiously served—and well-priced—fish and seafood. *Moderate.*

MARBELLA

La Hacienda (Carretera de Málaga): Country look notwithstanding, La Hacienda is the coast's principal outpost of *alta cocina*, appropriately translated into the French—given the style of the cooking—*haute cuisine.* You want to make a selection from each section of the ambitious menu—seafood terrines, or quenelles of eels—rather than the usual pike; lamb roasted in the Gallic manner or a broiled steak; fresh vegetables puréed or in other ways *nouvelle*; memorably delicious dessert pancakes. *Luxury.*

El Corzo (Hotel Los Monteros, Carretera de Málaga) is the subterranean grill of a *muy lujo* hotel. Go for late dinner—gents, wear a tie—and order a festive meal à la carte. *Zarzuela de pescados y mariscos*, a seafood casserole, is a specialty, along with *solomillo de buey*, a thick steak, and *soufflé de langostinos*, a crayfish marvel. The wine cellar is one of the finest on the coast. And note that this hotel's buffet lunches are standouts. *Luxury.*

La Meridiana (Camino de la Cruz)—located across the coastal highway from Hotel Puente Romano, atop a steep hill whose base is marked by the coast's sole mosque—is an airy pavilion of no especial esthetic significance, with what has proved to be, in my experience, an undistinguished albeit extremely costly à la carte, and a dressy clientele come primarily, it would appear, to see and be seen. Fare runs to salads, mousses and a not-bad garlic soup among openers, considerable seafood and veal as well as the obligatory *nouvelle*-type ravioli among entrées. Wines are so expensive as to be almost prohibitive—unless your name is Señor Moneybags. *Luxury.*

Le Nailhac (Hotel Byblos Andaluz, Fuengirola, east of Marbella) is an intimate space set amidst brick arches and painted tiles that fronts an open terrace, for dinners illuminated by starlight. Given Hotel Byblos's French roots, neither Le Nailhac's Limoges china or Gallic-accented cuisine should come as a surprise; there is a *nouvelle* lilt to it, but happily, it is not excessive. By which I mean you may open with good old fashioned Beluga caviar served with blinis, lobster terrine or cream of asparagus soup. Fish are fussed over: *pot au feu de la mer,* for example, or *suprème de saumon grillé* served with *sauce béarnaise.* But so is beef (*tournedos grillé*), chicken (*suprème de volaille au foie gras*) and veal (*médaillon de veau aux morilles*). *Symphonie aux trois chocolats et sa sauce pistache* stands out among sweets. Not surprisingly, the wine choice—French as well as Spanish—is exceptional. Arguably the finest French food on the coast. *Luxury.*

Marbella Patio (Calle Virgen de los Dolores 4) has both the look—painted tiles, a quietly flowing fountain, wrought-iron embellishments—and the taste of Andalusia. At lunch, your best bet is the three-course-and-wine menu, opening with gazpacho or a salad, continuing with garlic-scented chicken, fish or an omelet, and concluding with fresh fruit or ice cream. At dinner, the à la carte is more elaborate, and you do well to order paella or *zarzuela de mariscos,* a seafood stew. Fine wines. Charming service. *First Class.*

El Cortijo (Calle de los Remedios 5) is agreeably traditional in style, welcoming, and with a specialty of *paella*, temptingly tabbed (when ordered for two) and tasty. *Moderate.*

Cipriano (Puerto Banús): Make the rounds of the Puerto Banús promenade, as I have, and I suspect you'll agree that an alfresco table at Cipriano affords the most sweeping of port-and-harbor views. Waiters in striped shirts start you off with on-the-house carrot sticks and a blue-cheese dip. You do well to concentrate on seafood, opening with shrimp cocktail, oysters on the half shell, or lobster bisque. Dorado baked in salt is an entrée specialty, but you may have any of a number of fish simply grilled. And Cipriano's paella is the best I have had on the coast. Delightful service. *First Class.*

Marbella Club (Carretera de Cádiz): The coast abounds in buffet lunches served alfresco. Still, I defy you to find a more delicious and diverse selection of hot and cold dishes—vichyssoise and gazpacho, paella and lasagne, steak and baby lamb chops, cold roast beef and shrimp salad, to name some of the more than a score on display—than those constituting the daily buffet at this beautiful hotel. And everything is as tasty as it is good to look upon. *Luxury.*

Antonio (Puerto Banús) When a seafood restaurant packs in patrons, evening in and evening out, you know the fish is fresh. At Antonio's—where it's served to diners seated in white chairs surrounding tables set in rust linen—it's also tasty. Paella, too. *First Class.*

La Tortuga Feliz (Puerto Banús)—which translates as The Happy Turtle—may not sound Italian. But it is, indeed, with such *primi* (first courses) from the Peninsula as *carpaccio*, such pastas as *spaghetti carbonara, fettucini Alfredo* and *lasagne*; reliable veal entrées, and Italian wines. *First Class.*

Red Pepper (Puerto Banús) does not reveal its nationality through its name any more than does La Tortuga Feliz (above). It's Greek, with authentic assorted *meze*, or appetizers, and such traditional entrées as *moussaka* and roast lamb. Greek wines, too. Fun. *First Class.*

Picasso (Puerto Banús) simply has to be the only pizzeria—anywhere—so named. The pies come with something like a dozen toppings. And they're good. *Moderate.*

Old Joys (Puerto Banús) is a pubby café that draws crowds hungry for such specialties as chicken salad and omelets, as well as thirsty for—among other beverages—milk shakes and Irish coffee. *Moderate.*

Mesón del Garbanzo (Calle Buitrago, off Plaza Coronel Borbón) is as busy an after-dark spot as you'll find downtown. Ten kinds of pizza constitute the principal reason. Temptingly priced daily specials, too. *Moderate.*

Le Bistro (Calle Pantaleón, off Plaza Coronel Borbón) is an intimate, heart-of-town source of tasty French comestibles. *First Class.*

Mena (Plaza de los Naranjos): A table on the terrace in Marbella's principal plaza is not to be despised, especially if it's for dinner at Mena. Consider the paella, starting with the soup of the day and concluding, perhaps, with a pair of peeled-by-the-waiter Andalusian oranges. *First Class.*

Esquina de Antonio (Calle Sierra Blanca) is an agreeable, family-run place, smallish and smiling, with *claveles*—carnations—on the tables, and *pollo americano*—chicken grilled with bacon and served with broiled tomatoes and potatoes—a specialty. *Moderate.*

Cafetería Marbella (Avenida Ramón y Cajal at the park called Alameda José Antonio) packs them in, at both lunch and dinner, especially the latter, when it's cool at the tables on the terrace facing the park. Reasonably tasty fare at reasonable prices. *Moderate.*

TORREMOLINOS

El Copo (Playa de la Carihuela): If you're partial to fresh-as-can-be fish and seafood, simply prepared and equally simply served, in a modest beachfront setting, well, then, if you will pardon my metaphor, you'll be happy as a clam in Torremolinos. Consider an El Copo lunch or dinner, which might embrace a seafood salad (with *gambas*—large shrimp—and *camarones*—small shrimp), a superbly grilled sole, or *lenguado*, concluding with a mess of *chanquetes*—whole tiny whitebait, flour-dusted, deep-fried, and with good reason the most popular of the Costa del Sol's maritime specialties. With a carafe of the house's Valdepeñas wine accompanying. Service is swift and skilled if hardly white-glove, and tabs are nowhere in Spain more reasonable. *Moderate.*

Other Playa de la Carihuela seafood restaurants— similar in price and ambience, to El Copo (above)—include *Bernardo, La Jabega, La Langosta, Los Remos* and *El Rocquo.* And there are more: half a hundred all told. There is competition on a nearby street parallel with the beach, Calle San Ginés, whose *Restaurante Antonio* is but one of many restaurants, all even less expensive than those on the water, and more desirable at dinner—when it's cooler—than lunch, when there is no sea breeze to cool things off.

Antoxo (Carretera de Málaga) is away from the center, but indicated when you've a yen for a Basque dinner that's satisfying and fairly priced. *First Class.*

Don Pepino (Calle Antonio Girón 3) serves up tasty Italian favorites. Pizza is his most popular item, but there is pasta, as well, including ravioli, canneloni, and lasagna. *Moderate.*

Bagatelle (Calle de la Nogalera 108): You're hungry in late afternoon or mid-morning? Bagatelle comes to the rescue with pastries, ice cream concoctions, and, if you're up to it, *café Irlandés*, Irish coffee. *Moderate.*

SHOPPER'S COSTA DEL SOL

Málaga, the region's metropolis, draws shoppers to Calle Marqués de Larios, its Main Street—with such interesting stores as *Rocamar* (women's clothes) and *Rally* (menswear)—and to the area's sole major department store: modern, restaurant-and-supermarket-equipped *El Corte Inglés* (Alameda Principal). Moneyed *Marbella*'s principal thoroughfare, Avenida Ricardo Soriano, is browseworthy, with such boutiques as *Les Must de Cartier* (jewelry, gifts), *Charles Jourdan* (French shoes and fashions), *Giorgio* (pricey men's clothes), *Aguimar* (perfumes), *Roger & Fredy* (Lacoste sportswear) and *Cortefiel* (a Spain-wide mid-category men's and women's clothing firm). *Hiper*, a link of the national supermarket chain, is on the coastal highway just west of Marbella. *Puerto Banús*, the trendy yacht harbor (also to Marbella's west) is as notable for shops as for restaurants and cafés (see *Daily Bread*, above). As you amble about the crowded waterfront promenade of an evening (when Banús really comes alive, with everything open late), note such emporia as *Alexandra* (embroidered linens), *Gitana* (jewelry), *Rich Bitch* (men's as well as women's resortwear), *Big Bamboo* (women's clothing), *Mister* (costly men's duds), *Spirit* (amusing sweat and tee shirts), *Librería Salduba* (foreign-language [including English] periodicals), and *Trident* (luggage, in which to pack your purchases).

INCIDENTAL INTELLIGENCE ═══════════

The always-teeming international airport for the Costa del Sol is Málaga's; it is served in summer by Iberia on direct flights to and from the United States (the rest of the year, you change planes in Madrid); the airport lies between Málaga city and Torremolinos, from which it's just a few quick miles distant. Arrive as part of a group and chances are good that a bus will whisk you and your fellow-travelers to your hotel (buses back to the airport are also available). Arrive individually, and you take a taxi to your digs. Given the distances of some hotels from the airport—those in Marbella, for example—this can be pricey. If you'll be staying a while, rent a car, or try headquartering in, or at least close to, one of the towns. Note, also, that there is public transportation, with comfortable trains running regularly between Málaga, via

Torremolinos, and the town of Fuengirola, *which is as close as you'll get, by rail, to Marbella*. There is also good public bus service *all* along the coast. As in the rest of Andalusia, bullfighting is a spectator sport of consequence. If you can take in a fight at Málaga's immense downtown Plaza de Toros, you're in luck. The same applies to the bullring of little Ronda, which dates to the eighteenth century and was where the art of bullfighting was, in effect, codified. There are rings, also, in Marbella and Torremolinos. Casino Nueva Andalucía has its own entrance in Marbella's Andalucía Plaza Hotel; it's traditionally open from 7 P.M. until 4 A.M., for roulette, blackjack and other games, and you need your passport to get in, although passports aren't needed to play the slot machines in an adjacent hall. Disco-dancing is the principal after-dark diversion all along the coast; you'll learn soon enough at your hotel which places are currently favored. Flamenco dancing—*tablao flamenco*—is presented in the towns, and at some hotels; tabs, though they include a drink, are high, and you take your chances on the quality of the performers. Golf and tennis facilities are excellent. One can charter vessels for deep-sea fishing, go sailing, yachting, and, in winter, skiing at the not-far-distant Sierra Nevada points. Winters on the shore are mild, but not warm enough for sea-swimming, the seasons for which are generally spring through autumn. *Further information:* Oficina de Turismo de Málaga, Calle Marqués de Larios 5, with an airport branch; Oficina de Turismo de Marbella, Avenida Miguel Cano 1; Oficina de Turismo de Ronda, Plaza de España 1; Oficina de Turismo de Torremolinos, Calle de la Nogalera 517.

11

Cuenca

Hanging Houses,
Abstract Art

BACKGROUND BRIEFING

Cuenca is just far enough away from the major cities of Madrid (to the west) and Valencia (to the east) to be beyond the reach of one-a-day tour-buses, but just close enough to make a long day or, better yet, an overnight visit a distinct possibility.

Smallish Cuenca's roots are ancient. Romans were here, Visigoths came later, with Moors following. Castilian Christians gained the city in the course of the pan-Spanish Christian reconquest in the twelfth century.

If it was never fabulously rich—in the manner of other, smaller cities like, say, Salamanca—Cuenca amassed enough economic wealth and political clout over the centuries to have developed a still-substantial façade. And there is a geographic curiosity: nature made Cuenca's terrain special.

ON SCENE

Lay of the Land: What lures the visitor is the town's oldest quarter, at the northern tip of a rectangularly shaped town. That's where a concentrated cluster of towering houses perches above a rocky eminence with the waters of two converged rivers—Huécar and Júcar—way, way below. Photographs one has noted before arriving seem exaggerated, for the hanging houses, cliffside—*Casas Colgadas*, as they are translated—

appear as one-dimensional cut-outs from a schoolchild's building kit.

But the houses are believed to have silhouetted tops of the cliffs for some six centuries. Going inland, beyond Plaza Mayor and the neoclassic façade of the *Ayuntamiento*, or town hall, one arrives at a Cathedral that stuns with the richness not only of its architecture, but of its treasures—remarkable in a town so small. All about, on hilly streets paved with the cobbles of earlier centuries, are structures—both residential and ecclesiastic—as historic as they are handsome.

Modern Cuenca is a fairish distance to the south. Take a bus or taxi, if you haven't a car, via Calle Alfonso VIII to Plaza del Carmen with its landmark, octagonal-towered *Church of San Felipe*, downhill to *Parque de San Julián*, and a succession of thoroughfares leading to downtown shops and the railway station.

Museo de Arte Abstracto Español (Barrio de San Martín) is Spain's most unexpected, most unusual, and most ingeniously designed museum. It is, as well, one not only of national importance but—surprise of surprises in this provincial town—nationally operated. What happened was this: A contiguous group of three of the finest of Cuenca's *Casas Colgadas*, or hanging houses, had survived a variety of restorations and refurbishings over the centuries. They became municipal property in the eighteenth century, serving for a period as the city hall. There was a major restoration, a commendable municipal project, in the 1950s. At just about that time, a group of Spanish artists—La Generación Abstracta—began achieving international celebrity, to the point where its members' paintings were turning up in museums abroad. But there was no museum in all Spain where they could be exhibited collectively. A nucleus of the artists' group—Fernando Zobel, Gustavo Torner, and Gerardo Rueda among them—were brought together with Cuenca city fathers. In short order, Cuenca offered the houses as a home for the museum, which received national funding. The artists were as advanced in architecture and interior design as in painting. Retaining the best of the original architecture of the houses, and innovating with the latest in museum techniques, they created an art repository of extraordinary originality and beauty.

The visitor benefits, not only from the opportunity to see striking works by Spain's crackerjack contemporary painters and sculptors in a striking setting, but with the opportunity to take in, as well, a trio of Cuenca's cliffhanging houses, along with views of the gorge below from their balconies. Madrid's Museo de Arte Contemporáneo is infinitely bigger, and Barcelona's Fundación Miró—filled with works of that celebrated master—is more famous. But the Cuenca museum, combining today's art with yesterday's architecture in a unique setting, is one of a kind.

Cathedral (Calle Obispo Valero): Well, its tower toppled off at about the time the nineteenth century became the twentieth. But otherwise, Cuenca's 800-year-old Gothic Cathedral remains superbly intact. It impresses, as one approaches, with its massiveness. And goes on pleasing, with a nave at once handsomely vaulted and graced with a triforium (a gallery surmounting the nave's arches) dotted with a succession of splendidly sculpted saints. There is a chain of chapels; some, like the Muños, out of the later centuries of the Renaissance. And, considering Cuenca's modest size, the quality of the art surprises. There are, for example, a pair of El Grecos, an exquisite Byzantine casket for relics—enameled, bejeweled, and dating to the fourteenth century—sculptures by Pedro de Mena, a *Nativity* by Juan de Borgoña, even a *Crucifixion* believed to be by Gerard David.

Museo Arqueológico (Barrio de San Martín) is small but choice, occupying a clutch of chambers in a nicely restored structure adjacent to the Cathedral. The thrust is Roman Cuenca: coins, mosaics, sculpture, and pottery.

An Old Cuenca stroll: Cuenca from without is spectacular enough to warrant your saving time for a walk along the cliff towering above the Huécar River gorge, past the balcony-accented façades of the hanging houses and pretty little Plaza Mayor, through streets leading to the carved-stone façades of two houses and churches. Of the latter, *San Pedro* (Calle del

Trabuco), *San Miguel* (Calle San Miguel), and *Nuestra Señora de las Angustias* (Ronda del Júcar) stand out.

Rocky environs: With a car, you can take in the eerie rock formations of the Cuenca countryside. Americans, at least those who know the West, find this area of less interest than do Europeans, to whom it is positively exotic. Still, the view looking up on high to the *Casas Colgadas*, on the cliff above the Huécar River at the point called Hoz de Huécar, is smashing. And more distant *Ciudad Encantada*—the Enchanted City—is an Arizona-like maze of weirdly contorted rock formations.

SETTLING IN

Hotel Torremangana (Calle San Ignacio de Loyola 9) is a fair distance from the historic quarter, and, for that matter, from downtown. But you can walk to either, and you've virtually no other choice if it's a really good hotel you're after. This modern house—friendly, attractive, full-facility—is just that. Rooms, 112 in all, are lovely, and there are both a restaurant (about which more later) and *cafetería*, with a bar-lounge as well. *First Class.*

Hotel Alfonso VIII (Parque de San Julián 3) lies alongside an agreeable inner-city park, within walking distance of the old town. This is a very shaky No. 2, after the spiffy Torremangana, with half a hundred so-so rooms (the mattresses are among Spain's thinnest) and a *cafetería*. *Moderate.*

DAILY BREAD

Mesón Casas Colgadas (Barrio de San Martín) occupies two lower floors in the trio of splendidly restored hanging houses whose principal tenant is the Museo de Arte Abstracto Español (above). The street-level bar-lounge is fun for a drink-cum-*tapas*. Above, the restaurant proper—handsomely got up in period style—serves a generous and usually delicious *menú del día* that might, to give you an idea, run to cream of leek soup, veal-stuffed peppers, a dessert of *flan*, and a carafe of house wine. With memorable vistas of the Huécar River gorge as a bonus. *First Class.*

La Cocina (Hotel Torremangana, Calle San Ignacio de Loyola 9): The principal hotel's principal restaurant—contemporary with traditional touches—is the ideal spot for local favorites, including lamb roasted *zarajos*-style and roast *perdiz*, or partridge. Good steaks, and an interesting cellar, including the regional reds of Tarancon, and Cuenca's own *resoli*—a liqueur. *First Class.*

Figón de Pedro (Calle Cervantes 13) has a cheery traditional look to it, with the reasonably priced *menú del día* a good bet. Location is downtown. *Moderate.*

INCIDENTAL INTELLIGENCE

Cuenca makes for a long day's outing from either Valencia or Madrid; it's about midway between the two. You may go by public bus or train, but a more leisurely overnight stay is counseled. *Further information:* Oficina de Turismo de Cuenca, Calle Calderón de la Barca 28.

12

El Escorial

Bravo, Philip II!

BACKGROUND BRIEFING

It is surely safe to conjecture that any young man following a strong father to the throne of a powerful realm would want to prove himself. In the case of Philip II, that was a proposition in spades. Philip was not your run-of-the-mill minor-league species. His credentials are worth pondering.

His great-grandfather and great-grandmother were a team the world remembers as Ferdinand and Isabella, who united Spain through the merger of their respective kingdoms of Aragón and Castile; opened up the New World via the dispatch overseas of one Christopher Columbus; and—to weed out suspect Jews and Moslems who had converted to Christianity—instituted the Spanish Inquisition.

Philip's grandmother was a daughter of Ferdinand and Isabella, whom history identifies as Juana the Mad; she was wife to a Holy Roman Emperor's son, dubbed Philip the Handsome. He passed his good looks along. But his son by Juana had more than a classic profile. He grew up to be not only Charles I of Spain, but Charles V—the Holy Roman Emperor whose realm stretched from the vast Spanish territories in America through the Iberian peninsula to the Low countries (where he was born), beyond to much of Italy, along with the territory of the Hapsburgs (of which he was one) in then vast Austria. Titian was to paint Charles more than once (on horseback and again, with a pet dog—at Madrid's Prado, and seated at Munich's Alte Pinakothek).

Titian painted Charles's son, as well. The portrait of Philip II in the Prado delineates an elegant young man, one hand at his sword, the other on a plumed helmet, ready to do battle. Not to be outdone by the father whom he succeeded when the old man abdicated and retired to a monastery, Philip immersed himself in the politics of his far-flung territories (he used the Inquisition as a major weapon), in battles both on land and sea, in marriage (his four wives were, in succession, Maria of Portugal, Bloody Mary of England, Elizabeth of Valois—after England's Elizabeth I spurned him—and Anne of Austria), and, finally, religion.

An almost fanatic ascetic (he dressed in somber black most of his adult life) Philip conceived El Escorial first as a memorial to his pious father, second as a repository of the tombs of Spain's monarchs, and third as a first-of-its-kind combination palace-monastery, where he could live in isolation from his subjects, the while praying in the presence of a resident band of San Jerónimo priests. And so—not only to honor his father and forebears, but also as an act of thanksgiving for a substantial victory over the French in the Battle of St. Quentin that occurred in 1557 on the feast day of St. Lawrence, for whom El Escorial is named (its full title is San Lorenzo de El Escorial)—Philip set about his task.

Criticize him on other counts—reactionary social views, loss of his presumably invincible Armada to the same Elizabeth of England who had spurned his proposal of marriage, near-paranoid mistrust of associates and allies—but not in the matter of El Escorial. He chose two brilliant architects, Juan Bautista de Toledo, first, and after Bautista's death, Juan de Herrera. (The same pair was earlier commissioned by Philip to rebuild the royal palace at Aranjuez, as I indicate in the chapter on that town.)

The result was an almost revolutionary departure from the elaborately overdecorated, or Plateresque, style that had come to typify Spanish Renaissance architecture. Bautista, and later Herrera, came up with a clean-lined, neoclassic complex that, these many centuries later, remains elegant, functional, and a memorial not only to Philip's religiosity but to his impeccable taste.

ON SCENE

Lay of the Land: El Escorial is an architecture lesson, a history book, a gallery of Old Masters. It makes its first statement—on the majesty of monarchy, the power of religion—from without, by means of an almost unencumbered façade, high-walled and accented at its corners by the kind of towers still commonplace in Spanish building. View it from far enough away to afford perspective.

Within, the name of the design game has been symmetry. And on an astonishing scale. This is a great rectangular pile of granite, more than 500 feet wide, nearly 700 feet long, with no less than 16 inner courts, well over a thousand doors, and twice as many windows. Building time was two mid-sixteenth-century decades. (Although it is not generally realized that a number of Philip II's successors made contributions to El Escorial, beginning with his son, Philip III, and including Philip IV, Charles II, Charles III, Charles IV, on through Isabella II in the middle of the last century; two kings—the first two Bourbons, Philip V and Ferdinand VI—were exceptions; they boycotted El Escorial, to the point of directing that they not be buried in its pantheon.)

The main entrance leads into a glorious courtyard, *Patio de los Reyes*, at the far end of which is the monastery-palace's standout church, with royal apartments and principal picture gallery to the left, and the royal pantheon, sacristy, and chapter house (these last two containing additional paintings) to the right. El Escorial's monastery section is unvisitable, but every other major part of the complex is open to visitors. Here is how they break down, so you can take your pick:

Church of San Lorenzo could stand on its own in any substantial city. It is a largely unadorned exercise in gray granite, crucifix-shaped under a massive central dome in the manner of Rome's St. Peter's, with the principal decorative element a spectacular high altar, by co-architect Herrera.

Panteón de los Reyes: If it is not a cheery chamber, it is an impressive one. The Panteón's niches contain two dozen marble sarcophagi, with the remains of all the Spanish monarchs from the time of Philip II's father, Charles V, through to the late nineteenth century's Alfonso XII. (Only the earlier-mentioned first Bourbons, Philip V and Ferdinand VI, and later, elected King Amadeus are missing. The remains of Alfonso XIII, grandfather of the present sovereign, Juan Carlos, were taken to El Escorial in 1980.)

Habitaciones del Palacio: Most evocative are the rooms Philip II had designed for himself, especially his bedroom—severe but handsome—directly adjacent to the church and where he died, aged 71, in 1598. The throne room adjoins it, as does the small suite occupied by Philip's daughter, Isabel Clara Eugenia. The eighteenth-century Bourbon monarchs' quarters are something else again: sumptuous apartments in unrestrained Spanish rococo—salon with then stylish Pompeiian motifs; dining room, whose walls are surfaced with tapestries based on the works of Goya; opulent ambassadorial reception room.

Picture galleries: There are three principal ones; the paintings they shelter are in and of themselves reason for an El Escorial pilgrimage. Biggest collection is in a group of rooms called *Nuevos Museos*, whose Italians are breathtaking—a cluster by Titian, court painter to both Charles V and his son, the builder Philip, along with Veronese, Tintoretto, and Bassano, among others. El Greco leads the Spaniards (his *Martyrdom of San Mauricio* is memorable). And the Flemings are brilliantly represented—Bosch, David, van der Weyden among them. Note, too, the basement collection of drawings and other paraphernalia relating to the design and construction of El Escorial. But wait: there are additional paintings in the *Sacristía* by the likes of Spain's Claudio Coello and José de Ribera, and Italy's Luca Giordano.

Auxiliary palaces: Casita de Arriba, is a compact and charming residence: furniture, clocks, crystal, porcelain, textiles—all are highest caliber. Have a look, bearing in mind as you do so that a recent resident was King Juan Carlos, before he ascended the throne. Move along then, to *Casita del Príncipe.* Its interiors are unique in that they celebrate the light touch, often lacking in eighteenth-century Spanish palaces.

SETTLING IN

Hotel Victoria Palace (Calle Juan de Toledo 4) is the longtime leader—old-school, welcoming—in El Escorial town, fronting a garden-cum-swimming pool, with close to 90 rooms and a reliable restaurant. *First Class.*

Hotel Miranda y Suizo (Calle Floridablanca 20) has for long been No. 2 in town. Some 50 rooms, many with private baths, restaurant. *Moderate.*

DAILY BREAD

Mesón la Cueva (Calle San Antón 4) delights with *ambiente* in spades, and an invariably tasty *menú del día. First Class.*

El Parque (Plaza Virgen de Gracia 1) is indicated for warm-weather lunches, alfresco. Caveat: no credit cards. *First Class.*

INCIDENTAL INTELLIGENCE ══════════════

El Escorial is sometimes visited in tandem with neighboring *Valle de los Caídos.* This is a Franco-built tribute to the Francoist Civil War victory that centers around a chapel unfelicitously hewn out of a rocky mountain, with the tombs of Franco himself, of José Antonio Primo de Rivera, founder of the fascist Falangist movement; and—in a mammoth subterranean crypt—graves of masses of Civil War dead, the lot under a granite cross 492 feet high. *Further information:* Oficina de Turismo de El Escorial, Calle Floridablanca 10.

13

Extremadura

Mérida
Cáceres
Guadalupe
Trujillo

BACKGROUND BRIEFING

Extreme, indeed. Spain's most aptly named province—west-central, flanking Portugal's remote eastern frontier—is its most isolated, sparsely populated, and touristically neglected region. It's out of the way, minimally equipped with first-class hotels (although there are fine *paradores*), sizzling hot in summer, and most easily inspected by motorists. Still, there is access by long-distance bus and slow trains. The genuinely curious traveler with at least a fair command of the Spanish language (there is virtually no English spoken) rarely leaves this patch of Spain unsatisfied. Especially if he or she is from the New World. For it was in Extremadura—arid, table-flat, and without seacoast—that were spawned the *conquistadores*. They set out something like half a millennium back to explore and conquer great chunks of two continents, impelled as much by economic necessity (Extremadura was poor then as it is now) as by a sense of soldier-like adventure and intellectual curiosity, coupled with a near-passionate compulsion to Christianize the non-European peoples of the planet.

And so a special, Extremadura-reared breed of explorer—*hidalgos*, or gentlemen-soldiers—set off in small bands on frail ships and altered the course of world history. Their names take us back to history class: Francisco Pizarro, the conqueror of Peru; Hernando Cortés, whose name is synonymous with Mexico;

Hernando de Soto, who explored from Florida to Tennessee; and Vasco Núñez de Balboa, who traversed the Isthmus of Panama and discovered the Pacific Ocean, are the Big Four. But there were others, as well, including Francisco de Orellana, who made the first descent of the Amazon from the Andes to the Atlantic and is believed to have named the river, and Pedro de Valdivia, who, concentrating on southern South America, succeeded in subduing Chile.

A quartet of Extremadura towns—each in its distinctive way—reflects the remarkable conquistadores, their age, and the unique relationship between Spain and the New World. A visit to the Museo de América on the University of Madrid campus (see the Madrid chapter) is a good way of gauging the Spanish-American connection on soil of the Mother Country. But it pales in contrast to a first-person encounter with the region of Spain whose sons lost little time following in the footsteps of Columbus.

ON SCENE
Lay of the Land: Extremadura is by Spanish standards relatively vast, with Portugal to its west, Andalusia to its south, and Castile to its east and north. Each of the Extremadura towns of this chapter is eminently explorable. They are Mérida, the regional capital; Cáceres, the largest—and number two in population after Badajoz, from which it is some 50 miles northeast; Trujillo, nearly 30 miles east of Cáceres; and Guadalupe, another 30 miles eastward, and closest of the group to Madrid—120 miles distant. In these towns, and indeed throughout Extremadura—if you're traveling between February and mid-August—you want to look up whenever a church tower, or indeed *any* tower, looms into sight. Invariably, it will be the base of a stork's nest, more often than not with Mama Stork and a brood of youngsters in residence. *Las cigüeñas* are a special Extremadura treat.

MÉRIDA
If it is without the Extremaduran flavor of the other cities of this chapter, Mérida, the provincial capital, compensates in the area of antiquities. It was known in Roman times as *Emeritus*

Augustus, the first word of its title indicating its status as a settlement for war veterans; the second, the name of the emperor under whose reign it was founded a quarter century before the birth of Christ. Roman-built bridges still span rivers on the outskirts of this bustling little city. But the chef d'oeuvre—indeed it is one of the most spectacular of Roman remnants in Europe—constitutes the principal reason for a Mérida visit. It is *Teatro Romano* (at the foot of Calle Suárez Somonte) built only a year after the city's founding. Used to this day—visit Mérida in summer and you take in Greek as well as Roman plays—the theater's semicircle of a stage is fronted by elegantly arranged rows of seats in granite (original capacity was 6,000). But it's the stage that makes the theater special. It is framed by a two-level colonnade, the Corinthian capitals of its massed columns still in place, as indeed are sculptures of the type erected by Imperial decree as part of the original decor.

The adjacent *Anfiteatro Romano*, a 2,000-year-old arena, had more than double the capacity of the theatre, but is nothing like as spectacular a sight—at least contemporarily. What you do not, under any circumstances, want to miss is the neighboring *Museo Nacional de Arte Romano*, a bold and brilliant contemporary structure that opened as recently as 1986. Consider its daring architecture—a wing of mini-gables piercing the sky, a façade of square windows atop, but only atop, severe high walls; still another surface embellished with diamond-like designs; pale layered-brick interiors whose monumental proportions are inspired by those of ancient Rome but are adaptations, for contemporary displays, rather than emulations. It is as much fun ambling about—along ramps and runways, even an underground tunnel connecting the museum to *Teatro Romano*, as well as more conventional stairways that afford views of exhibits in vast spaces—as it is taking in remains of Roman Mérida on view. Not that these statues and busts, fragments and friezes, glass and coins—32,000 objects in all—are to be ignored. Still, when all is said and done, I don't know of another contemporary building in Spain that is more exciting. We are all in the debt of the gifted architect, José Rafael Moneo.

The eleven-century-old Moorish-built *Alcazaba*, or fortress, (at the terminus of Calle Sagaesta, edging the Guadiana River, where it is spanned by a Roman-built bridge) is visitable primarily for the Roman decorative elements of its interior. It's a hop and a skip from Mérida's impressive main square, *Plaza de España*, fountain-centered, fringed by low-slung structures of traditional design, and leading into *Calle Santa Eulalia*, the principal pedestrian shopping street.

CÁCERES

Cáceres is mood. It is as though its Old Town—elevated, walled, and turreted—wants merely to impress us with its advanced age and an underappreciated role in history. This is where New World explorers came home to retire, much as whaling captains lived happily evermore on the Massachusetts island of Nantucket. And, like Nantucket, Cáceres is plain but solid. The main pedestrian street, *Calle de los Pintores*, is strollworthy. But it is the eastern part of town—*Cáceres Viejo*—that beckons. Make your way up the hill from *Plaza Mayor* to elongated *Plaza del General Mola*, whose slim and somber towers pierce ancient walls enclosing the Cáceres of the conquistadores. What one wants first to do is amble about this old quarter, past mansions built four and five centuries ago by native sons returned to their homeland from the Americas. Look up over doorways at family coats of arms chiseled in stone. And note discreet balconies where the *hidalgos'* ladies took the air and surveyed the street scene.

Casa de las Veletas (Calle de Pereros)—longtime seat of a leading family—has been pressed into service as the *Provincial Archeological Museum*. Look over bits and pieces of Cáceres from Roman, Moorish, and more recent centuries; galleries are built around a charming patio. There are fragments of sculpture, weathered parchment documents, chests and coins, even a cistern of aged and ingenious design.

Casa del Mono (Calle Ancha) is a landmark fifteenth-century mansion; it's the province's *Museo de Bellas Artes* and as such brims with paintings; El Greco's *Jesus Salvador* is the most celebrated, with David Teniers and Luca Giordano also represented.

The sculpture is lovely, too. And the building itself is of especial beauty.

Church of Santa María (Plaza de Santa María) is essentially Gothic, triple-naved, with a carved high altar and tombs of distinguished native sons. Look at the square's façades, as you exit: They run an architectural gamut, Gothic through the Spanish Renaissance style called Plateresque (busily surface-decorated) on into baroque. Continue on through one elegant stone arch after another—to *Plaza San Mateo*—the most elevated part of the Old Town—and the *Church of San Mateo*. It's Plateresque—note the front door—with carved stone tombs. Take in, as well, the *Church of Santiago el Mayor* (Plaza de Santiago)—a Romanesque beauty and twin-towered, multi-epoch *Church of San Francisco Javier*, atop stone steps on the square named for it.

TRUJILLO

Cáceres, with a population hovering around the 60,000 mark, is a positive giant compared with Trujillo, one-sixth as large. This town gave its name to one of the principal cities of Peru, not surprisingly, for it's the hometown of the Pizarro family, and the seat of other conquistador clans as well.

Trujillo's severe, formidably walled *Castello*, a visitable Moorish castle-on-high (consisting only of battlements, and without residential interiors), protects the town, which appears to be built into a rocky mass. The core is completely enclosed *Plaza Mayor*, centered with an equestrian statue of Native Son No. 1—Francisco Pizarro—as interpreted by a team of twentieth-century American sculptors. There are lovely mansions all about the square. Ask to have that of Francisco Pizarro's half-brother, Hernando, pointed out; it has busts of both Pizarros on its façades. Inspect the square's *Monasterio de San Carlos*. Knock on the door and your guide—a resident nun—will appear, come to take you on a tour—through a spectacular patio—of those parts of the convent open to visitors.

Church of Santa María la Mayor is Trujillo's showplace church, a very grand Gothic work, with tombs of its conquistadores

(Pizarro's included) and pews of stone on which sat their Catholic Majesties, Ferdinand and Isabella, in the course of a fifteenth-century visit. Go up to the high altar for a look at the sublime paintings of Fernando Gallegos. Continue on to a pair of churches— Gothic, beautifully vaulted *San Martín* (Plaza de San Martín), and severely Romanesque *Santiago* (Plaza de Santiago).

GUADALUPE

Guadalupe is a very small town dominated by a very large monastery. It's the latter—which gave its name to New World pilgrimage churches (Mexico City's most especially) and to a Columbus-discovered French Caribbean island—that lures the visitor. Founded in 1300 on a site where the Virgin Mary is reputed to have appeared, the monastery—then operated by Hieronymite monks, but since the turn of this century under the control of friendly Franciscans, some 20 strong—developed as a pilgrimage destination, enriched by royal patrons. Later, pious conquistadores, upon returning to their homeland, made of the monastery a center for exchanges—cultural, political, spiritual—between Spaniards and the conquered of their New World territories, who share a common language and the same religion. Guadalupe was the site of ceremonies at which documents relating to Spanish America were signed. It was where Indians-turned-Christians were brought to be baptized. It became the principal site within the motherland of the colonization movement. It remains pre-eminent, as its official title—*Real* (Royal) *Monasterio de Guadalupe* indicates. And it continues to receive eminent visitors; Pope John Paul II, for example, paid a call in 1986.

There's a lot to see in this immense complex. Start with the Gothic church, officially designated a basilica by the Vatican, with its magnificent high altar (a work by El Greco's son is among its paintings) behind a splendid wrought-iron grille. Go on to the sacristy, where gilded arches frame a brilliant group of eleven white-robed clerics' portraits (they were priors of Guadalupe) by the great baroque-era painter, Extremadura-born Francisco de Zurbarán. Proceed to an adjacent chapel where the treasure—on a revolving altar—is the a statue of the much-venerated Virgin of Guadalupe, and—as a surprise—no less than nine paintings by the Neopolitan Baroque master Luca Giordano (who worked for a period in Spain, where he was styled Lucas Jordán). But there's more, most especially the *Sala Capitular*, with additional Zurbarán paintings; serenely beautiful cloisters both in the Moorish-Mudéjar style of the fifteenth century, and of later Gothic; and the *Museo de Bordados*—a repository of antique ecclesiastical vestments that is one of the best such in Europe, with exhibits including altar cloths from King Philip II (dating to 1547) and Portuguese-born Catherine of Braganza, consort of England's Charles II; as well as a cape of Columbus's mentor, Queen Isabella. Hope that the monastery's genial art expert, Father Tomás Patero, will be your guide. And when you've completed your tour (visitors are taken around in small groups, as they form), tarry for a meal or a drink in the restaurant or bar of the Franciscan-operated *Hospedería*, a hotel within the monastery complex (see below).

SETTLING IN

MÉRIDA

Parador Nacional Vía de la Plata (Plaza Queipo de Llano 3) is at once very old (it was built as a convent in the seventeenth century and was, of all things, a prison, before it was deftly transformed into a handsome *parador*) and very up-to-date (with a wing of new rooms that opened in 1987). But it is the venerable aspects of this house that offer special appeal. The baroque façade is among Mérida's handsomest, the patio remains serene, centered by a well, arcaded and plant-filled. The nuns' chapel, still with a wrought-iron grille that separated the altar from the nave, is the main lounge, and other public spaces are no less imposing. The bar is cozy, management congenial, staff friendly (not always the case in *paradores*), and the restaurant (below) one of the best in town. *First Class.*

Hotel Emperatriz (Plaza de España) has two pluses: advanced age (it went up as a wealthy citizen's *palacio* in the sixteenth century but gained a new façade in the seventeenth) and a situation on Mérida's handsome main square. The three-story patio, stone-walled main hall and original ceremonial stairway remain, there are 40 functional rooms with bath (some more impressive than others), restaurant and bar. *Moderate.*

Las Lomas Hotel (Carretera Madrid-Lisboa) is out of town and suitable principally for motorists. Withal, it's bright as a button, Y-shaped modern in aspect, with close to 140 full-facility rooms, reliable restaurant, relaxing bar, outdoor swimming pool that's a pleasure in summer. *First Class.*

CÁCERES

Extremadura Hotel (Avenida Virgen de Guadalupe) is not, alas, in the old town (no hotels are) but is not far from it, and is nicely equipped with just under 70 agreeable rooms in traditional style, pleasant public spaces that include a swimming pool in the pretty garden, restaurant and bar. *Moderate.*

Alcántara Hotel (Avenida Virgen de Guadalupe 14) is an across-the-*avenida* neighbor of the Extremadura (above), albeit newer. It too has just under 70 rooms (although its singles have showers only—no tubs, unlike those of the Extremadura). *Cafetería*, bar. *Moderate.*

TRUJILLO

Parador Nacional de Trujillo (Plaza de Santa Clara): It's not every *parador* that makes its home in a venerable convent, whose nuns moved out to make room for it—but only after authorities built the sisters a spanking new convent just next door. The Conceptionist order founded the old Convent of Santa Clara in the sixteenth century. Some four hundred years later, by which time their quarters had become mellow but antiquated, they moved into quarters with modern conveniences, the while their convent was transformed into a 46-room hostelry. It is the original architectural aspects of the convent that stand out in this link of the Parador chain—an utterly beautiful galleried cloister—most spectacularly. There are, to be sure, some rooms with canopied beds, but most, though comfortable, are plainly furnished in blonde wood, albeit with good baths. The tile-accented main lounge's plastic-upholstered furniture is disappointing, the bar small, the restaurant (below) by no means among the best in the network and the staff mostly grim-visaged. Location is atop a hill flanking the center, and there's an outdoor swimming pool. *First Class.*

Las Cigüeñas Hotel (Carretera Madrid, east of town) is a worth-knowing-about modern house, out of town, to be sure (you want a car), but with some 60 okay rooms with bath, capacious *cafetería* and big bar. Friendly. *Moderate.*

GUADALUPE

Parador Nacional Zurbarán (Calle Marqués de la Romana 10): Make no mistake: this is among Spain's most beautiful and—it is worth emphasizing—friendliest *paradores*. It went up in the fifteenth century as a hospital, to care for sick pilgrims come to worship the Virgin of Guadalupe at the neighboring monastery (see *On Scene*, above). Named for the great locally-born painter, many of whose paintings are on view in the monastery, the *parador* embraces a pair of superb structures, each enclosing a superb two-level patio. Arcades of one of these form an extension—delightful in warm weather—of the handsome restaurant (below), the lounge and bar are a pleasure, and the good-size swimming pool is set in a verdant garden. Those of the 40 rooms I have inspected—big double with a canopied bed, smaller twin with a huge garden-view terrace, among them—are a pleasure. *First Class.*

Hospedería del Real Monasterio (Plaza S. M. Juan Carlos I): Although my work has caused me—invariably with much pleasure—to inspect churches and monasteries operated by Franciscan friars in two hemispheres, I have encountered nothing elsewhere like the hospedería of the Guadalupe monastery. Under the astute professional direction of one of the monastery's 20 priests, Extremadura-born Father Juan Barrera, the Franciscans run a delightful, full-facility hotel within the monastery complex. And if you've a preconceived notion that it might be austere, be prepared for surprises. Public spaces include a traditionally-furnished lobby, intimate bar (where you want to order a platter of *tapas* with your sherry), reception area, and high-ceilinged lounge, as well as a pair of dining rooms (one for guests, below evaluated, the other for private parties, the monastery being a popular venue for weddings), and a sublime Gothic cloister, off of whose upper galleries are the 40 bedrooms. These include quite grand Royal Suite (with silver-framed photos of the present king and queen as well as Juan Carlos's grandfather, Alfonso XIII). But standard rooms are pleasant, too, and all are bath-equipped. Special. *Moderate.*

JARANDILLA DE LA VERA

Parador Nacional Carlos V: Toward the closing years of his event-packed life in the mid-sixteenth century, Holy Roman Emperor Charles V decided it was time to relax. He passed along the throne to his austere son, Philip II, and retired to a visitable-to-this-day monastery—Yuste, by name—some 75 miles northeast of Cáceres, at Jarandilla de la Vera. While Imperial quarters were being prepared at Yuste, Charles bedded down—over a period of several months—at a nobleman's castle that could be out of a Walt Disney movie—towered, turreted, romantic and contemporarily one of the most unusual of *paradores*. This is a 53-room house whose public spaces—lounge, bar, restaurant—evoke the long-ago presence of one of Europe's most celebrated monarchs. (While you're in residence, hop over to the nearby monastery to inspect Charles's personal quarters, the Gothic chapel and its pair of cloisters.) *First Class.*

DAILY BREAD

MÉRIDA

Nicolás (Calle Felix Lillo 13) caters to the Mérida establishment. At lunch, this centrally-situated spot hums; business types exchange the day's gossip, the while tucking into substantial fare. The *menú de la casa* is a good buy, and may run to a special soup or reliable gazpacho, grilled fillet of veal nicely garnished, *flan* or the day's special sweet, and house wine. But the à la carte is extensive, and with such specialties as trout *meunière* and roast partridge. Swift and cordial service. *First class.*

Parador Nacional Vía de la Plata Restaurante (Plaza Queipo de Llano 3): The handsome *comedor* of this handsome *parador* is at its best midday when you open the prix-fixe menu with assorted *entremeses*, or hors d'oeuvres. At any time, *caldereta de cordero*, an Extremedura variation on the theme of lamb stew, is a delicious bet. Commendable soups and sweets, too, and regional vintages among wines. *First Class.*

CÁCERES

Bodega Medieval (Calle Orellana 1) tries—and with success—to look as it should, given its evocative title. Setting is an atmospheric house dating back four centuries, with original ceiling, black and white tile floors which complement black Thonet-style chairs surrounding tables set in immaculate red and white linen. The staff welcomes you as if you were old friends. *Cochinillo*, roast suckling pig, is an entrée specialty of note, but grills—of pork and veal chops and fillets—are tasty, too. Or be adventuresome and try *tortilla Extremeña*—a local specialty. If you're pressed for time, settle for *bocadillos*—sandwiches—from the bar. Fun. *First Class.*

Figón (Plaza San Juan 14)—perhaps spoiled by its successful longevity—occupies not especially inviting—and quite cramped—quarters in a respectably aged house. The staff appears impatient to serve you and fill the table with other occupants—cordiality is not apparent—but fare is okay. There are two prix-fixe menus, with the pricier—concentrating on regional specialties based on fresh-water fish, eggs and pork—the more interesting. And the à la carte is extensive. *First Class.*

Trujillo

Pizarro (Plaza Mayor) is, at first glance, a small and unpretentious upstairs space. You warm to it, though, after an effusive welcome from the delightful owning couple. And you like the meal they bring you. It might open with assorted *entremeses*, a serving of Serrano ham, or the day's soup—ham and egg, perhaps. Stuffed partridge, a regional specialty; roast chicken and grilled veal served on a wooden plank are among entrées. *First Class.*

Parador Nacional de Trujillo Restaurante (Plaza de Santa Clara) is—like all *parador* restaurants—at its best midday when you open with a rich mix of assorted *entremeses*. Otherwise—unless, of course, chef and serving staff will have changed by the time you arrive—cooking is undistinguished (ask for the simplest grills, without sauces) and service is, by and large, unsmiling.

Guadalupe

Parador Nacional Zurbarán Restaurante (Calle Marqués de la Romana 10) is as delicious as it is good-looking and welcoming. You may open with assorted *entremeses* at lunch, but appetizers like seafood-stuffed avocado or shrimp and chicory salad are exemplary, too. Entrées include such regional specialties as *bacalao*—salt cod—prepared Extremadura style, surprisingly tasty roast kid, the lamb stew and stuffed partridge you may have enjoyed elsewhere in the area, and a simply but expertly broiled sirloin steak. Try a local dessert, *muegado de Guadalupe*, for example, or chestnut pudding. Carefully selected wines. *First Class.*

Hospedería del Real Monasterio Comedor (Plaza S. M. Juan Carlos I) Antique plates from the monastery's collection of local pottery decorate the walls of this grandly proportioned room, framed by a beamed ceiling. Fresh flowers center tables set in white linen, and prix-fixe menus—opening, perhaps with chilled gazpacho, following with fillet of fish or of veal, concluding with ice cream or *flan*—are good values. And the à la carte turns up such local specialties as lamb stew and fried pork, along with typical desserts. Gracious service. *Moderate.*

INCIDENTAL INTELLIGENCE

There are air-conditioned, reclining-seat buses to and from Madrid to the east, and Seville to the south, and some trains, with the buses to be preferred, slow as they are. Ideally, though, you explore Extremadura with a rented car, and, as I indicate earlier on in this chapter, a fair command of the Spanish language; English is very rarely spoken, even in better hotels, *paradores*, restaurants, shops, and transport terminals. *Further information:* Oficina de Turismo de Mérida, Calle Delgado Valencia 7; Oficina de Turismo de Cáceres, Plaza General Mola; Oficina de Turismo de Trujillo, Plaza de España.

14

Granada

*The Alhambra's
Ageless Grandeur*

BACKGROUND BRIEFING

Of the Spanish cities, Seville matches it in beauty. Still, nowhere more than in Granada does a single word more immediately evoke romance and grandeur. Or why, in other words, we budget our savings, pack our bags, and cross half a planet to experience Europe.

If Granada disappoints—and it can, in that it is a shabby city, more impoverished than most in Spain, save sadly ramshackle Cádiz—Granada's pluses outweigh a hotel plant that is wanting, restaurants rarely better than average, ubiquitous gypsy beggars-cum-babies, and aggressive, ambulatory bootblacks at every turn of every downtown street. Straddling a trio of hills beneath a ravishing snow-capped range of southern peaks, Granada has on its side the patina of history, and a sprinkling of relics great enough still—these many centuries later—for all Spain to respect.

Phoenicians, Greeks, Carthaginians, Romans: all were attracted to Granada's brilliant situation, beneath the snows on a fertile plain watered by the confluence of a pair of rivers, with the Mediterranean not far to the south. By the eighth century, Arabs had substantially settled in. But it was not until the thirteenth century that Granada's political fortunes peaked. A two-century Golden Age ensued, under a pair of alliteratively labeled dynasties whose names—Almoravids and Almohads—the

Granadines rattle off as we would Lincoln and Washington. Granada became synonymous with opulence, as much for its architecture, as for the fine and decorative arts.

The late fifteenth century saw dissent at the top. It had to do with the peccadilloes of a reigning caliph, which so angered his queen that the lady spurred a palace revolt in the name of their young son, dubbed El Rey Chico, the Boy King. This revolt so split the court that, lo! Christian forces moved in. The year is an easy one for New Worlders to remember: 1492. Ferdinand and Isabella took Granada, and in so doing ended Moorish power in Spain. The kingdom of Granada was at long last—after nearly eight Islamic centuries—Christian.

ON SCENE
Lay of the Land: Granada orients itself—perhaps as a onetime Moslem capital should—in the direction of the east, with the great bulk of the Alhambra looming above it, framed by the ever-snowy fringe of the Sierra Nevada. Calle Cuesta de Gomérez leads to Plaza Nueva, from which a principal east-west thoroughfare, Calle de los Reyes Católicos, continues into the core of the city and the towers of the Cathedral. Gran Vía de Colón is Main Street. The core of town is dotted with art-filled churches: *San Ildefonso, San Andrés, San Gregorio, Santos Justo y Pastor, San Matías, Santo Domingo,* to give you an idea.

One other point: whether to headquarter on the Alhambra heights or downtown? Selecting a hotel near the Alhambra tends to isolate one from the greater city. I suggest living below in the city, with the Granadines. For pilgrimages to the Alhambra, hop a cab up, and, if you like, walk down.

The Alhambra complex: I suspect you'll agree with me, if you know North Africa, that nowhere south of the Mediterranean shore are there monuments of the Arab genius at architecture and the arts any more brilliant than the Arab-built portions of the Alhambra. Indeed, there are specialists who opine that nothing in the Moslem world surpasses the walled gardens, pool-centered patios, and intricately embellished interiors of this medieval cluster.

Take it all in: arched gateways at the approach; patios (most es-

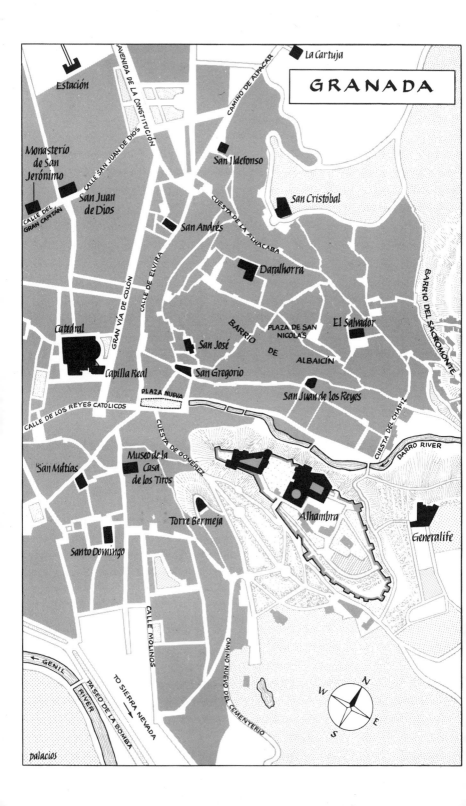

GRANADA

La Cartuja

Estación

CAMINO DE ALFACAR

AVENIDA DE LA CONSTITUCIÓN

CALLE SAN JUAN DE DIOS

San Ildefonso

San Cristóbal

Monasterio de San Jerónimo

San Juan de Dios

CALLE DEL GRAN CAPITÁN

San Andrés

CUESTA DE LA ALHACABA

CALLE DE ELVIRA

Daralhorra

GRAN VÍA DE COLÓN

BARRIO

PLAZA DE SAN NICOLÁS

El Salvador

BARRIO DEL SACROMONTE

Catedral

San José

DE

Capilla Real

San Gregorio

ALBAICÍN

CALLE DE LOS REYES CATÓLICOS

PLAZA NUEVA

San Juan de los Reyes

CUESTA DEL CHAPIZ

CUESTA DE GOMÉREZ

DARRO RIVER

San Matías

Museo de la Casa de los Tiros

Torre Bermeja

Alhambra

Generalife

Santo Domingo

CALLE MOLINOS

GENIL

PASEO DE LA BOMBA

TO SIERRA NEVADA

CAMINO NUEVO DEL CEMENTERIO

RIVER

N
W   E
S

palacios

pecially Los Leones, named for the not very fierce lions encircling its central fountain); arcaded galleries overlooking the city;
and interiors ranging from sumptuous baths through reception
rooms (including those of the harem) with walls tiled and
stuccoed, wood ceilings exquisitely carved and supported by
slim and elegant pillars. Everywhere, look carefully at the decorated plaster, which appears as light and lacy filigree.

By no means short-change the European part of this city
within a city: the palace built by Emperor Charles V, grandson
of Ferdinand and Isabella. What Charles wrought achieved a
still-maintained reputation as one of the great Renaissance
buildings of Europe, thanks most especially to its striking neoclassic façade and even more to its two-level circular patio.
Within are a pair of museums, about which I go into some detail
on a subsequent page.

Directly west of the Alhambra's core is what's left of the
Alcazaba, the fortress part of the complex, from one of whose
towers Isabella and Ferdinand flew the colors of Castile when
their troops secured Granada in 1492. A fair stroll east of the core
is the *Generalife*, a retreat-palace used mostly in summer by the
Moorish monarchs when they wanted to get away from the
Alhambra proper, in the manner of, say, Marie Antoinette and
her intimates escaping the main palace of Versailles to the adjacent Petit Trianon. Not that the Generalife was anything like as
small-scale as the Trianon: It was enormous, as you perceive
walking about its unfurnished rooms. But the treat today is its
formal, elongated garden—centered by pools, punctuated with
spraying fountains, made brilliant with flowers, and, atop the
city, affording memorable vistas of the lower Alhambra and of
downtown, far below.

One more Alhambra destination awaits. It's a onetime Franciscan monastery grafted onto what had been an Arab palace
dating back six centuries all told. It serves today as a *parador*
(see *Settling In*). No matter where you headquarter, step in to
see the plaque which explains that the then monastery was
where Ferdinand and Isabella were buried before their remains were moved to tombs in the *Capilla Real*—especially
created for that purpose—downtown.

Capilla Real (Calle de la Cárcel): What you want to remember is that the royal chapel is as much fine arts museum as church. Ferdinand's and Isabella's tombs—with sculpted likenesses of them above each—are almost alongside those of their daughter Juana the Mad and her Hapsburg husband, Philip the Handsome. The gilded, multi-tiered, sculpture-rich main altar, with figures of the royal pair flanking it, is masterful. So is the wrought-iron grille backing the tomb. One moves along to other objects: a gold crown of Isabella's, a gold sword of her husband's. And a collection of Flemish Primitive paintings: *Pietàs*, the dead Christ in the Virgin Mary's arms—both by Memling and van der Weyden; additional Memling *Virgins*; a Dirk Bouts of the head of Christ; with Spanish masters such as Pedro Berruguete represented too.

The Cathedral (Calle de la Cárcel): When one ponders its pedigree—leading Renaissance architect Diego de Siloé, creator of the golden staircase of Burgos Cathedral, among other works, was its leading light—the pity of Granada Cathedral is that it is not more impressive. Even if it were isolated, without competition from the next-door *Capilla Real*, it would disappoint, possibly because its original Gothic base doesn't blend as well as it might with de Siloé's Renaissance additions. Withal, proportions are massive—a score of columns support all of nine naves, with works of art by Granada-native master Alonso Cano in more than one of the ring of chapels, and in the Cathedral museum as well.

Church of San Juan de Dios (Calle San Juan de Dios): Skip the Cathedral (above) if you're pressed for time. But on no account miss St. John of God, the central city's most beautiful church, a dazzling example of what the Spanish species of baroque called Churrigueresque is all about. The façade is two-towered and severe. Within, one's breath is taken away by the gilded opulence: high and handsome main altar, equally elaborate altars of a quartet of chapels, exuberant frescoes of the nave's ceiling. Go next door, then, to the still-operating *Hospital de San Juan de Dios*, and walk through the main entrance to see the façade of its arched patio.

Monasterio de San Jerónimo (Calle del Gran Capitán): Not to be confused with the aesthetically unexceptional church bearing San Jerónimo's name nearby, this work of the sixteenth century, though still inhabited by monks of the San Jerónimo order, has friendly nuns of another order come from their convent to receive visitors, sell the delicious jams they make, and explain in Spanish—their only language—the principal wonders of the monastery and its chapel. Wonder No. 1 is a two-level cloister, one of the most imposing in the kingdom. Wonder No. 2 is the sculpture filling what must be more than half a hundred niches in the dozen levels of one of the great church altars of Spain. Not that the rest of the chapel—elegantly arched, strikingly frescoed, generously scaled—is any less impressive.

La Cartuja (Camino de Alfacar) is 10 minutes by car or taxi from the center, and as essential to a proper aesthetic appreciation of Granada as the Alhambra, Capilla Real, or San Juan de Dios. By which I mean to say, it's worth the cab fare, even if you have the driver wait. Inside, you find yourself in a seventeenth-century cloister, leading to a baroque church that just has to be one of the most beautiful to come out of the seventeenth century—plasterwork in pastels highlights a white-walled background, the lot set off by a golden altar. But there's more: a sacristy that is actually a chapel the size of the main church. It is late eighteenth century, with baroque plasterwork—on a series of high white columns lining each wall and framing a sublime altar—not dissimilar to the exuberant rococo in the churches of German's Bavaria. And that is going some.

Museo Provincial de Bellas Artes and Museo Arqueológico (Palacio de Carlos V, Alhambra) have in recent seasons kept such scandalously brief open-hours that I deal with them separately here, as distinct destinations that you may have to return to visit after you've seen the rest of the Alhambra complex. Of the two, Bellas Artes—with paintings by Granada-born Alonso Cano, sculpture by the Cathedral's principal architect-designer, de Siloé, and the tapestry-lined Sala de la Chimenes Italiana—is the more important. The Archeological Museum has Arab, Visigoth, and other venerable relics, academically if not artistically exciting.

Museo de la Casa de los Tiros (Calle de Pavaneras): This handsome Renaissance house shelters a delight of a museum; Granada's history is its thrust. Americans enjoy the Washington Irving room, chockablock with editions of *Tales of the Alhambra*—the little classic he wrote as a result of early nineteenth-century Granada residence, and which one sees for sale in major languages all over town. There's a memento-filled section dealing with Empress Eugénie, Granada-born wife of France's late nineteenth-century Emperor Napoleon III; a typically Granadine kitchen, almost on a par with counterparts in Valencia's Museo Nacional de Cerámica; a charming dining room, pottery-filled; and a gallery of Spanish monarchs' portraits. With the municipal tourist office's headquarters as a bonus.

Albaicín and Sacromonte districts: These barrios, both north of the Alhambra, overlooking town, could not be more disparate. The former, Albaicín, is residential Granada at its most Old World. Its cube-shaped houses, sparkling white and set off by verdant gardens, mostly date to Arab times. Amble about, using Plaza de San Miguel el Bajo as an orientation point. Sacromonte is something else again: the side of a cave-indented mountain, inhabited by Granada's gypsy populace. If you haven't had enough of the beggars downtown, Sacromonte offers more: flamenco dancers, these, who will perform at the drop of a handful of pesetas. Locales for the impromptu entertainment-cum-castanets-and-guitars are the caves, their whitewashed walls busily hung with tiny copper pots. "Showtimes" are whenever even a handful—or less—of tourists arrive.

Sierra Nevada: Mountain buffs, ski buffs, and panormic-scenery buffs like to earmark half a day of a Granada stay for an excursion to the modern *parador* (see *Settling In*), or inn, atop the snowy mountain range that backs the city. It's but 15 miles distant, the highway—dazzlingly engineered—is reputedly Europe's highest, and the views from the Picacho de Veleta lookout—at 11,246 feet—do not, believe me, disappoint; on a clear day you can see the Mediterranean. And if you go in winter, you can watch the skiers, or join them.

SETTLING IN

CITY CENTER

Hotel Meliá Granada (Calle Angel Ganivet 7) is the ideal Granada hotel: centrally situated, with 220 well-equipped rooms (my only quibble is that they could be larger), commodious lobby, attractive restaurant, convenient *cafetería* (worth knowing about this, no matter what your hotel), popular bar-lounge. One of the Meliá chain. *Luxury.*

Hotel Carmen (Calle Acera del Darro 62) should be at least twice as good as it is. I mention it here because downtown has not all that many decent hotels. This one is at least central, modern, clean, and with good beds in its nearly 170 unattractive rooms with baths. Facilities include a restaurant, *cafetería*, and bar, with the first two—so far as I can observe—keeping irregular hours. *First Class.*

Hotel Montecarlo (Avenida José Antonio 44) is a not-bad downtown house, conveniently situated, with some 60 rooms, most with private baths, pleasant lobby, good-value restaurant. *Moderate.*

Hotel Victoria (Puerto Real 3) must once have been quite grand. The distinctive dome above its well-detailed turn-of-century façade is a downtown landmark. But the Victoria has seen better days. Still, there are 90 rooms with bath, lobby, restaurant, bar. *Moderate.*

Hotel Luz Granada (Avenida de la Constitución 18) might well be at the head of my downtown selections if only it were central. It is, however, just far enough away from the core to be not quite walkable. Still, there are 175 agreeable rooms and suites, a welcoming lobby, very good main restaurant, *cafetería*, and—bear this in mind—a rooftop grill-cum-terrace that affords views not only of town but of the snowy Sierra Nevada. A link of the Spain-wide Hoteles Interhotel chain. *Luxury.*

ALHAMBRA

Hotel Alhambra Palace (Calle Peña Partida 1) is a mock-Moorish pile dating back perhaps half a century that has emerged from a recent, much-needed and really thorough refurbishing, stem to stern—including all 130 bedrooms and their baths. It went up as a hospital—King Alfonso XIII dedicated it—and its gracefully arched public spaces are high and wide. There's an attractive restaurant and bubbly bar, with the Alhambra but five minutes distant. *First Class.*

Hotel Washington Irving (Bosques de la Alhambra) is an elderly but handsomely maintained house right in the center of the Alhambra action—if, indeed, the Alhambra can be said to offer action. There are some 70 attractive rooms with bath, and a paneled bar-lounge. My only caveat is that (when I last checked, at least) no credit cards are accepted, a situation almost unique among hotels in Spain. *First Class.*

Hotel Guadalupe (Avenida de los Alijares) is more neighbor to the Generalife than to the Alhambra proper. But no matter. This is a very nice hotel in two distinct parts, each with its own entrance and *conserje.* There are 43 rooms all told (all with bath), attractive public spaces, a cozy bar, and a worth-knowing-about restaurant offering *menús del día* at good tabs. *First Class.*

Hostal América (Calle Real de la Alhambra 53) is a winner of a small house in attractive elderly quarters that puts one in mind more of a pension than a proper hotel. But, unlike at a pension, one need take no meals here other than breakfast, although demi- and full-pension arrangements are available. There are just over a dozen rooms (each with its own bath), a delightful lobby-lounge, and caring owner-management. You had better book by mail in advance. *Moderate.*

Parador Nacional de San Francisco uses simply "Alhambra" as its proper address. And well it might. This originally fifteenth-century Franciscan monastery is a significant enough historic monument for me to accord it space in *On Scene,* above. It was, as I mention, where Los Reyes Católicos—Ferdinand and Isabella—were buried before their bodies were moved to the Capilla Real, downtown; a plaque explains. There are, as well, an enchanting patio, mostly—albeit not entirely—antiques-filled public spaces (the dining room and bar are contemporary additions), and—here's the rub—just 39 rooms. Each of those I have inspected is lovely. But they're booked as much as a year in advance. That's a long time and that's why, with reluctance, the *parador* is near the tail end of my Granada hotels group. *First Class.*

Hotel La Bobadilla is not in Granada, but out in the country, near the village of Salinas, not far west of town in the direction of Seville. It's a motorists-only overnight splurge-stop, traditional in both architecture and decor (although relatively young—it opened only in 1986) set amidst an elevated forest, with 35 luxurious, no-two-alike rooms and suites all with lavish painted-tile baths, pair of restaurants (one, *nouvelle*-accented La Finca, is very grand indeed; the other has Spanish specialties and is informal), cocktail lounge, outdoor and indoor pools, solarium-sauna-fitness center-massage parlor, and tennis courts. A stunner of a complex. *Luxury.*

DAILY BREAD

CITY CENTER

Cunini (Calle de Capuchinas 14) is indicated for a lunch (it's a near neighbor of the Cathedral) or dinner of Granadian specialties. I am partial to *habas con jamón,* a delicious ham-and-beans combination. The *parillada de mariscos,* a seafood mixed-grill, is super, too. For dessert, it's wise to have each member of your party order a different one, concentrating on those of Granada-origin. Lots of locals in attendance. *First Class.*

Sevilla (Calle Oficios 12) is indicated for lunch in the course of exploring the core of the city. This is a gracious old restaurant just opposite the entrance to the Capilla Real in the Cathedral complex. Ask for a table on the terrace if it's a fine day, and order the well-priced *menú del día* (hope that *pollo ajillo*—garlic chicken—is available); tab is *Moderate.*

Torres Bermejas (Plaza Nueva 5): Granada has few luxury-category restaurants, the kind of place one picks for a grand splurge of a dinner. Torres Bermejas is among them, softly lit by shaded wall sconces, with alert waiters, and, traditionally, a choice of three *menús del día.* À la carte, as well. *Luxury.*

Los Leones (Avenida José Antonio 10) attracts budget-minded Granadines who appreciate the value of its thrifty *menús del día,* its good looks, and its chipper service. Central, too. *Moderate.*

Galerías Preciados Cafetería (Calle José Antonio): The Granada link of the kingdom-wide department-store chain serves a generous *buffet libre*—which means go back as often as you like—lunch in its third-floor *cafetería,* with both hot and cold dishes. Snacks, breakfast too. *Moderate.*

Woolworth (Calle Mesones 26): Woolworth's? Why not, especially if you're a mite homesick? Do not count on English being spoken, however, in its fast-service, low-priced *cafetería. Moderate.*

ALHAMBRA

Parador Nacional de San Francisco Restaurante (Alhambra): The preferred meal is lunch, if only because this is when one may choose from a selection of *entremeses,* or appetizers—some 20-odd, each in its own dish—as a first course of the set menu, as is the happy situation in units of the *parador* chain, kingdom-wide. At both lunch and dinner, there are regional specialties: *sopa de almendras,* a tasty almond soup; *omelet Sacromonte,* eggs Granada-style; or sardines up from the Mediterranean. Ask for a wine from the area: Albandón or Huetor, to name two. Reservations are not taken; go early and hope for a short queue. *First Class.*

Colombia (Antequeruela Baja, Alhambra): You're liable to collide with Cousin Dot or your neighbors from down the street, here on one of this big group-oriented restaurant's three levels. The food's authentic, the white linen crisp, and the guitar accompaniment agreeable. *First Class.*

INCIDENTAL INTELLIGENCE

It is an insult to Granada, not to mention one's own intelligence, to visit this city by means of a one-day commercial bus-excursion from the Costa del Sol, to the south. Like Toledo, because of its proximity to Madrid, Granada bears the cross of day-trippers. It cannot be done justice in so short a time. Do arrange to visit it properly, staying a couple of days. Iberia flies in; the airport is 10 miles from the center. As in cities throughout Andalusia, bullfights are big; try and take one in. Flamenco dancing figures mightily in the after-dark scene; as throughout Spain, flamenco *boîtes* are pricey and not always satisfactory, so that I make no recommendations. Ask your hotel concierge for the currently recommendable spots. Generally, the steep admission includes an initial drink with successive libations cheaper. *Further information:* Oficina de Turismo de Granada, Casa de los Tiros, Calle de Pavaneras 19.

15

Ibiza

Mediterranean Respite

BACKGROUND BRIEFING

Barefoot, tranquil, quaint, beyond the mainstream: Ibiza, it must be understood at the outset, is no longer any of these. Its airport has become one of Europe's busiest. It packs in a million sun-starved northern Europeans every summer, most of them on inexpensive packages. Its hotels—there are exceptions, of course—are the same species of resort hotel common to Majorca, Costa del Sol, and other mass resort areas the planet over. By that, I mean they're mostly big, multi-story, multi-facility houses, quite as modern as Ibiza—a veritable midget of an island compared with its giant Balearic neighbor, Majorca—is ancient.

For, make no mistake, Ibiza is old and still with sufficient souvenirs to prove it, despite an apparently no-holds-barred hotel-expansion policy that is the subject of frequent debate among its citizens. Phoenicians were on Ibiza as long ago as 1,000 years before Christians. Three centuries after the Phoenicians, colonists came from Carthage, on the shores of what is now Tunisia, across the Mediterranean. They called their capital—now Ibiza Town—Ebusos, and they developed a remarkably advanced society, not only fishing but wine-making and farming and mining. Not to mention thriving as artists and artisans. Indeed, enough of the Ibiza-Carthaginian art and artifacts have been found in the island's soil (they still turn up and are not unlike the pre-Columbian art of the New World) to serve as nucleus of what is one of the foremost museums of Carthaginian culture.

Romans eventually succeeded Carthaginians; remnants of their presence remain on the island. A half-millennium of incursions and invasions, many by the Vandals, followed the Roman exodus. In the eighth century, mainland Moors took over, governing with the same brilliance and vitality manifested in their larger domains. The Arabs left a strong cultural imprint, of which a good deal remains; most dramatic are the white cubes of houses that fill the landscape—three-dimensional exercises in the geometry at which the Moors were so proficient.

As Spain became Christian, in the post-Moorish era, so indeed did Ibiza: first as a part of Jaime I's Valencian kingdom, later under the Catalonians, a variation of whose distinctive language the Ibizans continue to speak, as do the Majorcans, from whose island (the biggest of the Balearics) modern Ibiza is administered. (Not happily, it should go without saying; the Ibizans want increased self-government.)

Contemporary Ibiza is nothing if not anomalous. Undaunted by the Germans, Britons, Scandinavians, Dutch, French, and Belgians that sweep in each summer on the tourist charters, it perseveres in remaining Ibizan. With hundreds of thousands of outlanders occupying ultra-mod hotels on an island 12-by-25 miles, this has not been easy for the native population of some 35,000. Withal, Ibizan country women still wear folk costumes of their forebears, dance traditional dances, and worship in the old whitewashed churches.

ON SCENE

Lay of the Land: Its size is just right, neither too large nor too small, with a single major town, Ibiza by name, on the southeast coast and a countryside with but two other towns of substance: Santa Eulalia del Río, due north of the capital on the east coast, and San Antonio Abad on the west coast. The interior—rugged and mountainous—knows few settlements; San José, with a precious antique of a church, is the main one. The coast is dotted with villages and a succession of beaches (called *calas* as well as *playas* on Ibiza).

Ibiza Town is a mostly ancient and atmospheric charmer, and warrants exploration by even the laziest of beachcombing vacationers. It embraces the elevated *D'alt Vila* quarter, sprawling around Plaza de la Catedral; the maze of venerable white cubes of houses comprising the fishermen's district to the west; the café-and-shop-filled marina district fronting the waters of the port, north of the *Cathedral*; and the southern, *Figueretas* district, whose hotel-flanked beach is worth noting because of its convenient urban position. Start with the chunky bulk of the on-high Cathedral, whose severe Gothic bell tower is Ibiza Town's sole skyscraper and whose interior bears signs of sadly infelicitous restoration over the centuries. Eminently more requisite is neighboring *Museo Arqueológico*, chockablock with souvenirs of the culturally exciting Carthaginian epoch, going back seven pre-Christian centuries. The museum building—originally Gothic but with architectural motifs through the baroque—is striking in and of itself, as are such Punic pieces as sculpted heads, oversized necklaces, ceramic animals. There are, as well, bits and pieces of later Roman Ibiza, coins especially. Additional evidences of Punic Ibiza? Trot over to the necropolis of Ereso at *Puig des Molins*, where the draw is a cluster of *hypoges*, or subterranean vaults, dating beyond the Carthaginian period to Phoenician times and embracing 2,000 tombs.

Santa Eulalia del Río, nine miles up the east coast from Ibiza Town, incorporates in its name the presence of the island's sole river. More visitable is an oddly beautiful fortress-church on the hill—or *puig*—called *De Missa*; it is sixteenth century, and adjacent to a cluster of similarly ancient houses, one of which, *Museo Barrau*, shelters the paintings of a local artist. Surrounding beaches are hotel-flanked.

San Antonio Abad, across-island from the capital, is the metropolis of the west coast, by Ibiza standards at least. This is a more substantial town than you might imagine, dotted with hotels, both in the interior and along the wide, sprawling, and beach-lined bay, where there are worse things to do, in late afternoon as the sun is setting, than stroll the coastal promenade, pausing in one of its cafés for refreshment. Multinational San

Antonio is kicky. No single resort town in Spain has a more cosmopolitan flavor.

SETTLING IN

Ibiza Town

Hotel Ibiza Playa (directly on the beach at Figueretas) is high, wide, and handsome—all 150 balconied rooms of it, with a capacious pool overlooking the sea, restaurant, bar, Spanish as well as northern European guests. *Moderate.*

Hotel Copacabana (Calle Ramón Muntaner in Figueretas) offers good value; a smaller house, not on but near the beach, with a restaurant, bar, and baths in all 110 rooms. Modern and *Moderate.*

Hotel Mare Nostrum (Plaza d'en Bossa, at Bossa) is a big, 500-room house with pool, restaurant, and bar. Not on, but near enough the beach to cause you no inconvenience. *Moderate.*

Hotel Argos (on the beach at Talamanca) is a welcoming house with 100-plus rooms-cum-baths, good restaurant-bar, and pool. *First Class.*

Santa Eulalia del Río

Hotel Fenicia is a mile from the center, smack on the beach called Ca'n Fita. Nearly 200 handsome rooms with balconies, seaside restaurant, bar-lounge, garden-fringed pool, tennis, and all the relaxation you would like. *Luxury.*

Hotel Tres Torres (Calle Seis Estaques) is an extremely comfortable, 110-room facility, nicely and quietly situated; pretty garden, pool. *First Class.*

Hotel Caribe (Playa Es Cana) has 270 modern rooms with baths in the doubles, showers in the singles, restaurant-bar, big outdoor pool, and calm swimmable waters fringing its beach. *Moderate.*

SAN ANTONIO ABAD

Hotel Palmyra (Avenida Fleming, directly on the bay) is far handsomer within than its prosaic façade would indicate. The 150 bedrooms-cum-terraces are among the most creatively decorated of any I know at Spanish resorts. Paneled bar-lounge; crisp white dining room; cozy, period-style lounges: all please. And a big pool complements the beach. *Luxury.*

Hotel Bergantín (directly on Playa de S'Estanyol) is a find, what with 250 full-facility rooms, a quiet environment, a pool as well as a beach, a few drinking spots, and a restaurant. *First Class.*

Hotel Tropical (Calle Cervantes) is a looker; center-of-town but quiet, thanks to its capacious grounds-cum-pool (with another for *los niños*—the kids), restaurant, bar-lounge, and a couple of hundred terraced rooms. *First Class.*

Hotel Orosol (Calle Ramón y Cajal) is a budget-category house of some 60 rooms with bath, restaurant, bar, and a heart-of-town situation that's a hop and a skip from Hotel Tropical (above), whose pool Orosol guests may use *sin recargo*, which means, of course, without charge. *Moderate.*

SAN MIGUEL

Hotel Hacienda Na Xamena is high in the hills, at San Miguel, north of San Antonio. It's smallish (there are just over 50 rooms) and stylish, based on traditional Ibizan house design, with top-of-the-world views all along the coast way, way, way below. All of the handsome rooms have terraces with vistas, and there's a top-category restaurant, bar-lounge, a trio of pools, and tennis. The Hacienda is Ibiza's poshest hotel, but, remember, you're quite a drive from the beaches. Member, Relais et Châteaux. *Luxury.*

DAILY BREAD

IBIZA TOWN

El Olivo (Plaza Luis Tur 8, Ibiza Town) is a charming Ibizan-decor spot, pleasant for lunch in the course of a day's in-town exploration. Order seafood. *First Class.*

El Portalón (Plaza Desamparados, Ibiza Town) has an authentic island look, good-value *menú del día*. *First Class.*

El Vesubio (Calle Navarra 19, Playa de Figueretas) will, if you smile sweetly, serve specialties from way up in the rainy northern province of Galicia. *Moderate.*

SANTA EULALIA DEL RÍO

Sa Punta (Calle Isidoro Macabich) is smart to look upon, with a fairly elaborate menu embracing international dishes and heartier local specialties. *First Class.*

SAN ANTONIO ABAD

El Refugio (Calle Bartolome Vicente Ramón 5) is traditional in decor, likewise with dishes both of the island and the mainland. The house's own wines are counseled. *First Class.*

El Patio (Calle Miramar 4) is well-located, heart-of-town, and well-priced. *Moderate.*

INCIDENTAL INTELLIGENCE

Both Iberia and Aviaco connect Ibiza's busy airport with such mainland cities as Madrid, Barcelona, and Valencia, and with Palma de Majorca as well. Other European carriers link the island with such continental points as London, Paris, and Frankfurt. Countless charters add to the confusion. The airport is six miles from Ibiza Town. There is regular passenger ship service, as well, between Ibiza and Barcelona, Valencia, Palma de Majorca, and the nearby little Balearic island of Formentera (an interesting excursion destination). *Further information:* Oficina de Turismo de Ibiza, Calle Vara de Rey 13.

16

León

What King Ferdinand Hath Wrought

BACKGROUND BRIEFING

Pronunciation, first. If you say "lee-on" you're not going to be comprehended. In Spanish, the "lee" becomes "lay," and that accent mark over the *o* means that the word comes out as "lay-own." It counts for something both in Spain—where it's the name not only of our subject city but of a contemporary Spanish province and an ancient Spanish kingdom—and in the New World as well; there are Leóns both in Mexico and Nicaragua.

The name of the game in today's Spanish León is trade and commerce. This is, essentially, a humming, medium-sized city at the foot of a range of northwest mountains, where a pair of rivers, the Bernesga and Torío, meet up. One doesn't go out of one's way for a pleasure visit. Still, if you are in the neighborhood—en route, for example, to Santiago de Compostela, as were countless religious pilgrims who stopped in León centuries ago—you want to lay over, for what remains of old León is worth encountering.

The pity, as with so many cities, is that not more of the historic town has come through to our era. What León has to show is of impeccable pedigree: a quartet of monuments of as many epochs of its past.

Like so much of Spain, early León knew Roman colonists, later, Germanic Visigoths, still more recently, Moors out of North Africa. It was during the eighth century—with reconquest by the Christians from the Moors—when matters became more complex. One doesn't envy Spanish school children having to sort out when León was (a) under kings of Asturias, (b) under kings ruling the combined kingdom of Asturias and León, (c) under kings of Castile and Navarre, in tandem, (d) under a unitary Castile, and, ultimately, (e) as a monarchy united with that of Castile, under the remarkable Ferdinand III (later to be sainted), who managed to bring together all of Christian Spain, Granada excepted, by the time he died in 1252.

ON SCENE

Lay of the Land: For the short-term visitor, intent principally on an inspection of León's major monuments, the city is not as compact as it might be, and seems much larger than it is in population (about 100,000). The railway station is out of the way, on the west, or minor, bank of the Bernesga River. The city's leading hotel—which doubles as one of its major historic monuments—is toward the northern fringe of the core, on the river's east bank. Two principal destinations, the *Cathedral* and the *Basílica de San Isidro*, lie to the east of the center. The traditional heart of the city—Plaza Mayor, dominated by the Renaissance-era *Consistorio* (town hall), and still a marketplace—is to the south, while its contemporary counterpart, Plaza de Santo Domingo, is toward the center. It marks the eastern terminus of Calle Ordoño II, the bustling, shop-and-café-lined main street that continues west to the square grandly labeled Glorieta de Guzmán el Bueno. A substantial fragment of the city's medieval walls remains in the area of the Cathedral. Still other pieces of old León are to be found in the Plaza Mayor district: the Romanesque *Church of San Martín* in a barrio that takes its name, and equally aged *Church of Santa María del Mercado* flanking a square with its name.

San Marcos (Plaza de San Marcos): If you're wise, your León home away from home will be the stunning luxury hotel that is a major sector of this extraordinary complex, and about which I go into detail on a later page. Suffice it to say, at this point, that I hope you'll stay here, and begin your León explorations without even having to leave the premises. San Marcos dates back a millennium to the time when pilgrims, en route from France and other countries to the east, were on their way to the shrine of St. James the Apostle at Santiago de Compostela (the subject of a chapter in this book). The original San Marcos was a monastery-hostel-hospital for religious pilgrims. Later, though, King Ferdinand II, husband of Isabella I, initiated plans for a new structure that would house the elite Knights of the Order of Santiago, of which he was the titular leader and to whom he was indebted for their military prowess in the course of the successful Christian reconquest of Spain. By the time Ferdinand's grandson, Charles, had become king (and Holy Roman emperor), the new San Marcos opened. It was worth waiting for. The intricate and exquisite façade, to begin, is one of the great Plateresque exteriors extant. The cloister, with two levels of arched galleries, is serenely beautiful. The early Gothic church—with a spectacularly high nave—was retained and embellished with a carved-wood choir and sacristies, which now house a more recent addition to the San Marcos complex: León's separately administered *Archeological Museum*, with such treasures as ancient Iberian coins, mosaics from the Roman period, Romanesque capitals and crucifixes, and sculpted saints of the later Middle Ages. The old chapter room—with a geometric-design Mudéjar ceiling—is now a lounge of still another part of the San Marcos complex that is the basis of one of the most extraordinary hotels in Europe.

The Cathedral (Plaza de la Catedral) is one of Spain's great ones, an enchanter right up there near the top level of the cathedrals in Toledo, Seville, and Burgos. León's is pure and elegant Gothic, mostly out of the thirteenth century. Look about without: at the twin-towered façade, the high-flung flying buttresses, and, worthy of special study, lavishly carved portals of the side entrance. Its scale alone is recommendation enough for the interior, but the stained-glass windows of this cathedral put one in mind of those of Chartres, in France. There are 125 windows, the achievements of artists from the thirteenth century right up to our very own. Works of art are dotted all about, but there is a rich concentration in a multi-chamber museum of paintings, crucifixes (especially in ivory), and sculpture. Before you exit, visit the cloister, and pass by the choir, whose 110 black-walnut stalls were executed 500 years ago.

Basílica de San Isidro (Plaza de San Isidro) is one of the ranking specimens of Spanish Romanesque, with few superiors anywhere in Europe. This is a generously proportioned church with a wealth of carefully designed detail: arches of its doors, vestibules, and windows, capitals of its columns, proportions of its apses and its patio. Not to mention sumptuous frescoes, as vivid today as when they were painted eight centuries ago, in its pantheon. As at San Marcos and the Cathedral, there is a separate museum, with illuminated manuscripts, enameled chests, polychrome saints, and—among other things—a golden coffer of St. Isidore's relics, covered and lined with centuries-old silks.

An excursion to Astorga, 25 miles southwest of León, can be rewarding, especially if the visitor has become fascinated with the route followed—a millennium back—by pilgrims come from France and the east, en route to the shrine of St. James at Santiago de Compostela, tó the northeast, and the subject of a chapter in this book. As I indicate above, the monastery of San Marcos was a major stopping-off place for these travelers. At little Astorga, the bishop's palace—*Palacio Episcopal*—adjacent to the Cathedral, has two things to recommend it. First, the building itself is the work of the turn-of-the-century Barcelona architect Antonio Gaudí. Not surprisingly, to those familiar with Gaudí's work, it's a variation on the theme of a turreted and towered medieval castle-chapel, and is now dubbed *Museo de los Caminos*. Second, it is filled with art and artifacts of Santiago-bound pilgrims: polychrome saints, finely detailed gold crosses, paintings and documents, the lot rewarding and insightful, especially if one is en route to, or has come from, Santiago de Compostela. The next-door Gothic cathedral is a surprise of consequence in so small a town; its high altar is splendid. So, for that matter, is the town's Baroque-era Plaza de España, with its light and lively *Ayuntamiento*, an especially appealing town hall.

The even smaller town of *Villafranca del Bierzo*—another 25 miles to the east—is nicely combined with Astorga in the course of a day's outing. It's a pretty mountain village with half a dozen extraordinarily handsome churches, tiny Romanesque ones to giant baroque *San Nicolás*. And, as a special treat, the restaurant (and accommodations) of Alberque de Carretera, a relatively modest unit of the government-run chain of *paradores*.

SETTLING IN
Hotel San Marcos (Plaza de San Marcos), as I indicate above, is a part of the away-from-the-counter San Marcos monastery complex. To sleep, eat, drink, lounge—and just plain walk about—this palace-like compound begun by King Ferdinand the Catholic and completed in the reign of Emperor Charles V is not an easily forgotten experience. Earlier on, in this chapter, I allude to that portion of the complex operated as a museum. Other public spaces—including a ravishing cloister and a series of high-ceilinged, antique-accented galleries—double as lobby, cocktail lounge, television room, and restaurant. There are, as well, nearly 260 modern-decor rooms and suites in a contemporary wing. A link of the Paradores de España chain. *Luxury.*

Hotel Conde Luna (Calle Independencia 5) is, unlike the San Marcos (above), conveniently central and popular with returning visitors who've experienced the monastery and want to be closer to things. One hundred and fifty comfortable rooms, in an attractive environment, bar-lounge, indoor pool, and the commendable Restaurant El Mesón. *First Class.*

Hotel Quindoes (Avenida José Antonio 24) is an agreeable house on the street linking the San Marcos with the center of town. Convenient location. Nearly 100 rooms, with private baths. Restaurant. *First Class.*

DAILY BREAD
Novelty (Calle Independencia 2) is a novel name for a restaurant in Spain. This one has a zippy contemporary look to it, a central situation, and exemplary fare, including the Basque veal specialty, *zancarrón vasco*. *Luxury.*

Bodega Regia (Plaza San Martín 8) is a traditional-style foil to the Novelty (above) with attractively priced specialties, including pan-fried trout from nearby streams. *Moderate.*

Emperador (Calle Santa Nonia 2), in the center, is homey, welcoming, and serves local dishes. Ask if the Leonese version of the stew-like *cocido* is on the menu. *Moderate.*

INCIDENTAL INTELLIGENCE

Oficina de Turismo de León, Plaza de Regla 4.

17

Madrid

Expert at Elegance

BACKGROUND BRIEFING

Though it may not like to think of itself in this way, Madrid is quite the upstart among the Latin capitals. Rome conquered the ancient world. Lisbon traded with the Phoenicians and became the seat of Portugal's crown in the early twelfth century. Paris had a patron saint of its own as early as the fifth century, but had been a town since Caesar's conquest. And though not a national capital, it might be added that Spain's No. 2 city, Barcelona, counts the Carthaginians as ancestors. Madrid, smack in the barren interior, without so much as a proper river running alongside it, was little more than an obscure fortress until the fourteenth century.

At that time, in 1329, the *Cortes*, or Parliament, of Castile honored it by meeting there. And a century later Ferdinand and Isabella took up occasional residence; Emperor Charles V did likewise. But it was not until the middle of the sixteenth century—in 1561—that Charles V's son, cool and cruel Philip II, made Madrid the capital; although only after Philip's son, Philip III, became king did it begin to be built up as such.

Philip II's remarkable palace-monastery at El Escorial (worthy of a chapter of its own in this book) is exurban. But Plaza Mayor—constructed during Philip III's Golden-Age reign—is surely the major Renaissance monument of Madrid. And there are other remnants of Old Madrid that are called to your attention in later pages of this chapter. Still, one must go elsewhere in Spain—Córdoba, Granada, Seville, Toledo, Burgos, Santiago de Compostela, Barcelona, León, Salamanca (all subjects of chapters in these pages)—to view the country's great architecture. So indeed must one look elsewhere for the beginnings of the nation that became great only after it united to fight a brilliant Afro-Arab enemy: the Moors.

The earliest Spaniards didn't have Spain to themselves for long. Romans took them over two centuries before Christ, and they became Christianized in succeeding centuries. Germanic Visigoths followed, remaining as overlords for some time. But in the eighth century, Spain was to know a new conqueror. Moors came from across the Mediterranean in North Africa. They might well have taken all of Europe had not the Franks contained them in 732. Still, they held onto their Spanish territory despite internal squabbling—enough to weaken them to the point where northern Spaniards could realistically consider ousting them.

It took time—several centuries—for this to happen, during which the Moors implanted their rich culture, as did the highly skilled and gifted Jews. Both groups lived amicably alongside the Christians. Eventually, the two major Spanish kingdoms, those of Castile and Aragón, were united in the fifteenth century when Ferdinand II and Isabella—*Los Reyes Católicos*, as they came to be called—were married. Then came 1492. Isabella sent Christopher Columbus off to find a new route to India, and Spain had the good luck to be the power that discovered a new world. At the same time, Ferdinand and Isabella's troops captured Granada, last remaining Moorish stronghold. In their zeal to create a united Christian kingdom, Ferdinand and Isabella expelled the Jewish community, which took its skills and capital to the Netherlands and other countries. This move was to the detriment of Spain, for the Jews had been of substantial cultural and commercial importance. Later, many Moors—who had been forced to convert to Christianity—were expelled, and constituted another loss of significant importance.

Still, Spain had its New World—almost all of South America (Brazil went to Portugal), Central America, the southern part of North America (including Mexico), and the Philippines, as well, became Spanish territory in the sixteenth century. Spain was the New World's first power. Emperor Charles V concentrated on unification of the country. His ambitious son, Philip II, went a step further. Although he did not begin the Inquisition, Philip was fanatic enough to have made it an ugly force, not only in Spain but also in the Spanish Netherlands, where his policies were so oppressive that the northern area—now Holland—successfully revolted. Dutch losses were as nothing compared with what followed. After his wife—England's stubborn and unhappy Catholic Mary Tudor ("Bloody Mary")—died four years after they were married at beautiful Winchester Cathedral in the south of England, he proposed to Mary's half-sister Elizabeth I and was turned down. In 1558, he sailed his "invincible" Armada against the fleet of the queen who had spurned his hand—and was defeated. The loss of the Armada signaled the start of a bad-luck period for the Spanish empire.

Madrid, rather paradoxically, blossomed culturally under Philip III in the baroque seventeenth century: Miguel de Cervantes created his immortal *Don Quixote*, Lope de Vega wrote his plays, El Greco and Zurbarán painted; and the distinctive Spanish baroque, or Churrigueresque, style evolved in architecture and decoration, crossing the Atlantic to the colonies of the Americas to have a lasting effect.

The succeeding reign saw Philip IV serve as patron of such luminaries as Flemish Rubens and Seville-born Velázquez. (Indeed, because of the attendance of Velázquez at his court, few rulers in history were painted more often than the fourth Philip.) Monarchs of the Bourbon dynasty were the first to live in Madrid's mammoth, still eminently visitable Royal Palace; they ushered in a French-influenced era of decadence, bigotry, and corruption in high places, and an impoverished peasantry; attempts at reform were futile.

In 1808, Napoleon humiliated Spain by occupying it and installing his brother Joseph Bonaparte on the throne. With the help of the first (the Iron) Duke of Wellington's British forces, the French were ousted a half-decade later, but another decade saw virtually all of the South American colonies independent. The Spanish-American War at the end of the last century ended with the loss of the Philippines, Cuba, and Puerto Rico.

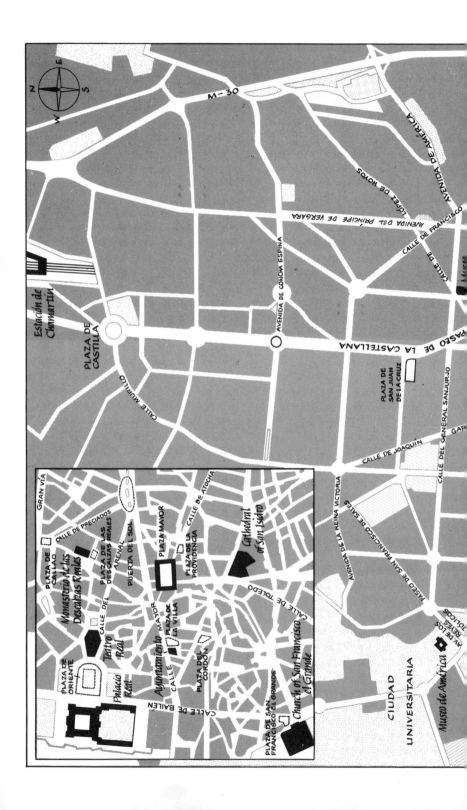

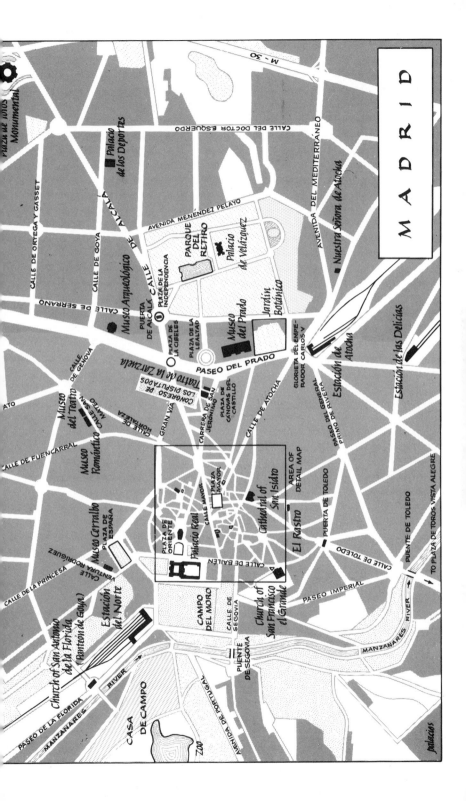

The twentieth century brought few improvements; strikes and demonstrations were forcefully repressed. General Primo de Rivera's military dictatorship ruled from 1929 to 1930 and finally, in 1931, the last king to reign for four and a half succeeding decades—Alfonso XIII—departed. Next came a republic whose first president, Alcalá Zamora, resigned in protest against extreme anticlerical legislation enacted by the Cortes.

In 1936, the Popular Front—composed of liberal republicans working with socialists and communists—won the national elections so overwhelmingly that reactionary forces led by General Francisco Franco precipitated a rebellion that plunged the country into a bloody three-year civil war that took more than one million lives and helped set the stage for World War II.

Franco's insurgents received substantial help from Nazi Germany (whose bombing of the defenseless Basque village of Guernica is immortalized in the monumental Picasso painting, for long at New York's Museum of Modern Art, and now in an annex of Madrid's Prado) and Fascist Italy. However, Loyalist republicans—led by Catalonian nationalists in Barcelona and by the Basques—had little outside help except that of an international brigade (in which some 600 Americans served) and token support from the Soviet Union. The Loyalists made a remarkable stand. They managed to hold Madrid until the end of the war: a feat, considering their inferior numbers and their internal differences.

Its own war over, Spain remained neutral in World War II, although its partiality toward the Axis powers resulted in the United Nations initially turning it down for membership in 1948, finally admitting it almost a decade later.

Post-World War II decades saw a government—dictatorial well into the Seventies—make commendable albeit cautious efforts to bind up the wounds of a bitterly divided land, at the same time ever so gradually lessening oppressive controls to the point where the press was a mite less restricted, and conversational criticism was tolerated, even if public opposition was not. Generalísimo Franco made a point of bypassing the pretender to the throne, Don Juan, son of Alfonso XIII (even though he wanted the job), in favor of Don Juan's son, Prince Juan Carlos. (See *Royal Family*, Chapter 1.) The transition from totalitarian state to constitutional monarchy has been, by and large, smooth and peaceful, though hardly without problems like strikes (Spanish labor was able to express itself after a powerless three and a half decades), and terrorism (especially by a fanatic Basque group).

ON SCENE
Lay of the Land: Madrid's beauty lies in its style. It is expert at elegance. What it lacks in individual monuments of architectural greatness it compensates for with the sweep of its boulevards, the dramatic fountains and heroic sculpture of its circles, the splendid proportions of its plazas, the emerald lawns and rainbow hues of flowers in the parks and gardens, the smartness of the shops and cafés, and, surely the most important, the modish Madrileños who populate them. Say what one will about Spain's earlier monarchs, there is no gainsaying the care and skill and attention they lavished on their capital. Post-Civil War Madrid— the city was severely damaged during the insurgents' siege— manifests the same good Spanish architectural sense of earlier eras. There is a solid, important, built-to-last quality about contemporary office towers and apartment houses that is in refreshing contrast to their counterparts in virtually every city of the world, from Philadelphia to Paris.

Think of Madrid's two super-important thoroughfares as forming a cross. The vertical artery, as Paseo del Prado, becomes Paseo de la Castellana, concluding en route north in a recently developed and substantial section of the city. Madrid's handsome modern railway station, *Estación de Chamartín*, is out in this area, near Plaza de Castilla, and a considerable distance from downtown and the other main railway stations, much older *Estación de Atocha*, on the square grandly called Glorieta del Emperador Carlos V at Calle de Atocha, and *Estación del Norte*, just west of Plaza de España.

Return to our cross-shaped main arteries: The horizontal artery—crossing east to west—begins as Calle Mayor, but for the great bulk of its length it is Calle de Alcalá. The point where the Paseo and Alcalá intersect is Plaza de la Cibeles, a circle identified by a statue of the goddess Cybele, in a chariot powered by lions, the lot fountain-surrounded. Cibeles is an important crossroad because Madrid's principal shopping street leads from it: This is Gran Vía. Note that it continues northwest as Calle de la Princesa to its terminus, skyscraper-surrounded Plaza de España.

Return to Calle de Alcalá, take it east a bit to another circle of a square, Plaza de la Independencia, and go north. The wide street you enter—Calle Serrano—is also important, for its shops are the smartest in town. Return to Cibeles and walk south on Paseo del Prado; in a few blocks you reach Plaza Cánovas del Castillo, around which are not only the *Palace* and *Ritz* hotels, landmarks both, and the city's main Iberia Airlines office, but, more important, the *Prado Museum*. *Jardín Botánico*, the Botanical Garden, is due south, and *Parque del Retiro*—one of the most beautiful parks in Europe and worthy of as leisurely an inspection as you can afford to give it—is to the east.

Return again to Cibeles, and head west on Calle de Alcalá. First major square you reach is ebullient, people-packed Puerta del Sol, in more ways than one the heart of Madrid. This is not only a shopping quarter—popularly priced shops and the big department stores' (*El Corte Inglés* and *Galerías Preciados*) Madrid outposts are hereabouts, on and surrounding pedestrians-only Calle de Preciados, which cuts north into Plaza del Callao and Gran Vía. This is also where Spain quite literally begins, for all principal highways going into northern, southern, eastern, and western Spain emerge from the *Kilómetro 0* point in the center of the elliptical square.

But there's more to central Madrid. Continue west on Calle de Alcalá, and it now becomes Calle Mayor (Main Street). Take your time, for you are approaching Philip III's early seventeenth-century Plaza Mayor, entered through a series of archways and, within, a coordinated grouping of superb Renaissance structures. Continue west on Calle Mayor—the extension of Calle de Alcalá—and you reach the southern extremity of the massive *Palacio Real*, the Royal Palace that is known also as *Palacio de Oriente* after Plaza de Oriente, fronting and separating the palace from the opera-house-turned-concert-hall, *Teatro Real*, with a formal French park, *Campo del Moro*, due west.

THE BIG TWO: PRADO AND PALACE

Museo del Prado (Paseo del Prado): Think about it: In no other principal world city is an art museum the undisputed No. 1, beeline-above-all-else visitor destination. Not in Paris, with the Louvre and the Beaubourg (there's the Eiffel Tower); not in London, with the British Museum (there's the changing of the guard at Buckingham Palace); not in Rome, with the Vatican Museums (there's St. Peter's); not in New York, with the Metropolitan Museum (there's the Statue of Liberty); not in Amsterdam, with the Rijksmuseum (there are boat tours of the canals).

No, Madrid's Prado is special. Newcomers for whom art galleries may be of secondary interest elsewhere, automatically accord this gallery priority. There are two reasons. First, Madrid has no other absolutely socko, globally reputed attraction; not an ancient city, it is more attractive because of ambience in toto than specifics, exciting as many of them are. Second, the Prado is indeed worthy of attention.

An unspectacularly graceful building in neoclassic style, the Prado—or Museo Nacional de Pintura, to use its secondary title—goes back to the late-eighteenth-century reign of Charles IV, when the idea of it as a natural history museum was hatched. Ferdinand VII changed the subject matter from science to art, and it opened in 1819 as the Museo Real, with a nucleus of 300 paintings from the royal collection. That quantity has been increased tenfold.

But it is quality as well that distinguishes the Prado. Not that the heavy representation of Spanish masters is to be discounted. There are no less than half a dozen immense galleries of Spain's all-time national hero of a painter, Velázquez, fourteen rooms devoted to Goya, three galleries of El Greco. Besides the Big Three—Velázquez, El Greco, and Goya—Murillo, Zurbarán, Sánchez Coello, Cano, Gallego, Juan de Juanes, and Morales are also represented.

But this is hardly to the exclusion of foreigners. Indeed, no other museum in all Spain comes anywhere close to the Prado. Seville and Valencia's Museos de Bellas Artes, Barcelona's Colección Cambó and Madrid's sadly under-appreciated Real Academia de Bellas Artes de San Fernando and Museo Lázaro

Goldiano (both enthusiastically called to your attention on later pages of this chapter) are among the leaders in this regard, but do not match the Prado.

The Italians appear in glorious profusion—Titian and Tintoretto most especially, but Bellini, Veronese, Boticelli, Fra Angelico, Lotto, Tiepolo, Giorgione, and Raphael as well. Dating from the time when Spanish Hapsburgs ruled the Low Countries are such Flemish and Dutch masters as Rubens (who worked for a period in Spain), Van Dyck, Rembrandt, Jordaens Teniers, van der Weyden, and Memling; the great Germans, including Dürer, Cranach, and Holbein; French immortals, such as Poussin and Watteau; even English portraitists like Gainsborough, Lawrence, and Reynolds.

The Prado is big. Plan on a couple of half-day visits. There are two massive floors of galleries, not to mention a café (see *Daily Bread*, below).

Painting not to be missed? See if you agree with my baker's dozen of personal favorites: Velázquez's *Las Meninas*; Zurbarán's *Defense of Cádiz Against the English*; El Greco's *The Adoration of the Shepherds*; Murillo's *The Good Shepherd*; Goya's *The Family of Charles IV*—tough choices to make from among the Spaniards; and—from among the foreign schools—van der Weyden's *Pietà*; Fra Angelico's *The Anunciation*; Raphael's *The Cardinal*; Titian's *The Emperor Charles V at Mühlberg* (along with the same painter's portrait of Charles V's son, Philip II); Veronese's *Venus and Adonis*; Rubens's *The Three Graces*; Dürer's *Self Portrait*. Antonio Moro's riveting study of sad-eyed "Bloody" Mary Tudor—Philip II's second wife—is also in the running, along with Lorrain's *Burial of St. Sophia*, Parmagianino's *Dama y Tres Niños*, Memling's *Adoration of the Magi*, and Van Dyck's *Countess of Oxford*.

Palacio Real (Plaza de Oriente): Public inspection of European royal palaces is a tricky proposition, with little consistency in the pattern. London's Buckingham—most celebrated of the lot—never is open to the public, except for two of its appendages, which are museums; one must travel to exurban Windsor to see how the British royal family lives. The Danish crown is equally private, in the case of Copenhagen's Amalienborg; we must settle for state reception rooms in the building also housing the Danish Parliament. Norway's Royal Palace in central Oslo is eternally out of bounds. The Dutch open Amsterdam's rarely used Royal Palace, but not the palace in The Hague, where the queen actually lives. Which brings us to Brussels and Stockholm. In the former, we find Belgian sovereigns, not unlike Spanish counterparts, living out in the country, using the in-town palace for ceremonials, and occasionally opening it to visitors. The Swedes, with their still royally inhabited Royal Palace in Stockholm's Old Town, lead the lot, with regular open-hours, and, moreover, superbly furnished, treasure-filled interiors. If the Spaniards cannot match Swedish aesthetics, they are at least as obliging as regards open-hours. Like King Baudouin and Queen Fabiola of Belgium, King Juan Carlos and Queen Sofía live in the suburbs. But diplomats are officially received in Madrid's Palacio Real and it is used for other state occasions. If the palace is a case of quantity over quality, there is no denying its lavishness, nor its easy accessibility, which makes it possible for the most casual visitors to see how pompously the royals lived.

It is as though the eighteenth-century Bourbon kings wanted to say to French cousins that Madrid could play the palace game, too. And did it ever! It is more than too big. It was built and decorated with a heavy hand, at its best from without, an enormous pile, its façade colonnaded, and complemented by the formal Campo del Moro to one side and the Plaza de Oriente to the other. It's questionable whether even the palace's regal tenants—Charles III was the first in 1764—ever saw all of it. There are close to 3,000 rooms. But rest easy; you'll see only the best 50 on the regular guided tours, usually departing hourly.

Make no mistake, there are considerable treasures to be encountered: paintings by Velázquez, Tiepolo, and Goya, priceless objects fashioned of silver, crystal, stone, and wood, some fine specimens of Spanish rococo furniture, brocades, chandeliers, carpets, tapestries, paneling. Most spectacular rooms include the Gasparini Salon and its anteroom, the chapel, Queen María Cristina and Queen María Luisa's quarters, state dining room (usually set for a gala dinner), and throne room. If the library is open, go in; it's full of beautiful books and other treasures. If you are not exhausted and undone upon exiting, consider three museums in connection: one displays more royal coaches of yore than you may want to observe (*Museo de Carruajes*); another is equally generous is its display of royal armor (*Armería Real*); the third was the royal pharmacy. And just out back, completing the architectural palace-park ensemble, is the *Church of Nuestra Señora de la Almudena*—a not entirely felicitous mix of classic and baroque, twin-towered.

EXPLORING OLD MADRID

Plaza Mayor: Make your initial entry by means of a brief walk westward down Calle Mayor from Puerto del Sol, until you reach a series of arches on your left that leads into the plaza. Designed for pedestrians only, this is Old Madrid's masterwork, an elegant exercise in symmetry for which Madrileños remain eternally grateful to the seventeenth century's King Philip III, who masterminded it. The most sumptuous building, *Casa de la Panadería*—Bakery House—combined the function for which it's named (on the main floor) along with royal lodgings above, from which monarchs watched the city's principal ceremonials. The twin to the Panadería, just opposite, was an equally grand butcher shop, while mercantile guilds occupied quarters behind the arcades on all four sides. There are cafés in the square today, ideal coffee stops, preparatory to a stroll about what remains of the city's historic core—a region largely unknown to and neglected by contemporary visitors. Stop in at the municipal tourist office (Oficina Municipal de Información)—it's right on Plaza Mayor—for a map and orientation, so that you can more easily become acquainted with the area mostly to the south of Plaza Mayor.

Ayuntamiento (Plaza de la Villa): It is to Madrid's great credit that, large as it is, it retains a relatively small Renaissance-era palace, *Casa de la Villa*, as its city hall. The square of the same name just a little west of Plaza Mayor, off Calle de Mayor—embraces a mix of architectural styles. It is small and charming. Pop inside the Ayuntamiento, if only to see the frescoed cupola of what had been a chapel.

Church of San Miguel (Calle Sacramento): Few Spanish churches are as Italian as this baroque, convex-fronted beauty out of the eighteenth century; you believe you're in Rome as you step in to view the rich interior.

Church of San Francisco el Grande (Plaza de San Francisco el Grande): *Grande* indeed; this eighteenth-century giant makes the city's Cathedral (nearby) appear a simple parochial church in contrast. Squat towers frame its fat dome 105 feet in diameter. Within, seek out the chapel of San Francisco—for a Goya mural, chief treasure, along with the choir stalls.

Capilla del Obispo (Plaza del Marqués de Comillas): This chapel dates back almost half a millennium, and is art-filled; note the main altar and the sculpted tombs.

Capilla de San Isidro (Plaza de San Isidro) dazzles. As how could it not? The chapel's dome is almost as big as the oddly square bulk of the structure it tops. See the painted altar.

Church of San Pedro el Viejo (Calle del Nuncio): St. Peter the Old is just that. Or at least its fine tower is, dating to the fourteenth century in the Mudejar style. The church proper, from the later Renaissance, has a graceful altar.

Church of San Nicolás de los Servitas (Plaza de San Nicolás) has a Mudéjar tower even older than San Pedro's (above): twelfth century. (In fact, this is reputed to be the oldest building in Madrid.) Again like San Pedro, the church proper is newer. Look up: the ceiling is super.

Church of San Plácido (Calle del Pez): If you haven't become acquainted with the painting of baroque artist Claudio Coello, well, then, this is the place. A Coello *Annunciation* is framed by a golden altar.

Church of San Antonio de la Florida (Paseo de la Florida), away from Old Madrid to the northwest of Plaza de España, is pilgrimage-worthy because of its cupola. This is a late-eighteenth-century construction whose royal builder, King Charles IV, commissioned Goya to decorate the cupola. The master's theme, essentially that of the miracle of St. Anthony of Padua, is ingeniously interpreted. Watching the haloed saint are the people of Madrid as Goya saw them, a cross-section of the city's men and women on the street: laughing workmen, lovely ladies, frisky youngsters. Very special.

Cathedral of San Isidro (Calle de Toledo): Madrid's cathedral was originally a Jesuit-built baroque-era parish church. Its simple twin-towered façade does not belie its even plainer interior. Indeed (irony of ironies, here in the capital), no bishop's seat in Spain is less elaborate. One reason is reconstruction after a 1936 fire.

Plaza del Cordón: A neighbor-square to Plaza de la Villa, serene Cordón hasn't a single public building. But it's framed by beautiful town houses. You want to enjoy their façades, most especially that of the one called Casa de los Alfaros, with the cord-like embellishment that gave the square its name.

Ministerio de Asuntos Exteriores (Plaza de la Provincia): Doesn't Ministry of Foreign Affairs sound imposing in Spanish? As well it might, given its home—a masterful Renaissance palace that you do well to enter somehow or other, if only for a peep at the patio.

Palacio de los Diputados (Carrera de San Jerónimo): The relatively modest albeit handsomely detailed neoclassic building you pass by as you walk west on Carrera de San Jerónimo from Plaza de Cánovas del Castillo, en route perhaps to Puerta del Sol, houses the lower chamber of the Spanish Parliament. It went up in the middle of the nineteenth century during the romantic-era reign of Queen Isabella II. Were it to be erected today, when the legislature of the kingdom is functioning at full force, it might be a larger, more imposing building. It's not generally open to visitors, but if for no other reason, you'll want to pause for a glance at the sculpted pair of lions guarding it. When the king and queen open Parliament, a red-and-gold canopy covers a carpet for them from the door down the steps to the street.

El Rastro is the time-honored and collective name of a cluster of streets, in and about Calles Ribera de Curtidores, Mesón de Paredes, Lavapiés, and Embajadores, that is at its most visitable on Sunday mornings when it's the locale for the capital's flea market—Madrid's counterpart of Paris's Marché-aux-Puces, Rome's Porta Portese, and London's Portobello Road. There are antiques or would-be antiques in an area more or less their own, and nonantiques (which can mean just about anything) in adjacent quarters. Fun to scout, even if you're not a serious purchaser. If you are, and legitimate antiques interest you, this barrio's proper shops—open the week long with regular hours—can be worth your consideration. The Rastro begins at the foot of Calle de Toledo, south of the Cathedral of San Isidro.

BEYOND THE CENTER

Zoo de la Casa de Campo: As good a reason as any to sample Madrid's subway, the away-from-the-center zoo, in the pretty park known as Casa de Campo, is noteworthy not only for a diverse population of species usually encountered in such places, but for its pair of black-and-white giant pandas—Chang-Chang and Shao-Shao—a gift to King Juan Carlos and Queen Sofía from People's China, and—who knows?—cousins, perhaps, of Ling-Ling and Hsing-Hsing, China's gift to the U.S., in residence at Washington's National Zoo.

AFTER THE PRADO:
MADRID'S DOZEN BEST MUSEUMS

The Spanish capital surprises with the extraordinary diversity—and excellence—of its museums, the great majority of which are sadly devoid of visitors, who mistakenly believe that there's only the Prado. On the contrary, Madrid is one of Europe's great museum cities. Beginning with a pair of art museums that—along with the Prado—are absolute requisites for paintings buffs, here are the 12 I think are the most important:

Real Academia de Bellas Artes de San Fernando (Calle de Alcalá 13, near Puerta del Sol): When you consider that this academy was created as long ago as 1752 by King Fernando VI— some eight decades before the Prado opened—its relative lack of celebrity, as a repository of a paintings collection of the very first caliber, is difficult to fathom. But now that it is back in its palatial quarters after a closure for refurbishing that extended from the late 1970s into the late 1980s (while some of its treasures were on show at the Biblioteca Nacional) there is little excuse for any visitor with even minimal interest in the fine arts to pass it by. The building itself is a stunner, with, among other features, a monumental entrance hall, the elaborate auditorium in which the Royal Academy conducts its deliberations, a range of handsome galleries, and I might add, an absolutely knock-'em-dead marble men's room, no less impressive, I am told, that its female counterpart.

The collection is heavily—but by no means entirely— Spanish. Still, you do not want to miss Velázquez's paired portraits—unusually small for this master—of Philip IV and Queen Mariana of Austria, his second wife. A quintet of Zurbarán priests, white-robed and life-size, dazzles. So do such Murillos as *St. Francis of Assisi* and *The Resurrection of Christ*. But there is so much more Spanish work: an entire room hung with Goyas (with his palette in a gilded frame), Ribera's *St. Anthony of Padua*, Alfonso Cano's *Jesus and the Samaritans*, Valdés Leal's bearded *St. Peter*, Juan de Juanes's *Holy Family*, and a gallery of nineteenth-century portraits, including a pretty young *Isabel II*—painted in 1844, just after she ascended the throne, seven years after her contemporary Queen Victoria, whom she appears to resemble.

Foreign schools are no less riveting: an enormous *Susannah and the Elders* by Rubens—one of a number by that artist; a Giovanni Bellini of Jesus, Corregio's *San Jerónimo*, Van Dyck's *Los Santos Juanes*—of the two Saints John, and a rich group of eighteenth-century works by the likes of Fragonard and Mengs, Tiepolo and Battoni. With a bonus of ever-so-comfortable sofas upon which to recline in the course of exploration.

Museo Lázaro Galdiano (Calle Serrano 122) houses a remarkable collection—in the donor's own opulent *palacio*—embracing the arts (and not only paintings) of Europe. Every Galdiano visitor has his or her own favorites. I think of an exquisite collection of Italian Renaissance miniature bronzes, of chairs and settees crafted in late eighteenth- and early nineteenth-century Spain as Iberian counterparts of France's Louis XVI and Empire styles, of lavish church vestments and medieval swords, of Rococo-era fans and the richly brocaded walls and frescoed ceilings of the thirty galleries. And paintings: They include such foreign works as a tiny portrait of a woman with long curls and a green mantle by Leonardo da Vinci, a small but searing Tiepolo of Christ carrying the Cross; portraits of Britons by the likes of Hoppner, Raeburn, Gainsborough, Reynolds and Lawrence; Caravaggio's *Madonna and Child*, a Clouet *Knight in Armor*, the Virgin Mary as variously interpreted by David and Isenbrandt, Dürer and Metsys; Dutch greats by Rembrandt, Hobbema and Cuyp; even a pair of landscapes executed in the early nineteenth century by England's John Constable. And remarkable groups of Spanish canvasses: El Greco and Zurbarán, Murillo and Goya, the last named in considerable quantity. And a special nod to the guards: among the kindest and most knowledgeable in town.

Museo de América (Avenida de los Reyes Católicos): I can't imagine any American—North, South, or Central—not being intrigued with the Museo de América. It occupies a big building of its own (in the style contributed to Spanish Colonial America) at Ciudad Universitaria, the modern campus of the University of Madrid. It's best taken in with the Museo Español de Arte Contemporáneo (below), also on the campus. The América's collection embraces all of the indigenous cultures of Spanish America as they related to the culture of Spain, with which they were combined, upon the arrival of the conquistadores and missionaries. One sees maps, paintings, tiles, tapestries, religious objects, all manner of Spanish Americana, the lot giving us an idea, on home ground, of the tremendous cultural debt we in America owe to this former mother country.

Museo de Artes Decorativas (Calle de Montalbán 12, just off Calle de Alfonso XII, near Parque del Retiro): You do well to hike up to the fifth floor of this elegant mansion and work your way down, through three score extraordinarily handsome rooms. Nowhere can one perceive more effortlessly the genius of Spanish interior design: a tiled Valencian kitchen of the eighteenth century; a Renaissance chapel, leather-walled, with a Mudéjar ceiling; a Toledo reception room, with tapestried walls and green velvet chairs; red damask walls with matching canopy in a baroque bedroom; exquisitely carved cabinets and framed embroideries surrounding the formal table in a sixteenth-century dining room; a toy-filled nursery and sitting room in the century-old Isabelline style, the counterpart to our Victorian. Beautiful.

Museo Arqueológico (Calle Serrano 13): The city's smartest shopping street has other lures, among which is the collection of prehistoric Iberian artifacts of this top-rank museum. Star of the show is the fine-featured *Dama de Elche*, one of a number of statues carved in stone during the rich Iberian period four and five centuries before Christ. There are eye-filling remnants of Roman Spain as well—busts, architectural fragments, mosaics, jewelry. And additional treasures from the Christian era, those from the Middle Ages the most spectacular. (Calle Serrano has still another museum-treat; read on.)

Casón del Buen Retiro (Calle de Felipe IV, behind the Prado and opposite Museo del Ejército, below): If, like me, you were among those who enjoyed the tranquility of this sole remaining fragment of the seventeenth-century Buen Retiro Palace, the while enjoying relatively uncelebrated post-Goya paintings of the nineteenth century, well, forget it. The quiet ambience of this annex of the Prado changed when the Spanish Government negotiated the transfer of the Picasso mural-masterwork, *Guernica*, from the Museum of Modern Art, in New York, where it had long hung.

Picasso painted it, in 1937, while in self-imposed exile (he was an avowed opponent of Francoist forces, during the Spanish Civil War), as commentary on the bombing of the innocent northern village of Guernica by German planes aiding Franco's insurgents. A vast mural in grays, blacks and whites, it is sheathed—for security reasons—in a giant frame of clear plastic, with a pair of the master's preliminary sketches flanking it, in a setting which could not offer more dramatic contrast: the one-time royal palace's gala reception hall, its ceiling a sumptuous baroque fresco, out of the seventeenth century, by Italy's Luca Giordano (Lucas Jordán, to the Spaniards). Notice, on the wall opposite *Guernica*, plaques commemorating placement of works of art in the *casón*, by three kings—Felipe IV, for early work by Alonso Carbonel; Carlos II, for the Jordano ceiling fresco; and the reigning Juan Carlos I, who was present at the installation of the Picasso, on October 25, 1981.

Before departing, have a look at works of the last century by such artists as López, Rosales, Fortuny, Esquivel, Becquer, as well as Sorolla, who lived in the 1920s, and was so prolific—and so talented—that his attractive home (Paseo General Martínez Campos 37) is now *Museo Sorolla*.

Museo Cerralbo (Calle Ventura Rodríguez 17) occupies the late-nineteenth-century town house of the seventeenth Marqués de Cerralbo. The rooms themselves are more palatial than residential: a grand foyer and even grander staircase, a beaux-arts ballroom that will knock your eye out, and, if you please, the marqués's personal armory. Collections run to furniture, porcelain, antique clocks, and jewelry. Then come paintings: Spaniards like Ribera, Zurbarán, and El Greco, and such foreigners as Titian, David, Giordano, Tiepolo, Snyders, Veronese, Van Dyck, and Poussin. Smashing.

Museo del Ejército (Calle Méndez Núñez 1, almost opposite Casón del Buen Retiro, above): If, like me, you're a nut for tattered military pennants, colorful uniforms of earlier centuries, caissons and cannons, medals and muskets, commanders' field tents and seal-embossed documents, well, then, you'll find the Spanish army museum (all the guards are soldiers) absorbing and not unlike France's, at Les Invalides, in Paris.

Museo Español de Arte Contemporáneo (Avenida Juan de Herrera, on the Ciudad Universitaria campus and nicely combined with Museo de América, above) occupies an appropriately contemporary building, the better to show off an extra-large collection of modern art, not only by Spanish household-name masters like Picasso, Miró, Dalí, and Gris (who are well represented), but by less-celebrated talents, many of whose works delight and please.

Monasterio de las Descalzas Reales (Plaza de las Descalzas Reales) is a still-operating convent that was founded by Princess Juana, daughter of Emperor Charles V (and not to be confused with Queen Juana the Mad, her grandmother). The building had earlier served as a royal residence—indeed, Princess Juana was born in it. But even after it became a religious house, it sheltered royal ladies other than its founder, and thus the name of the order: *Descalzas Reales*, or Royal Unshods. Decor is appropriately regal. Paintings include works by such masters as Brueghel, Titian, and Antonio Moro, not to mention numerous Spaniards, including Sánchez Coello. The grand foyer and staircase are positively Renaissance-palatial, with a memorably decorated ceiling. The chapel is a beauty. Location is Old Madrid, north of Calle Mayor.

Monasterio de la Encarnación (Plaza de la Encarnación) is an Old Madrid convent partially open to the public. Like Descalzas Reales (above), it had royal beginnings. Though with nothing like the splendor of Descalzas Reales, there are paintings (Ribera is represented), standout sculpture, a fine choir in the chapel, and a remarkable room—the *relicario*—in which saints' relics, reposing in jeweled caskets, line the walls.

Museo Romántico (Calle de San Mateo 13) embodies the Madrid of the romantic nineteenth century. It is at once the most imaginatively conceived and the most charmingly executed of the capital's museums. (By charming I mean a grinning museum guard who operates an 1850 children's music box for you, as you approach.) Setting is the town house of the late Marqués de la Vega Inclán. Rooms of the house are museum enough for anyone: a chandelier-lit, musical-instrument-filled ballroom where you can just imagine gala festivities, a dining room with a decorated ceiling and Spain's equivalent of English Regency dining chairs, to give you an idea. There are, as well, exquisite paintings of aristocratic Madrileños and their families, and the kind of memorabilia of the era that is not easily come by. A sheer delight.

Centro de Arte Reina Sofía (Calle de Santa Isabel 52), though not a proper museum, is so outstanding both architecturally and for the caliber of the temporary modern-art exhibitions which it shelters, that I call it to your attention, with the hope that a show will be in progress during the course of your stay in Madrid, and that you'll pop over (location is near the Prado) to have a look at the splendidly vaulted corridors and starkly handsome galleries (the former wards) of a five-story eighteenth-century hospital imaginatively transformed for its current use in the late 1980s. There are plans for a permanent collection, and moreover, for the transfer to the Reina Sofía, from Casón del Buen Retiro (above) of the giant Picasso mural, *Guernica.*

SETTLING IN
Because Madrid offers the widest hotel choice of any Spanish city—there's rarely a visitor to the kingdom who does not visit the capital—I present evaluations of some 40 hotels all around the city, *Luxury, First Class,* and *Moderate,* in order of my personal preference within each group. A single caveat: Reread *Lay of the Land,* earlier in this chapter, and you'll perceive what enormous areas Madrid embraces. If your mission is exploration, as a pleasure-visitor, I recommend selecting a centrally situated hotel so that you may walk about and absorb the flavor of the core of Madrid, where, for the most part, its appeal lies. Business visitors, at least those whose work will take them to the newer area of the city in its northern reaches, may find hotels in that area—remote from the center though it is—of value.

LUXURY

Hotel Ritz (Plaza de la Lealtad 5): It's all well and good that the leading hotel of Seville (Chapter 4) is named for King Alfonso XIII. Still, it would not have been remiss to have called Madrid's indisputably top hostelry after the very same monarch. It was, after all, his idea. Well-traveled, he came to appreciate in the early years of this century that his capital lacked hotels of the caliber of those founded by César Ritz in both Paris and London. (See *France at Its Best* and *Britain at Its Best.*) And so a company was organized, and Monsieur Ritz, along with French architect Charles Mewès were called in, in 1908, two years in advance of the opening by the king of what has remained Spain's principal monument to the Beaux-Arts style. Although the Ritz has been the capital's *Número Uno* all of these years—I first knew it under the directorship of the late and legendary Alfonso Font in the early 1970s—there was no denying that it had begun to show signs of wear. When the global, Britain-based Trusthouse Forte chain bought it in the early eighties, they hired multi-lingual, Gibraltar-born John Macedo away from London's Savoy. As new managing director, he supervised a meticulous multi-million-dollar refurbishing completed in 1984, wherein the architecture of the building, interior as well as exterior, (brass-fitted marble baths for each room the sole exception) was refreshed rather than altered. Original furnishings and accessories—Louis XV and Louis XVI-style chairs, lamps and chandeliers, tapestries and sconces, chests and clocks, sculpture and mirrors—were retained albeit refinished. The hotel's precious carpets, the lot of them custom-made by the Royal Carpet Factory, were either restored or hand-woven replacements were made in their stead (every carpet in the hotel is signed and dated). And the new color scheme—walls, brocaded draperies, silk upholstery—is based on hues of the carpets, room by room by room. You are impressed from the moment you approach the circular entrance hall, its walls punctuated with pilasters capped by gilded capitals, the traditional bowl of red carnations on its center table. The contiguous Upper Hall is arguably one of the handsomer public spaces in the kingdom—for morning coffee, premeal drinks or afternoon tea. (Don't approach without jacket and tie after 11 A.M., gents!) The adjacent restaurant (supplemented by a garden for warm-weather meals) is evaluated on a subsequent page. Accommodations are more a case of quality than quantity; there are but 170 no-two-alike rooms and suites. The Royal Suite—two living rooms (one of them circular), two sumptuous bedrooms, two extraordinary baths—is, to understate, special. But junior suites are lovely, and so are less pricey doubles, and for that matter, singles. Which leaves service. Relatively recent change in ownership-management notwithstanding, the staff remains chockablock with old-timers, as skilled as they are smiling. A Trusthouse Forte Exclusive Division hotel that is affiliated with Leading Hotels of the World.

Hotel Palace (Plaza de las Cortes 7): Only two years younger than its across-the-square neighbor, the Ritz (above), and like the Ritz, constructed on the initiative of King Alfonso XIII, the much-bigger Palace (520 rooms and suites vs. the more intimate Ritz's 170) exudes big-city bustle. Its marble-floored lobby (most spectacular in its nether reaches, when it becomes an elegant rotunda, with a dome of Art Nouveau stained glass) was lightened and brightened in connection with the hotel's 75th anniversary in 1987. The same period saw many of the accommodations refurbished, as well, as part of an ongoing program. (Refurbished rooms overlooking the playing fountain in the square go first). The Neptuno Palace Grill, long popular with members of the across-the-street Parliament, retains its splendid coffered ceiling although a touch of *nouvelle* has modified its menu. A newer second restaurant, the Ambigu, edges the lobby and is reviewed on a later page. The Palace does a better job with breakfast—choose a very good buffet or order à la carte in the handsome breakfast room—than any other hotel with which I'm familiar, in the capital. There's a busy bar, concierges are alert and knowledgeable, there's a business center (telex, secretarial services, photocopying), and genial Director Juan J. Bergés is on scene morning into the evening, seeing that his guests are happy. Member Leading Hotels of the World.

Hotel Castellana Inter-Continental (Paseo de la Castellana 49): If you're of a certain age, you may remember the Castellana Hilton—a history-maker because when it opened, several decades back, it was Hilton International's pioneering first hotel on the continent of Europe. Well, *tempus fugit*. A few seasons back, after an in-between period of hiatus, "Hilton" was replaced by "Inter-Continental" in the hotel's title; another top-rank, U.S.-based chain had taken over. And did they ever set to work refurbishing and redecorating. A consequence is one of the handsomest hotels in the kingdom. Retaining original generous proportions—massive, high-ceilinged circle of a marble-floored lobby, capacious suites and bedrooms, good-sized baths—Inter-Continental designers and architects have fashioned a hotel of this very moment, albeit with agreeable overtones of an earlier era. The lobby bar is inviting. There's a smart restaurant—Continentes—mellow with paisley-print walls and framed antique prints, that's evaluated on a later page. On upper floors—there are 311 rooms and suites—accommodations are bright and welcoming; small-patterned fabrics have been used for draperies, spreads and carpeting, against white grounds and baths are typically up-to-the-minute Inter-Continental. Moreover, the staff is a pleasure. You feel welcome immediately upon arrival.

Hotel Villa Magna (Paseo de la Castellana 22): Of the city's relatively new ranking hotels—it opened in the 1970s—the Villa Magna stands out as the most elegant. Diplomats, top politicos, and international business brass have been attracted to it from the start. And with reason. It's a class act. Decor is in the neo-classic style of the late eighteenth and early nineteenth centuries, never excessive, with crystal-chandeliered lobby covering a broad expanse; Mayfair Bar appealing in tones of black and brown, restaurant—Rue Royale, by name—at once white-glove and delicious; such appreciated amenities as a barbershop and beauty salon; just under 200 attractive, beautifully accessorized rooms and suites with exceptional baths; and a staff of knowing pros. Member, Leading Hotels of the World.

Hotel Husa Miguel Angel (Calle Miguel Angel 29 at Paseo de la Castellana), another of the newer luxury hotels, greets visitors with a vast clean-lined lobby whose principal embellishment is a pair of superbly crafted, contemporary-design crystal chandeliers. Amenities stand out here: big and comfortable bar-lounge vaguely Victorian in its look; attractive Florencia Restaurant, with substantial four-course prix-fixe menus; super indoor swimming pool, sauna, alfresco terrace-café that's nice in summer, and just over 300 thoughtfully-planned rooms and suites.

Location is the newer section of the city favored by affluent *Madrileños*, if not that convenient to the center for visitors. One of the major links of the Husa chain. Friendly.

Hotel Tryp Fenix (Paseo de la Castellana 2 at Plaza de Colón) reopened in 1987 after a long period of closure, the while it was treated to a thorough stem-to-stern refurbishing, you might almost say rebuilding from within. Conveniently located and architecturally impressive (it dates originally to the early 1950s), the restyled Fenix has indeed risen, not unlike the mythical bird whose name it takes. Its new decor, traditional in style, may be faulted its fussiness. But there is no denying that this is an agreeable, skillfully operated, full-facility house. Those of the 226 rooms and suites I have inspected are state-of-the-art—with light-dimmers on lamps, telephones with memory (and, of course, in baths as well as bedside), safes with electronic systems, TV with video and satellite channels, and, in the case of the dozen suites, special security doors and windows. There are both restaurant (the look is Louis XV, in tones of pink and white) and *cafetería*, with breakfast served buffet style; and an inviting English-look pub with comfy chairs in red leather. Very nice indeed.

Hotel Princesa Plaza (Calle Princesa 40) is a graceless, relatively contemporary 400-room complex several blocks northwest of Plaza de España that is, to be sure, full-facility, but whose chief attribute in my view is a giant outlet of the El Corte Inglés department-store chain in the same building. Groups are a specialty.

Hotel Meliá Madrid (Calle Princesa 27) is a near-neighbor of the Princesa Plaza (above), a little closer to Plaza de España (thus a bit more central), and some years older. It is, to be sure, a full-facility, 250-room skyscraper, but doubles tend to be small and decor jazzy. All told, the least enjoyable link—of any that I know—in the generally exemplary Meliá chain.

Hotel Luz Palacio (Paseo de la Castellana 67) is an agreeable contemporary house, with a capacious lobby-lounge in traditional style. Two hundred and fifteen generous rooms and suites, restaurant, bar-lounge. A part of the Interhotel chain. Location is beyond the Miguel Angel (above), a fair distance out, on the Castellana.

Hotel Eurobuilding (Calle Padre Damián 23) is considerably north of the center. Some 550 rooms and suites, contemporary in design, and adequate, with a range of places to dine, drink, and shop. But, my goodness, what a long way from town!

Hotel Meliá Castilla (Calle Capitán Haya 43) is a thousand-room tower, with all the conveniences of a city within a city (and considerably newer than the chain's other Madrid property, the Meliá Madrid, above). Which is just as well, since its location is even more distant from the center than that of the Eurobuilding (above), its nearest competition.

Hotel Barajas (Avenida de Logroño, Barajas): This one's to be considered only if you're stuck at the airport, for overnight. Not that it's disagreeable. On the contrary, it is among the handsomer of the luxury houses, with 230 inviting rooms, a swimming pool, and delightful public spaces for meals and relaxation. But you're nine miles from town, which means fairly steep cab tabs back and forth.

FIRST CLASS

Hotel Arosa (Calle de la Salud 21 at Gran Vía, near Plaza del Callao): Once you've ascended from the tiny vestibule to the lobby up a flight, you like the Arosa. It's possible to fault its traditional decor for being a bit vivid, still, this is a well-located house, with 120 rooms—mostly papered in a variety of designs—and a bar-*cafetería*.

Hotel Emperador (Gran Vía 53): Traditional in style, this is an updated old-timer with a smallish lobby and 230 rooms. Restaurant and pool-sundeck are on the roof.

Holiday Inn Madrid (Avenida General Perón) is among the city's newest (it opened in 1987) and, not unlike sister Holiday Inns the planet wide, is well equipped, with a pair of double beds per bedroom, good baths with good showers, convenient places to eat and drink. Location, way out at the Palacio de Congresos, is okay if you're attending a convention and want to be near the hall, but you're quite a distance from the center.

Hotel Suecia (Calle Marqués de Casa Riera 4): The name means Sweden, and the Suecia does not lack Scandinavian touches, including contemporary decor both in public spaces and some three score rooms, and the smorgasbord served Thursday and Friday, May through September, at both lunch and dinner in the restaurant. Bar-lounge. Heart of downtown location, just off Calle de Alcalá, next to Teatro de la Zarzuela, Madrid's opera house.

Hotel Los Galgos (Calle Claudio Coello 139) is well-situated on the street directly parallel to shop-lined Calle Serrano. This is a tastefully contemporary house whose 360 rooms vary in size; lobby bar, subterranean *cafetería*.

Hotel Alcalá (Calle de Alcalá 66) is near the attractive Calle de Velázquez shops and cafés. There are 100 good-sized plaid-look rooms (although the singles can be small), bar-lounge, and a restaurant (serving interesting Basque specialties), as well as a *cafetería*.

Hotel Velázquez Tryp (Calle Velázquez 62) offers 150 rooms and suites in a congenial setting that attracts locals from the stylish quarter in which it's situated. Restaurant, bar.

Hotel Wellington (Calle Velázquez 8): This is a contemporary house with traditional touches—wrought-iron grilles are common—in its decor; there are 325 rooms and suites, restaurant, bar.

Hotel Emperatriz (Calle López de Hoyos 4, near Paseo de la Castellana) features 170 well-equipped rooms with a restaurant and bar-lounge leading from its lobby, the lot in vivid-hued modern style.

Hotel Mayorazgo (Calle Flor Baja 3) is at its best as regards location: just off the Gran Vía, north of Plaza del Callao. Two-hundred-plus comfortable rooms. Very well-regarded restaurant, bar.

Hotel Menfis Tryp (Gran Vía 74) is a longtime Gran Vía house. There are 120 balconied rooms; the front ones afford super views, but the higher up you are, the quieter. Bar and breakfast.

Hotel Washington Tryp (Gran Vía 70) is the Gran Vía neighbor of the Menfis (above) and not dissimilar, with about the same number of rooms. Bar and breakfast.

Hotel Coloso (Calle Leganitos 13) is a modern house, intimate—rather than *coloso*—in scale with about half a hundred pleasant rooms—that's near both the Gran Vía and Plaza de España. *Cafetería*, bar.

Hotel Torre de Madrid (Plaza de España)—Tower of Madrid, to translate—does indeed tower over Madrid. There are 120 units of varying size (some have half a dozen beds), with smashing views if you're up near the 32nd and top floor. Restaurant, bar.

Hotel Plaza (Plaza de España) is an elderly house, with more than 350 rooms, *cafetería*, bar, swimming pool, and a sweeping landmark of a Plaza de España façade that I am considerably more partial to than the interior.

Hotel Chamartín (Estación de Chamartín) abuts the capital's newest railroad station, whose name it takes, near Plaza de Castilla, way away from the center of town, in the newer northern sector. There are several hundred neat rooms, *cafetería* and bar-lounge. Ask to be high-up, looking southward, for a super view of the city.

Hotel Florida Norte (Paseo de la Florida 5): You have to want to be opposite the North Railway Station to be happy at the Florida Norte. Location is west of the Royal Palace, on the other side of Campo del Moro park. This is a good-sized hotel, with some 440 modern rooms, restaurant, bar.

MODERATE

Hotel Tryp Rex (Gran Vía 43): This is a renewed old-timer with a central, Gran Vía location, 144 rooms with bath or shower, and bar-lounge. Breakfast only.

Hotel Gran Vía (Gran Vía 25) embraces 162 neat rooms with bath, many of them really good-sized, as well as a capacious bar-lounge and a *cafetería*-bar.

Hotel Montesol (Calle Montera 25): Once you're past the narrow lobby and in one of the bright corridors upstairs, you begin to like the Montesol. Half a hundred rooms with bath. Breakfast only. Location: Puerta del Sol, heart of town.

Hotel Capitol (Gran Vía 41): What it lacks in style, the Capitol compensates for with location and spotless rooms, all with baths. Breakfast only, but there's a convenient branch of the Manila Cafetería chain next door.

Hotel Opera (Cuesta de Santo Domingo 2) is a near-neighbor of the Royal Palace (just to the west) albeit hardly palatial; the lobby is small, the rooms likewise compact, but immaculate. Breakfast only.

Hotel Alexandría (Calle San Bernardo 29) is just off the Gran Vía and is central and modern, with 69 rooms, each with bath or shower. Breakfast only.

Hotel Asturias (Carrera de San Jerónimo 11, on Plaza Canalejas, east of Puerta del Sol) must once have been very grand. The old patina remains in high-ceilinged lobby and generously scaled rooms with French windows leading to mini-balconies.

Mattresses could be thicker, but there's a restaurant and bar, and location is good. A Tryp hotel.

Hotel Paris (Calle de Alcalá 2, at Puerta del Sol) is center-of-the-action. Like the Asturias (above), it too has known an epoch of glory. Again like the Asturias, mattresses are thin. Restaurant.

Hotel Mercator (Calle de Atocha 123) is convenient to Atocha railroad station, Gran Vía, and the Prado; 90 rooms, snack bar, lounge. Breakfast only. So-so.

Hotel Principe Pío (Paseo de Onésimo Redondo 16) is at its best in the case of those of its 160 smallish but otherwise okay rooms that overlook Campo del Moro park and the Royal Palace. Restaurant, bar. North Railway Station is to the rear.

Hotel Regina (Calle Alcalá 19) is blessed with a super location—on a major street and near Puerta del Sol, Gran Vía, and Plaza de las Cibeles—and is well equipped with just over 140 clean-lined rooms with bath, bar-lounge and *cafetería*. Good value.

Hotel San Antonio (Paseo San Antonio de la Florida 13) fronts the North Railway Station and Casa de Campo park, is next-door to pricier Hotel Florida Norte (above), and contains nearly 100 unglamorous rooms with baths. Restaurant, bar. Downtown is to the east and south.

Hotel Claridge (Plaza Conde de Casal 6) is southeast of Parque del Retiro and a subway ride into the center of town. There are 150 modern rooms with baths, as well as *cafetería* and bar. But you're likely to feel isolated.

Hotel Puerta de Toledo (Puerta de Toledo 2) is in an interesting quarter of Old Madrid, south of Plaza Mayor and the Rastro flea market. It's named for a superb eighteenth-century, royally erected triumphal arch—as is the square on which both hotel and arch are situated. The hotel is modern, with 150 compact rooms with bath and a restaurant-bar.

DAILY BREAD

Barcelona is a strong second, but there is no doubt about it: Madrid is Spain's restaurant city. Madrileños enjoy eating: grandly as well as moderately. They like a drink—dry sherry (*fino*) or a glass of beer for that matter—but always in the company of something solid, the bite-sized nibbles or *tapas* purveyed by bars that are nowhere else more delectable in Spain. And they are snackers at *cafeterías*—both at the chains named for American states (Nebraska, California) and at one-of-a-kind cafés, where they might fortify themselves with hot chocolate and *churros*, finger-shaped fritters designed for dunking. Meals are nowhere later in all Spain. Breakfast is when you want it, but lunch is never served before 1 P.M., and dinner is between 10 and 11 P.M., with 9 acceptable in the case of foreigners, in the typical restaurants, and even 8 in the hotels where we stay in quantity, and which become accustomed to our desire for the evening meal at an oddly premature hour. Not that the Madrileños abstain from nourishment for excessive periods. The lunch-dinner span is punctuated by the afternoon snack called *merienda* or by aperitifs and *tapas*.

Madrid restaurants embrace local specialties: *cocido Madrileño* (a casserole of sausages, poultry, meat, and chickpeas), *pollo a la chilindrón* (special fried chicken), *fabada* (ham-and-bean-based stew), *cochinillo a la Segoviana* (whole roast suckling pig), and *perdiz a la Toledana* (roast partridge). And regional dishes—Basque, Catalonian, Andalusian, Galician, Valencian—as well: the cold soup from Andalusia called *gazpacho* through the classic *paella Valenciana*. With area wines, and vintages from the major wine regions, Rioja especially.

Here are evaluations of some two score restaurants, cafés, bars with especially interesting tapas, *cafeterías*, and snack spots. I classify the restaurants as *Luxury, First Class,* or *Moderate* (these last are called *tascas* or *mesones*) with the order in each category following my personal preference. *Buen apetito!*

LUXURY

Zalacaín (Calle Alvarez de Baena 4) is nothing if not celebrated as an all-Spain restaurant leader. It is smart to look upon, with a traditional decor based upon hues of brown and rust, service is subtle (watch the way captains keep their eyes on things), and fare (take your time inspecting the cold buffet, as you enter) solid Spanish with Basque overtones combined with *nouvelle* influences out of France. You may order as straightforward an entrée as *steak au poivre*, or experiment with the likes of a clam-flecked artichoke mousse. Zalacaín is for a splurge dinner; sample the menu, appetizers through desserts, with a good Rioja accompanying. Location is a quarter-hour taxi-ride north of the center.

Alkalde (Calle Jorge Juan 10): There's more than at first meets the eye in this unassuming-looking place that begins with a lively street-level bar (whose *tapas* are among the best in town and are dealt with in a later paragraph) and continues to a subterranean series of cave-like rooms in which food that is nowhere else any better in Madrid is served to an affluent, sophisticated, mostly local clientele. Everything is delicious: bread and wine, *entremeses variados* (mixed hors d'oeuvre openers), on through to exceptional egg, fish, and meat specialties. Why not the veal triumph, *medallón Alkalde*? Fine wine list. Skilled and rapid service.

Jockey (Calle Amador de los Ríos 6): There's an air of understatement at Jockey that goes down well, and has these many years. You like the club-like environment, attractive international clientele, quietly expert service, and French-accented fare: seafood-stuffed crêpes to begin, sole *meunière*, champagnesauced chicken, steak Bordelaise. And the light and lemony *coronel de limón* for dessert. Study the wine card with care; it's extraordinary.

Hotel Ritz Restaurant (Plaza de Lealtad 5): I don't know of a more unabashedly beautiful restaurant environment in town than the high-ceilinged dining room of the Ritz, whose pale paneled walls pick up tones of its magnificent hand-woven carpet, and are punctuated with antique tapestries and brocade-draped windows giving onto a fountain-centered garden. (Lunch at a garden table surrounded by blue-cushioned white wicker chairs is a warm-weather Madrid treat). The menu is international in the best sense—lobster salad, stuffed Dover sole, roast lamb, filet of beef, masterworks from the house's *patissier*—but the Ritz takes pride in Spanish specialties: smoked Serrano ham or fresh Galician oysters as openers, a super chicken dish called *pollo salteado chilindrón*, hake Catalán style or, depending on the day of the week, favorites like *paella Valenciana, fabada Asturiana* or *cocido Madrileño*. There's a changed-daily prix-fixe menu to supplement the à la carte, a cellar that is one of the kingdom's finest, and a skilled serving staff, many of whose numbers are long-on-scene. (House guests, note: Of course you may order breakfast from room service, but at least one morning, go downstairs; it's beautifully served in the restaurant.)

El Cenador del Prado (Calle Prado 4) makes its home in an aged heart-of-town house to which you are warmly welcomed. Coral is the dominant tone, with caned Louis XV-style chairs at tables set with Art Nouveau-patterned porcelain, and illumination from discreet, silk-shaded lamps. Tuxedoed captains seem as much in supply as white-jacketed waiters. There's an enormous wine list (Riojas are especially prevalent) and the attractively presented fare is essentially—and deliciously—*nouvelle*. Go with the four-course menu, opening with, say, a chilled melon soup, shrimp-flecked, continuing with the day's fish in a green sauce, or octopus in its own sauce, and following, a well-prepared *solomillo*, or steak, and a super sweet. Very nice indeed.

Rue Royale (Hotel Villa Magna, Paseo de la Castellana 22) is the smart restaurant of a smart hotel, with agile tuxedoed service and a well-composed à la carte, with such appetizers as smoked Scottish salmon (or the chef's special salad based on it), and the house's pâté, chicken in a whisky sauce or truffled tournedos (as well as always-available paella) among entrées, a *salade niçoise* much appreciated in summer; luscious sweets, and wines from an extensive list.

El Bodegón (Calle Pinar 15) is a longtime leader in relatively new quarters—which, like the old ones you may remember, are named for the three-dimensional still life, or *bodegón*, at the entrance. If you're a stranger to partridge, this is the place to become an *aficionado*.

O'Pazo (Calle Reina Mercedes 20): There's nothing Irish about O'Pazo. It's Galician to a turn, with the accent on seafood. You want to indulge yourself in specialties created from such ingredients as crayfish, scallops, lobster, and a variety of fish, hake especially. Pretty marine-motif decor.

Charlot (Calle Serrano 70) is not for a casual lunch in the course of shopping in Serrano's boutiques. Plan for a festive meal here. Don't neglect the pâtés. Move along to *salpicón de mariscos*—spicily sauced seafood salad—and, say, *pichón relleno*—stuffed pigeon, as you surely have not experienced it heretofore. With standby roasts and grills. Amusing turn-of-century decor, amusing crowd.

Club 31 (Calle de Alcalá 58): Not a branch of Jockey (above), but a handsome variation on the Jockey theme, with a shared management and equally delicious fare. Agreeably bouncy and busy at both lunch and dinner, with the beef masterwork—*tournedos marchand du vin*—memorable.

Clara's (Calle Arrieta 2) is indicated for a post-Teatro Real dinner in a festive setting. Location is just opposite the theater, in a fine mansion with a fine pedigree and furnishings in keeping. The staff is discreet but alert, the fare as international or as Spanish as you would like.

L'Hardy (Carrera de San Jerónimo 8) occupies the early-nineteenth-century house that's been its home since Queen Isabella II reigned. The lower floor vends cakes, chocolates, and *tapas*—the latter so super that I recommend them at a later point. Restaurant is up a flight, with decor, I suspect, mostly original, and a staff spoiled from the attention of influential admirers—Queen Isabella was an early one—over so long a period. Snooty waiters or no, the ambience is one-of-a-kind and the *cocido Madrileño* delicious.

Horcher (Calle Alfonso XII 6) has been a Madrid institution since the turn of the century, packing in affluent visitors to smilingly serve them outrageously expensive food that is neither especially German (the nationality of the founders), nor especially Spanish, nor, for that matter, especially tasty.

FIRST CLASS

Casa Lucío (Calle Cava Baja 35)—core of town, near Plaza Mayor—occupies unassuming quarters on two floors of a very old and atmospheric house, with reproduction paintings on stuccoed walls, leather chairs around tables set with white linen, a humming main-floor bar, and, despite (or possibly, because of) its unpretentious ambience, a distinguished clientele which has included King Juan Carlos and Queen Sofía, government ministers, captains of industry. But the waiters are nice to everybody, and the food they serve up is superlative. *Solomillo parillado*— thick and juicy grilled steak served on wooden planks—is the most popular entrée, but garlic-scented grilled chicken is super, too, as are the omelets served with fries. Open with tasty *sopa Castellana*, and if they're in season, conclude with a giant serving of fresh cherries presented atop a bowl of ice.

Botín (Calle de Cuchilleros 17): The address, first: The street takes its name from the landmark Arco (arch) de Cuchilleros of the landmark Plaza Mayor, from which it emerges. Botín, just below the arch, is still another landmark, on scene since 1725 and furnished quite as it has been since opening day. Everything is mouth-watering: soups, meats (including roast suckling pig and roast baby lamb), and game birds (partridge stew in particular). Atmospheric, delicious, fun.

Ambigú (Hotel Palace, Plaza de las Cortes 7) occupies an atmospheric alcove giving on to the stained glass-domed rotunda, in the lobby of a landmark hotel (above). Go anytime between 11:30 A.M. and 2:30 A.M., for a drink or a snack, lunch or dinner. The look is casual but service is smart, via tuxedoed waiters, with the range of comestibles soups and salads, pastas (spaghetti is prepared *al dente* and expertly sauced) and grills, pastries and sherbets; afternoon tea, sandwiches and coffee.

Continentes (Hotel Castellana Inter-Continental, Paseo de la Castellana 49) mixes good looks and good eats, with cuisine a creative mix of Spanish (host country), French (consulting chef's national origin) and American (Inter-Continental is a U.S.-operated chain). Open with seafood salad in a crab shell, foie gras, or gazpacho; continue with salmon-flecked scrambled eggs, shrimp casserole, duck-breast, or a U.S.-style prime sirloin, terminating with chocolate mousse, Spain's own *flan*, or house-baked pastries. Smiling service.

La Toja (Calle Siete de Julio 3) distinguishes itself for its seafood—fresh, uncomplicated and with the accents of northerly Galicia. Select either a fish of the day, or for that matter, the shellfish. There's an agreeably busy ambience, and agreeably kind staff.

Príncipe de Viana (Calle Manuel de Falla 5) is no-nonsense Spanish-authentic, with a northern accent. By that I mean you come here for seafood ragouts, cod—*bacalão*—prepared the way Basques like it, tasty bean specialties. There's always a crowd.

Horno Santa Teresa (Calle Santa Teresa 12) occupies smallish but very pretty white-and-red beamed quarters. A crew of waitresses—in starched black and white—serves up perfectly delicious comestibles, starting with *entremeses* on a groaning trolley, with roast veal among the entrées that follow. Have a baked fresh peach for dessert. Caveat: no credit cards.

Taberna del Alabardero (Calle Felipe V) is just across Plaza de Oriente from the Palacio Real. It dates to 1871, and has retained the charm of its original decor, both in the front bar-lounge and the *comedor* (dining room) out back. *Cazuela vasca*—a Basque-style fish casserole—or the *entrecôte* are ideal choices.

La Gran Tasca (Calle Ballesta 1) is a longtime downtown favorite, unpretentious, welcoming, and with hearty fare, especially its superior *cocido Madrileño; cochinillo* (roast pig) and *perdiz* (partridge) are tasty, too. Good house wines and a value-packed *menú del día.*

Edelweiss (Calle Jovellanos 7) only sounds like the hit song from *The Sound of Music.* You may order Teutonic and even Alsatian dishes (the *choucroute garnie* is recommendable) and drinks, but, by and large, you are in Spain, with Spaniards, here. Daily specials are good bets, and the house wine is inexpensive. Near the Calle de Alcalá.

Aroca (Plaza de los Carros 3)—in an interesting and aged part of town, a nice walk south from Plaza Mayor—appears low-key upon entry, consisting of an unadorned bar-room and a likewise plain dining area. But management and staff are cordial (most clients appear to be regulars) and what you're served—assorted *entremeses*, or appetizers, half a fried chicken, garlic-seasoned or grilled lamb chops, a dessert of fruit or cheese—is corking good; ditto the house wine, a carafe Valdapeñas.

El Puchero (Calle Larr 13, in the center) matches red-checked curtains with red-checked tablecloths, lines its walls with brightly shined copper, and greets you with smiles. If it's warm, opening with a chilled and tasty gazpacho is a good idea. Grilled veal chops are delicious, as are the fries accompanying, and an order of roast pork with the beans called *judías* is a novel and satisfactory idea. Torremilanos, a red from northerly Burgos proves a sound wine.

Taberna del Prado (Calle Marqués de Cubas 23, near Plaza de las Cortes) accords main-floor space to its bar, with the brick-walled restaurant down a flight. Your best bet is the *menú del día*, opening, perhaps, with hearty *sopa Catalán*, a prelude for such entrées as roast chicken or veal scallop, with ice cream a reliable sweet, and Torresilla, from Navarra the satisfactory house red. Service is swift but cool.

El Schotis (Calle Cava Baja 11) is an unpretentious but commendable choice of a solid meat-and-potatoes meal, in the neighborhood of Puerta del Sol. Try *solomillo* (a thick steak) with *papas fritas* (French fries) or the roast of the day.

St. James (Calle Juan Bravo 26): This is not an English tea shop, although it sounds as though it might be. The thrust here is paella—traditional Valencian-style, and in a number of other ways, invariably tasty. With sound wines to accompany. And in a handsome setting.

Drop (Calle Silva 24): There comes a time when, even in Spain with its fine cuisine, one craves pasta. Or pizza. Drop into Drop, just off Plaza del Callao.

Bellman (Hotel Suecia, Calle Marqués de Casa Riera 4) represents the Scandinavian alternative. At least on Thursday and Friday, when a Swedish-accented smorgasbord is served both at lunch and dinner in this Swedish-accented hotel.

La Barraca (Calle de la Reina 29) is packed with Americans and Japanese devouring *paella*, a house specialty, as if it were the greatest ever. It's adequate, but Madrid abounds in restaurants where that dish is equally good—or better—and which are more populated with locals, offering service that is more cordial, swifter, and more spontaneous.

Valentín (Calle San Alberto 3, up a flight) is so central—between Gran Vía and Puerta del Sol—and so well known over so long a period that it's a pity to report that the food is no longer recommendable, at least on the basis of two recently sampled dinners, friendly waiters notwithstanding.

MODERATE

Casa Paco (Puerta Cerrada 11) is an Old Madrid steak house of long standing, packed with Madrileños who know good beef at good prices. The *menú del día* is one of the best buys in town, but you do well too on an à la carte order of *solomillo*, or steak (you order it by weight), or on extra thick lamb or veal chops, all of which are so good that they compensate for the gruff service.

La Corralada (Calle Villanueva 21) has a fresh, bleached-oak and tan-linen look, and is packed with contented locals (the barrio is the smart one that is in and about Calle Velázquez, near the center) feasting on the good-value *menú del día*, which might embrace leek soup, a grilled fresh trout, and the house pudding.

Casa Vasca (Calle Victoria, just off Carrera San Jerónimo near Puerta del Sol) is unassuming, smiling, and with rib-sticking Basque fare on a *menú del día* that might include garlic and egg soup, a well-prepared fillet of hake, a sweet, and house wine.

Mejillonera la Ría (Calle Victoria 12) is a neighbor of Casa Vasca (above), and, as its name indicates, a source of mussels (*mejillones*, as they are called in Spanish) prepared in a multitude of manners, invariably delicious. Fun.

Plaza de Monterrey (Calle de Alcalá, up a flight) is a near-Puerta del Sol establishment of considerable seniority, refreshing simplicity, and good Galician nourishment—grills, seafood, casseroles—at fair tabs.

Casa Ciriaco (Calle Mayor 24): If you're to dine on Main Street, why not at Ciriaco? Especially if you favor chicken. *Gallina en pepitoria*—chicken fricassee—is the specialty.

Casa Mingo (Calle Echegary 27) is among the more popular of several worth-knowing-about *mesones* (inexpensive eateries) on this street leading south from Carrera San Jerónimo. Go for the bean-based stew, *fabada Asturiana*. Super.

Casa Maxi (Calle Toledo 123) is on the street leading south from Plaza Mayor with the Cathedral of San Isidro its major landmark, and the Puerta de Toledo fish market not far south. Which leads to Maxi's specialty: seafood.

Le Bistroquet (Calle Conde 4): French food in Old Madrid—and at a price? *Mais, oui.* Sample *soupe à l'oignon* at Le Bistroquet, south of Plaza Mayor.

Luarques (Calle Venura de la Vega 16, off Carrera de San Jerónimo) has the virtues of a central situation and a moderately-tabbed three-course-and-wine menu, which might open with chicken soup, offer grilled trout as the entrée, and conclude with ice cream or *flan*. Unlike at most core-of-Madrid restaurants, the staff speaks Spanish only, and credit cards are not accepted.

BARS, CAFÉS, CAFETERÍAS

Alkalde (Calle Jorge Juan 10) is earlier recommended as an extraordinary restaurant. I bring it up at this point because its bar is an extraordinary source of *tapas*—the drink accompaniments adored by Spaniards, Madrileños especially. This is a perfect spot to get hooked. Order a glass of beer or a sherry and select a plateful: shrimp, cubed fish, mussels and clams (both hot and cold), cubed Serrano ham, crumbled Mantega cheese, ham or chicken croquettes, finger sandwiches, cold but tasty omelet wedges, slivers of sausage. Eat enough and you can skip dinner. Or, consider a Madrid variation on a pub-crawl by wending your way on a *tapas*-tour.

Blanca Paloma (Calle del Carmen at Calle de Tetuán): The White Dove, to translate, is an attractive *cafetería* near Puerta del Sol for a snack or a casual meal.

Café Gijón (Paseo de Recoletos 21, off Plaza de las Cibeles) attracts a good-looking crowd, trendily albeit smartly attired, youngish as well as older, male with a smattering of females, gay and straight, Spanish and foreign. With a full-service—and moderately tabbed—restaurant in the basement.

Café Hispano (Paseo de la Castellana 76) is a principal congregating spot on the modishly-populated Castellana—mid-day, late afternoon through the wee hours. Amusing.

Café Plaza Mayor (Plaza Mayor 2) is one of a number of options on Madrid's most beautiful square, for coffee or wine and a snack.

Café de Oriente (Plaza de Oriente 2) affords views from its outdoor tables of the Royal Palace in one direction and the Royal Theater in the other. Good things to eat (it's a proper restaurant as well as a café) both alfresco and under cover.

Galerías Preciados (Calle de Preciados): The mother house of the nationwide department-store chain bids you for nourishment in its big and buzzy *cafetería*, with the range a multi-course meal, a sandwich, or an ice-cream concoction.

La Torre del Oro (Plaza Mayor 26): The lure here is hot and cold running *tapas*, fun pre-dinner in this classic Old Madrid setting. For what to order, see Alkalde, above.

L'Hardy (Carrera de San Jerónimo 8) is accorded space above as a restaurant of repute and antiquity. I call it to your attention here because it's on its main floor that are sold a delicious range of *tapas*, served in near-regal style, with either hot consommé or sherry to accompany.

Los Motivos (Calle Ventura de la Vega 10, south of Carrera de San Jerónimo, near Plaza Mayor): Your motive here should be pre-dinner *tapas* (see Alkalde, above, for specifics).

Lucky (Calle de Montera 24), near Calle de Preciados and the department stores, is one of a small chain of *cafeterías*, where the *churros y chocolate* combination—finger-shaped fritters eaten after you dunk them in hot chocolate—is commendable.

Manila (Calle del Carmen at Puerta del Sol, and at several Gran Vía and other central Madrid points) is a large, multi-room, well-operated *cafetería* ideal for sandwiches, snacks.

Nebraska (Puerta del Sol and other central locations) is still another chain of *cafeterías*. I especially like the Puerta del Sol outpost, which embraces a bar, café, candy counter, bakery, hot dog-hamburger section, and—upstairs—a waiter-service restaurant, complete with linen tablecloths and a full menu.

Serrano 50 (Calle Serrano 50, adjacent to and connected with Celso García department store) within—and I repeat, within—is a moderately priced *cafetería*. If you order at a table on the street, the better to watch the good-looking shoppers trot by, you'll pay for the observation-post location.

Museo de Jamón (Carrera de San Jerónimo 6): Don't take the name seriously; this is a stand-up spot for *bocadillos*, or sandwiches, of *jamón* (ham) and *chorizo* (sausage), with pastries, as well, and wine among the beverages.

La Oficina (Calle Preciados 10), a well-located *cafetería* with a counter that appears to be a block long, is indicated for on-the-run nourishment; cakes are good, ditto *churros* with hot chocolate. Breakfast, too.

Parque Retiro Café edges an idyllic lake in core-of-the-city Retiro Park, entered from the intersection of Calle Antonio Maura and Calle Alfonso XII. Relax with a cold drink and something to eat, from an outdoor table, as you watch Madrileños at their leisure, strolling and traversing the lake in rented rowboats. The setting is lovely.

Museo del Prado Café (Paseo del Prado) is a relatively recent installation in the nation's premier museum: sleekly contemporary in black and white, cafeteria-style. Opt for snack-food—sandwiches, pastries and the like—or more substantial dishes. Location is the ground floor; follow the signs.

SHOPPER'S MADRID
Barcelona (Chapter 4) is a substantial second, but Madrid—as national capital and principal metropolis, with an innate sense of style and relatively sensible geography—is Spain's premier shopping town. Shopping areas, not surprisingly in a city so

large, are dotted about, but the short-term visitor does well to concentrate on the two that are the most central.

The elder of these is the popular-priced downtown district, centered in a landmark square, Puerta del Sol, with the mother houses of the two national department-store chains on Calle Preciados, satellite shops on surrounding streets extending north, through Plaza de Callao, to the broad thoroughfare—no longer as smart as in former days but still to be reckoned with—known simply as Gran Vía; and still more shops leading west from Puerta del Sol along Calle Mayor which, passing architec-turally splendid Plaza Mayor (above) extends west through Old Madrid to the Royal Palace complex (above).

Smarter and correspondingly pricier, by and large, is the more modern shopping quarter based on Calle Serrano, extending north from the monumental gate, Puerta de Alcalá (just east of Plaza de las Cibeles and its familiar fountain), and including such neighborhood streets as Calle Goya, Calle Velázquez, Calle Claudio Coello, Calle Hermosilla, and Calle Ortega y Gasset, the lot eminently strollable.

The area known as the Rastro (south of Plaza Mayor) is a cen-ter for antiques, with Calle del Prado and Plaza de las Cortes also sites of antiques shops. Specifics? Here are some, by category:

Department Stores: Each of the Big Two chains has a number of stores in Madrid. They're both longest-on-scene downtown on Calle Preciados, where *El Corte Inglés* has the edge, in my view, with quarters more modern and sprightly. Be-sides a big men's shop in a detached building called Lainez, El Corte Inglés has an additional men's department on the third floor of its main building (along with a worth-knowing-about barber shop and an Iberia office, as well as a giant basement su-permarket, with wines); women's clothing and a beauty parlor on four; kids' togs on two; porcelain, crystal and housewares on one; a seventh floor *cafetería*/restaurant; and an information/ interpreters desk on main, with excellent gratis maps of Madrid. Other big El Corte Inglés outlets are on Paseo de la Castellana, Calle de Goya and Calle de la Princesa. *Galerías Preciados* (which has taken to shortening its name upon occasion simply to *Galerías*) occupies two Calle Preciados buildings. The most interesting-to-visitors department of its Hogar (for-the-home) Building is the main-floor china department with an excellent stock of pottery from the various regions of Spain. The Main Building's seventh-floor *cafetería* (along with a good cheese and wine shop) is counseled in Daily Bread (above); other departments are women's clothing on two, men's clothing on one, kids' duds on four, shoes and souvenirs on the mezzanine and Mr. Minit shoe repair on main. Of Galerias' other Madrid stores, the one you want most to know about is at Calle Serrano 47—very smart and streamlined, with women's, men's and children's clothing, gifts and an attractive *cafetería* in a two-floor-and-basement building. Though an exclusively-Madrid operation, still another department store, *Celso García* is not to be overlooked. It has outlets in three Calle Serrano points; two of them are relatively small one-floor stores (one each for women and men), while the third is multistory and modish, with a street-floor café (see Daily Bread); gifts, books and perfumes-colognes on main, women's clothing on one, men's on two and children's on three.

Antiques: The Rastro quarter—demarcated by Catedral de San Isidro, Puerta de Toledo and Glorieta de Embajadores, is at its busiest Sunday mornings, when Madrileños by the thousands mill about its myriad stalls and shops. These include *Romaya* (Galerías Ribera) for eighteenth- and nineteenth-century furniture, *Los Andes* (Galerías Piquer), for Roman and other antiquities; and *Luis Carabe* (Nuevas Galerías), for porcelain, to name but a trio.

Antique Auctions: *Sotheby's* (Plaza de la Indepencia).

Candy: *La Violeta* (Plaza de Canalejas) is a beloved old-timer; specialties are violet confections and gumdrops, handsomely wrapped, that make nice gifts. *Santa Croce* (Calle Serrano) vends fine chocolates.

Children's wear: The department stores (above) have well-priced selections; consider also *Lencería Ideal* (Calle Hermosilla) and *Friki-Tílburi* (Calle Velázquez).

Handicrafts and ceramics: *Artespaña* (Gran Vía) is one of a nationwide chain; *El Patio de Claudio Coello* (Calle Claudio Coello), *Cerámica de Talavera* (Calle Lagasca).

Jewelry: *Luis Gil* (Calle Serrano), *Yanes* (Calle Goya) and *Aldoa* (Gran Vía) are among the leaders.

Leather (including handbags, wallets, luggage): *Loewe* (which is the German for *lion*, and which Spaniards pronounce as *Low-EH-vah*)—with shops on Gran Vía and at two near-each-other points on Calle Serrano (with men's and women's clothing and accessories, as well)—might be termed an Iberian counterpart of Italy's Gucci, at once high-style, *very* costly, and with foreign branches. *Gucci* is a nearby Calle Serrano neighbor of Loewe. *Manuel Herrero* (Calle Preciados) is an old-reliable; *Go* (which also vends shoes) and *Orlan* (both on Calle Serrano) are commendable, too.

Men's clothing: *Rafael y Salvador, Alba,* and *Fancy Men* (all on Calle Serrano), *Darric* (Gran Vía) and *Eduardo Arroyo* (Calle Claudio Coello) are a representative handful, among many.

Men's and women's clothing: *Loewe* (Calle Serrano and Gran Vía) is especially modish. *Cortefiel* (Gran Vía) is kingdom-wide, mid-category, with both men's and women's wear in this outlet, and others (on Calle Serrano and Calle Preciados, for example) for women only. *Gianfranco Ferre* (Italy-origin), *Alfredo Caral,* and *Gancedo y Gonzalez* are all on Calle Serrano; *Elysardo* (Calle Velázquez); *Zarauz* (Calle Goya); *Chispa* (Calle Preciados) and—among many other sources—the major department stores (*El Corte Inglés* and *Galerías Preciados*), with extensive ranges and frequent good-value specials.

Women's clothing: No dearth in this fashionably dressed capital. A few examples: *Zorilla* (Calle Preciados and Calle Serrano),

Pepa Nieto and *Valentin Amupero* (both Calle Serrano), *Donaña* (Calle Claudio Coello), *Palão* (Calle Velázquez), and *Choren* (Calle Goya).

Perfumes, colognes and soaps: *Myurgia,* one of the leading Spanish makes (and widely exported), has its own retail shop on Plaza de las Cortes, opposite the Palace Hotel. The other top make, *Puig* (*Agua Brava, Agua Lavanda,* other labels) can be found in department stores' main floors, and such *perfumerías* as *Rosi* (Gran Vía).

INCIDENTAL INTELLIGENCE

Bullfights: Madrid is the big time for Spanish bullfighters (Barcelona and the Andalusian cities, especially Seville and Granada, follow in this regard.) There are two *plazas de toros*: *Plaza Monumental de las Ventas,* northeast of the center, at the extreme end of Calle de Alcalá with its *Museo Taurino,* a museum of bullfighting; and *Vista Alegre* (Avenida Matilde Hernández), with fights Sunday afternoons and certain Thursdays, spring through fall. Ask your hotel concierge to get you tickets on the *sombra* (shady) side of the ring.

Flamenco dancing, not easily come by as a quality proposition, is probably best observed at such *tablaos flamencos* as *Los Canasteros* (Calle de Barbieri 10), and *Café de Chinitas* (Calle de Torija 7), which doubles as a First Class restaurant, so that you might want to combine dinner with the show. Otherwise, go at about 11 P.M. for a drink—expensive, since it includes the admission charge—and the performance.

Opera, concerts, theaters, movies, casino: *Teatro Real* (Plaza de Oriente) is the longtime opera house, now converted to use for concerts: symphony, classic guitar (which Madrileños are fond of), and the like. This is a beauty of a gilded and multi-tiered traditional-style house. *Teatro de la Zarzuela* (Calle de Jovellanos 2, off Calle de Alcalá) is Madrid's opera house, turn-of-century, horseshoe-shaped. There is no resident company, but rather, an annual spring season, with mostly imported artists, with the singing far surpassing the cheap productions. There are, as well, a couple-of-dozen legitimate theaters where plays and musicals (always, of course, in the Spanish language) are presented with a generally high degree of professional skill. And a dozen *café-teatros* with musical comedy on their stages. Performances are usually twice daily at the standard theaters, at 7 and 10:30 P.M., while the *café-teatros'* lights dim later for shows, at 11:30 P.M. and 1:30 A.M. Movies are mostly dubbed into Spanish, but there are cinemas where the original versions of films are shown; ask your hotel concierge. Madrid's *Casino* is out of town, on Highway N-VI, but you may reach it via free buses from Plaza de España; hours are 5 P.M.-4 A.M., games include roulette and blackjack, as well as slot machines, foreigners must present passports for entry, gents must wear jackets, and there are restaurants and a nightclub with entertainment; phone 859-03-12. Finally, check the what's-on or *Cartelera* (billboard) pages of the papers—*ABC* and *Ya* are two such.

Aeropuerto de Barajas is seven miles from the center, to which it's connected by regularly scheduled airport buses (terminating in town at Plaza de Colón) and taxi. Iberia operates a convenient shuttle service between Madrid and Barcelona, and connects the capital with other Spanish cities, as does the exclusively domestic carrier, Aviaco. Avoid the Barajas cafés unless you are absolutely famished or about to perish from thirst; prices are exorbitant, even for an airport.

Further Information: The Spanish Government's Secretaría General de Turismo operates an information office—answering questions and providing gratis leaflets and the like about destinations throughout Spain—on the street floor of its headquarters at Calle María de Molina 50. Madrid's Oficina Municipal de Información is at Plaza Mayor 3 and at Calle Sres. de Luzónlo. Its friendly staff is helpful but not necessarily multilingual. There are other municipal information-office branches at the airport and Chamartín railway station, and a second all-Spain information center at Torre de Madrid, Plaza de España. Iberia's eternally hectic main city ticket office is at the rear of the Palace Hotel, on Plaza de Cánovas del Castillo.

18

Majorca

Of [George] Sand
and Sunshine

BACKGROUND BRIEFING

The dispelling of misconceptions is nowhere else in Spain more necessary than in the case of the principal Balearic island. Majorca, it should be understood from the outset, is big time. It is a century and a half since George Sand took her tubercular lover, Frédéric Chopin, to spend a cold and rainy winter in a deserted monastery high in the Majorcan hills. They had a dreadful stay. But they were Majorca's first modern-age tourists of note.

It took some time for successors to come in numbers. They began arriving in trickles in the decades after World War II when news of the balmy Majorcan sunshine penetrated all the way north to lands like England and Sweden and Holland, where even the summers can be gray and chilly. An invention called the charter flight speeded matters along, while Spanish entrepreneurs poured pesetas into the construction of hotels all along the island's coast.

Today, the half-million native Majorcans play host to some three million visitors annually. A decade or so back, when I first visited Majorca, there were 1,000 hotels. That figure has now more than doubled.

The wonder of it all is that, once one leaves Palma's ever-frenetic international airport (among the planet's busiest the year round), the pace slackens. There are crowds in the bigger resort clusters, to be sure. But this gorgeous, 53-mile-long, 1,400-

square-mile Mediterranean island is big enough—uninhabited interior mountain regions notwithstanding—to absorb the mobs, and retain enough of its placid character to afford visitors the relaxation they crave.

Then there is the matter—largely neglected by northern Europeans who want little more than sun, surf, and disco dancing—of Majorca's ace in the hole: a capital city that is at once engaging, culture-rich, hotel-filled, beach-fringed, and a testament to the grandeur of a onetime island kingdom with roots as respectable as those of any region on the mainland peninsula.

Everybody has gotten into the Majorcan act. There were prehistoric Iberians, and later Phoenicians, Greeks, and Carthaginians. The Romans established a substantial colony here a good century and a quarter before Christ. Vandals replaced them, and Byzantines came all the way from Constantinople and incorporated Majorca into their glittering empire, only to yield to invading Moors in the eighth century. The Moors had staying power, remaining some 500 years, and eventually establishing their own monarchy on the island. During this time Majorca-based pirates were feared throughout the region.

In the early thirteenth century—Majorcan schoolchildren rattle off the year: 1229—King James I of Aragón seized the Balearic Islands (and eventually Valencia) from the Moors. His conquest paved the way for a Christian Majorcan kingdom to succeed that of the Arabs in 1276. James I of Aragón's son became James I of Majorca, the first sovereign of a trio to rule the island. Majorca was absorbed by the pan-Spanish kingdom of Ferdinand and Isabella. Subsequently its history was not unlike that of the mainland provinces (although, unlike most, it is today the seat of a royal residence: King Juan Carlos and Queen Sofía habitually spend much of each summer in Majorca). Like several of those provinces, though—Catalonia and the Basque regions, especially—it takes a special pride in its culture and its language, Majorquín, which is a close relative of Catalán.

ON SCENE

Lay of the Land: Simplify Majorca's geography by dividing it into Palma—the capital and sole metropolis with roughly half the population of half a million—and the rest of the island. The capital snuggles into the northernmost point of the immense and beautifully beach-fringed bay, *Bahía del Palma*, that takes its name, on the southwest coast. The most built-up resort areas flank the city to the west—*Cala Mayor, Illetas, Palma Nova,* and *Magalluf*. East of Palma there are also substantial resorts—*Ca'n Pastilla, Las Maravillas,* and *El Arenal*—all on the long beach stretch, *Playa de Arenal,* as well as others to the northeast. The popular areas of *Paguera* and *Puerto de Andraitx* are west of Palma. If you've a map before you, look now to the diagonal that constitutes the magnificently mountain-backed northwest coast, running from *Sant Telmo* to *Cabo* (Cape) *de Formentor*, Majorca's northernmost point, past destinations of consequence along the way, such as inland *Valldemosa* (where Chopin and Sand lived), the port and inland city of *Sóller, Puig Mayor* (the island's highest peak), the thriller-diller roller coaster highway linking coastal *Torrent dei Pareis* and the inland (and dull) *Monasterio de Liuc,* and *Puerto de Pollensa,* just below *Cabo de Formentor's* bay and beaches.

The small towns of *Inca* and *Manacor* (where tourists are lured to a pearl factory) are the only settlements of consequence in the interior of the island. And the east coast, though not without fine beaches, is most often visited for a pair of monasteries—*San Salvador,* a mostly eighteenth-century complex at an elevation of 1,600 feet, with a view, and the Franciscan *Monasterio de Cura,* even older and farther inland—along with a trio of caves spectacularly decorated by nature. Of the caves, *Artá* and *Drach* (with an underground lake) are perhaps the most requisite.

At this point, I suspect you've a question. I've anticipated it. You want to know, given the choice of possibilities for headquartering on this island, where to bed down. It works this way: Visitors select their homes away from home more or less by nationality. Wealthy international yachtsmen tie up at Palma's Paseo Marítimo. The French tend to congregate in and about Puerto de Sóller, on the northwest coast. Germans and Dutch are found in quantity at heavily congested Playa de Palma hotels, southeast of the capital, while the British settle in to the southwest of town, in and about Magalluf and Palma Nova, about as sardine-packed as Playa de Palma. More Germans populate the hotels on the distant east coast, where beaches are at their widest.

That leaves Americans. Because their Majorca stays tend to be shorter than Europeans'—a few days instead of a few weeks—they mostly put up in the capital.

Palma is not why sun-starved northern Europeans go to Majorca. If they don't avoid it—you'll find them dining, drinking, and discoing there after dark—they neglect it, much preferring bouts around the pool and naps on the beach to daytime exploration of what is one of Spain's most charming cities.

The city more or less chops itself in two. The older sector lies to the east, extending inland from the bay, and the modern half to the west. The high, handsome façade of the Cathedral is the landmark of Old Palma. From the rear of the Cathedral it's an easy walk north past ancient mansions with elegant patios, on Calle Morey, to Plaza Santa Eulalia (with a landmark church) along Calle Colón to Plaza Mayor, or, continuing east on Calle General Mola to Plaza Pío XII and Calle Jaime III, the main shopping street. More contemporary is Palma's west end. Paseo Bajo, which fronts the bay to the west, changes its name to Paseo Marítimo as it extends east all the way to the town's older section. It skirts a network of waterfront hotels and the restaurant-encircled Plaza Gomila, just in from the harbor, and goes past Club Náutico to the passenger ship terminals, with the busy beaches—*Cala Mayor, San Agustín, Camp de Mar,* and *Las Illetas*.

The Cathedral, known locally as La Seo and situated on a waterfront plaza by that name, is a Majorcan spectacular. It was the first structure of consequence to rise, back in the thirteenth century when the Christian forces of King James I of Aragón came from the mainland to wrest the island from Moorish control. It is light and lovely, big and bountiful, a joyous Gothic monument—its great flying buttresses and high, fortress-like walls visible for miles around—to the Catholic cause. The rose window over the choir, some 14 yards in diameter, is an exuberant mosaic in glass, with flower-like clusters of yellow, red, and blue. Needle-like pillars of the central of three naves support severe Gothic vaults. The Cathedral's treasures are in its separately entered *Museo*

Diocesano: a medieval St. George slaying the Dragon, against a backdrop of the Bay of Palma; ancient books and documents; coins and tiles; pottery and portraits; golden monstrances and baroque candelabra.

La Almudaina and La Lonja, waterfront neighbors to the Cathedral (they are due west) are a pair of dazzlers that, traditionally, have been open to visitors as museums, but in recent seasons have been closed more often than not. If you see the doors to either one open, pop in posthaste. Moors built the Almudaina before King James's conquest. Originally a military bastion, it was transformed into a residence for the Majorcan monarchs; throne room, chapel, and patio stand out. *La Lonja* is as imposing from without—a pure Gothic box, elegantly scaled—as from within, where it constitutes a single albeit very grand chamber that, centuries back, was headquarters for the town's merchant princes. The fluted columns supporting a vaulted ceiling are noteworthy.

Museo Marítimo (Paseo de Sagrera, next door to La Lonja) occupies a honey of a galleried Renaissance palace that is at least as exemplary as the contents of the museum within. You will have seen choicer maritime museums. Still, this one—by means of captains' portraits, bosuns' wheels, compasses, ship models—evokes the seafaring flavor of the city.

Museo de Majorca (Calle Lulio 5, an extension of Calle Morey): This is Majorca's best-kept secret, and, without question, it ranks as Palma's most requisite destination after the Cathedral. First, because it occupies a two-story Renaissance palace-cum-patio—*Ayamans* by name—beautifully and authentically restored by the Spanish government, which opened it in 1976 following acquisition from the City of Palma. Second, because of Majorcan works of art—exclusively Majorcan—that grace its galleries. There are a series, from the Middle Ages, of portraits of the prophets; richly hued altarpieces; a couple of rooms full of saints' heads sculpted in the fourteenth century; coats of arms and portraits of Renaissance Palma gentry; extraordinary specimens of the island's own majolica pottery; even capitals and fragments of stonework dating back to Roman Majorca. An all-Spain sleeper of a museum.

Museo de Palacio Vivot (Calle Zavella 4) is almost as unknown to outlanders as the Museo de Majorca (above). A core-of-Old Palma mansion, with a beautiful patio, it gets even better inside, with mostly seventeenth-century furniture, tapestries that bring the Renaissance to life, and paintings by, among others, Spain's Ribera and Belgium's Brueghel.

Church of Santa Eulalia (Plaza de Santa Eulalia) is Gothic, with a baroque altar at the end of its three-aisle nave.

Church of San Francisco (Plaza de San Francisco): Don't let the Plateresque façade (by noted architect Francisco de Herrera) throw you off. San Francisco, within, is essentially Gothic but with modifications from later eras. Beeline for the cloister, an all-Majorca beauty spot, with pencil-slim columns supporting its arches, and painted Renaissance beams the surprise of its gallery.

Ayuntamiento (Plaza de Corte): The town hall, with its ebullient baroque façade, bespeaks strength and security. Step right in, and one of the veteran attendants on duty is bound to motion you upstairs to the council chamber. Follow along; it's not only a nifty room—the woodwork is masterful—but there's a treat: a Van Dyck portrait of San Sebastián.

Castillo de Bellver (Parque de Bellver), begun in the fourteenth century, is high above the city, a good two-mile drive from the center. But go. It was to Bellver—with its cool, elevated situation—that the Christian Majorcan monarchs moved each summer from winter quarters at the Almudaina castle downtown. You don't make the trek to Bellver so much for the *Museo Municipal*—with bits and pieces of historical Palma its exhibits—as you do for the building itself. This doughnut-shaped masterpiece encircles a two-level patio, and is itself surrounded by a quartet of circular towers. Views of Palma—the bay and the open sea in one direction and the mountains in the other—are smashing.

Pueblo Español (Paseo Ecuador, northwest of the center) is no more to my taste than its counterpart in Barcelona. Why seek out contemporary copies of architecturally interesting old buildings in a country so full of super originals? No matter; you might enjoy seeing artisans at work in the shops, watching street dancers, and hearing the Babel-like decibel count emanating from the multinational crowd taking it all in.

Valldemosa—a mountain village 10 easy miles due north of Palma—is the classic Majorca excursion. And rightly so. It is, after all, more than 140 years since the 34-year-old French writer George Sand, her 15-year-old son Maurice, 9-year-old daughter Solange, and tubercular 28-year-old Polish lover, Frédéric Chopin, spent not quite eight cold and wet winter weeks in a three-room cell with a garden, in little Valldemosa's sprawling Carthusian monastery. The wonder of it all is that both the village (lovely) and the monastery (imposingly beautiful) are little changed since that time. There's not a waxworks or a fast-food joint or a plastic motel in sight. Instead, multilingual village women, dressed in typical Majorcan folk costume, act as guides to the seven sections of the museum with the umbrella title *Real Cartuja de Valldemosa*. If the single-shot admission fee is Spain's steepest (I know of none as high anywhere else in the kingdom), value received is substantial. By that I mean you see the mostly eighteenth-century monastery complex—including an authentically restored and furnished monks' pharmacy, library of the monastery's abbot, mini-palace of a long-ago Majorcan king, and sacristy—and its collection of ancient religious objects, plus still other rooms housing the village's historical mementoes.

When all is said and done, of course, it's the VIPs' cell-suite that you came for. It does not disappoint. The three contiguous rooms are furnished quite as they might have been when the trio of Sands and the ailing composer-genius inhabited them during that unseasonably damp and cold winter. There are personal mementoes, two paintings of Sand, and another of Chopin. But the locally made upright piano at which Chopin worked—and worked hard—until just before departure (when his own piano, held up by Majorcan customs, arrived) is Exhibit No. 1. Music buffs will be interested to know that on that instrument he composed the series of short works designated as Preludes (some of which he had begun, but not polished, before arrival), as well as a pair of Polonaises (A Major and C Minor), the Mazurka in E Minor, and—music historians are inclined to believe—the Sonata in B-flat Minor and two Nocturnes.

The pity of the Sand-Chopin tenancy at the *Cartuja* was their rotten luck with weather. When the sun shines, which is much of the time in Majorca—even in elevated Valldemosa—nothing is more idyllic than the view of the valley below, from the garden, still meticulously tended, fronting the monastery cells. Even George Sand, who wrote so critically of Majorcans she encountered and of the trials and tribulations of her "invalid," enthused over the lovely setting: "It is one of those views which overpower the spectator because they leave nothing more to be desired, nothing to the imagination."

It is perhaps worth pointing out that the monastery was the fourth home for the party in their 96-day Majorca winter. They lived briefly at first in a Palma pension, moving successively to a suburban Palma villa from which they were evicted (the landlord was fearful of Chopin's cough) and to the Palma home of the sympathetic French consul before moving up to their *celda*, or cell, in the *Cartuja*. *Cartuja* shops sell two fascinating, locally published paperbound books you'll want to pick up: Sand's minor classic, *Winter in Majorca*, translated from the original French and annotated by longtime Majorca resident Robert Graves, and an English translation by R.D.F. Pring-Mill of *Chopin and George Sand in Majorca* by Bartomeu Ferra.

SETTLING IN

PALMA

Hotel Son Vida Sheraton: I'm stretching it a little when I locate the Son Vida Sheraton in Palma. Actually, it's several miles to the northwest, in its own verdant park, high on a hill with views of the city and the sea way, way below. This is among Majorca's more luxurious hotels, an essentially modern 170-room house, built upon an ancient nucleus and smartly traditional in style, with contemporary accents. Everything is big and bold: lobbies, lounges, bars, restaurants, and bedrooms, from most of which there are striking panoramas. (This is an upside-down hotel; it descends a hill, with the room floors below the public spaces. Remember, when booking, that the higher up your accommodations, the better the vista from your room's terrace.) Son Vida's thrust is golf—an 18-hole course is adjacent, and there's tennis, too, along with a pool around which lunch is served to an attractive, moneyed, multinational clientele, with heavy German, French, Spanish, and—not surprising, given its affiliation with U.S.-based Sheraton—American overtones. *Luxury.*

Hotel de Mar (Playa de las Illetas) is my choice for a beachfront house on sands just next door to the city, going west on the Bay of Palma. This is an understatedly handsome house, from glazed-tile façade to baths with telephones and stall showers as well as tubs in the 150 good-sized rooms and suites. The public spaces—one dines and drinks indoors and without, swims at a pool or from the beach—are a pleasure. *Luxury.*

Hotel Valparaíso (La Bonanova) is around the bay, minutes from the center of town, with sumptuous views of the city and harbor from its 150 elaborate rooms and suites. Everything is overblown, which is not to say that anything is lacking: restaurants and bars in variety, an atmospheric *boîte*, indoor and outdoor pools, resident swans afloat in garden pools. *Luxury.*

Hotel Victoria Sol (Avenida Joan Miró 21, at Paseo Marítimo) is Palma's traditional harborfront leader: with 170 good-sized rooms and suites with terraces, bay-view restaurant (which moves outdoors for dinner on fine evenings), bar, jumbo pool, and sun terrace, pretty garden. *Luxury.*

Hotel Palas Atenea (Paseo Marítimo): The contemporary design of the Palas Atenea is prosaic but ever so functional. There are 370 well-equipped rooms (with terraces), fine pool, convenient restaurant, and bar-lounge: *cafetería*, too. *First Class.*

Hotel Saratoga (Paseo Mallorca 4) is not going to put you in mind of the upstate New York resort for which it's named. Which is not to say you won't be content in this medium-sized, medium-category house, just inland from the harbor. All rooms have terraces and baths; rooftop and ground-level pools, restaurant, bar. *Moderate.*

Hotel Jaime III (Paseo Mallorca 14b) is a well-priced, near-the-harbor house. Rooms are good-sized and with terraces and baths; restaurant, bar, *cafetería. Moderate.*

Hotel Palladium (Paseo Mallorca 40) is at once quiet and conveniently situated. All of its pleasant rooms have baths. Breakfast room and a bar that serves snacks as well as drinks, but no restaurant. *Moderate.*

BAY OF PALMA

Hotel de Mar Sol (Illetas) is set in its own sprawling, impeccably landscaped garden, with a honey of a pool to complement still another indoors, and the wide white-sand beach. Rooms are full-facility, terraced and sea-view the lot of them. There are congenial places to drink and to dine, including around the pool at lunchtime. *Luxury.*

Hotel Cupido (Playa de Palma) is a no-frills, 200-room (all with baths and terraces) house, with a big pool, restaurant, and adjacent shopping mall with *cafetería*, bar, and shops; and best of all, the beach just across the street. *Moderate.*

Hotel Los Tordos (Palma Nova) offers 300 fully equipped rooms, restaurant, *cafetería*, bar, and a capacious pool, with the beach close by. *Moderate.*

Hotel Antillas (Magalluf) is tall, tasteful, and with a full range of amenities, including a pair of pools and the beach adjacent. *First Class.*

Hotel Guadalupe (Magalluf) is a kind of multinational, multilingual Catskills come to Majorca: Fun and games galore, with group activity the thrust. Everyone has a good time, and that's a lot of people; there are nearly 500 comfortable rooms, and all facilities. *Moderate.*

OUT-ISLAND

Hotel Formentor (Formentor) is the ultimate Majorcan retreat: queen bee of the out-island hotels, with only its own lovely gardens separating it from one of the most idyllic beaches on Majorca. Elongated, sleek, and white-walled from without, the look and atmosphere within are traditional and conservative. Rooms tend to be understated, if lacking in no amenity. There are table d'hôte and à la carte restaurants, with still another eatery—for buffet lunches—down at the beach. Two pools (one for kids), riding, tennis, nightly movies, billiards. Gents, please note: both jacket and tie for dinner. Hotel Formentor—populated mostly by Britons, Germans, French, Swedes, with sprinklings of Spaniards and Americans—has style. *Luxury.*

Hotel Miramar (Puerto de Pollensa) is at once cozy, charming, and with a central situation in the heart of one of the island's prettiest villages. There's an elderly main building, with inviting lobby, bar, lounges, and a honey of a dining room in crisp white, green-accented. And a newer, adjacent wing. Rooms in both parts are delightful, with views of sea and mountains. You swim just across the street at the beach, and sun on the hotel's pier. *First Class.*

Hotel Espléndido (Puerto de Sóller) is a worth-knowing-about beachfront hostelry in this strikingly situated north-coast town, near Sóller (with its Museum of Majorcan Ceramics), and Valldemosa. There are 100 agreeable rooms, restaurant, and bar. *Moderate.*

Hotel Villamil (Paguera) wraps itself around a crenellated mock-medieval tower, and is situated in a brilliant garden that's fringed by a beach and punctuated by a big pool. The 100 rooms are extra-large and with super baths; dining—both indoor and alfresco—is exceptional. A link of Britain's Trusthouse Forte chain. Elegant. *Luxury.*

Hotel Golf Santa Ponça (Santa Ponça) is quite the most imaginatively designed and decorated of Majorcan hotels. And it's tiny as regards capacity: less than a score of contemporary terraced rooms. The rattan-furnished public spaces—lounge, bar, posh indoor-outdoor restaurant, *cafetería,* pair of pools (one with a bar half in, half above the water)—have wit and charm. You go here if you love golf; the club's 18-hole course is internationally reputed. *Luxury.*

DAILY BREAD

PALMA

El Faro (Paseo de Sagrera 4) is an apt choice for a seafood lunch in the course of in-town sightseeing. Setting is a canopy-covered terrace, on the bay. Order the well-priced *menú del día. Moderate.*

Penélope (Plaza Progreso 19) is heart-of-town with a smart look—graphics on the walls, fresh flowers on the tables, swift service—and lobsters (from a big tank) a specialty, along with less pricey seafood and paella, too. *First Class.*

Plat Plat (Avenida Joan Miró 50, near Plaza Gomila) is a trendy downtown choice for Majorcan specialties: the chicken specialty *pollo escalduns,* for one. *First Class.*

La Pizzeria (Calle Bellver 9, near Plaza Gomila) is indicated if you're homesick for pasta and pizza, somewhat Spanish-accented, but tasty. Attractive. *Moderate.*

El Beccoro (Calle Bellver 11, near Plaza Gomila and just opposite La Pizzeria above) serves the hearty Spanish steak called *solomillo* with baked potato and a salad. And the house's own red wine. *Moderate.*

El Patio (Calle Consignatario Schembri 5 at Plaza Gomila) is good-looking and with an international flair to its menu—paella, pasta, pork chops, to give you an idea. *First Class.*

Coco Loco (Plaza Gomila) is a mob scene, but an agreeable one. All hands tuck into steaks, grilled chicken, or hamburgers, and end with Irish coffee. *Moderate.*

Olas Steak House (Plaza Gomila) is a whimsical touch of Denmark—all in red and white, the Danish national colors—that packs in the hungry, feeding them T-bone steaks with baked potatoes, or, as a variation, *steak au poivre flambé.* Fun. *Moderate.*

Celler Premsa (Plaza Gomila) is a hearty tavern of yore, with stout wine casks lining its walls. Crêpes are the lure—the menu describes them in a dozen languages. *Moderate.*

Bar Bellver (Plaza Gomila) is this ever-lively square's ever-lively congregating spot for coffee, wine, or what have you. Watch the world go by. *Moderate.*

OUT-ISLAND

Bon Aire (Avenida Adelfas, Playa de las Illetas) is not nearly as simple as it looks. The typical Majorcan decor, smartly understated, includes a seaview terrace (perfect for lunch) and beamed, brick-walled interiors. Seafood. *Luxury.*

Ca'n Pedro (Avenida Archiduque Luis Salvador, Valldemosa) is a neat traditional-style spot—not unlike the ancient village in which it's situated—serving nicely priced *menús del día.* Indicated for lunch, in the course of a pilgrimage to the *Cartuja.* *Moderate.*

Hotel Formentor (Formentor): The main restaurant or the beachfront pavilion—the former for a copious *menú del día,* the latter for the cold buffet—of this extraordinary hotel (see *Settling In*) are relaxing choices for midday respite while touring this scenic area. *First Class/Luxury.*

Hotel Miramar (Puerto de Pollensa): Crisp white napery, contemporary oils on the walls, ladder-back chairs, and a tasty *menú del día*. *First Class.*

Gran Tortuga (Carretera de Cala Fornells, Paguera) is at once scenic and delicious; try the fish of the day. *First Class.*

El Patio (Calle Burdils 35, Porto Cristo) is worth knowing about when you're hungry at midday, while on an expedition to Drach Caves, on the east coast. Start with gazpacho, with a poultry or a fish entrée following. *First Class.*

INCIDENTAL INTELLIGENCE

Palma's Son San Juan Airport, seven miles east of town, is rarely serene. Prepare for long check-in queues and a fair share of confusion, arriving for departure as early as you can. Iberia connects the island with points on *la península*—as the mainland is called on the island—and other European carriers, both scheduled (including Lufthansa, Air France, British Airways, KLM Royal Dutch Airlines, Scandinavian Airlines, and Swissair) and charter, connect it with the continent. Ships depart Estaciones Marítimas, on Paseo Marítimo in Palma, for Barcelona and Valencia, as well as Ibiza and Port Mahón on the Balearic island of Menorca. There is ship service all the way to Genoa, Italy, too. Frequently departing buses connect Palma with nearby beaches, and with more distant island points. Trains, from Palma's Estación Ferrocarril (Plaza España) to Sóller on the north coast, Inca in the interior, and other points. *Further information:* Oficina de Turismo de Majorca, Avenida Jaime III 10, and at the airport.

19

Pamplona
Basques and Bulls

BACKGROUND BRIEFING

The influence of fiction on tourism is not to be underestimated. When Ernest Hemingway chronicled the madness of each summer's Running of the Bulls in the northern Spanish town of Pamplona in *The Sun Also Rises* half a century ago, he set in motion an annual touristic pilgrimage.

Only the terrorist tactics of fanatic Basque nationalists in recent seasons have cut into the attendance at Pamplona's merrymaking during part of each July, occasioned by the traditional observance—*Sanfermines*, it is called—of the Feast of San Fermín. The dates, not unlike our July 4, are fixed: July 6-20.

Starting early, at 7 o'clock each morning of that fortnight, hundreds of Pamplona's young blades, wearing scarves of scarlet, the color of bullfighters' capes, dash through a maze of narrow streets, somehow or other managing to keep ahead of a pack of bulls that have been tapped to perform later that very day. The procession—*encierre*, the Pamplonans call it—moves from the beasts' corral to Plaza de Jonnos, the bullring located on a square named, appropriately enough, for Hemingway in the center of town.

The ritual has centuries of precedent, as well it might in a city with Pamplona's advanced age. Still medium-sized, and strongly Basque as regards language and culture, this ancient capital of the province of Navarre started defending itself from attackers as long ago as the fifth century, when Visigoths coveted it in the course of their expansion into the Iberian peninsula.

Other invaders, Moors and troops of Charlemagne included, raised their colors in Pamplona. But never for very long. The strong-willed Basques of the town and province invariably prevailed, creating their own kingdom of Navarre early in the ninth century.

And a thriving kingdom it was for more than half a millennium, when most of its territory became a part of the united kingdom of Navarre and Castile. Although modern in many respects, Pamplona adores tradition. Ancient walls still frame the northern half of the core of town. And a star-shaped fortress looks down upon it from the south.

ON SCENE

Lay of the Land: Pamplona is, in proportion to its size, not a whit less grand than sister Spanish cities. Life revolves around massive and magnificent Plaza Mayor (that goes as well by its proper name, Plaza del Castillo). A neoclassic bandstand occupies its center, and double rows of trees line each side, with cafés lying between the greenery and shops of the galleried arcades. Calle Estafeta connects Plaza Mayor with Plaza Hemingway and the bullring to the east, and Plaza de los Burgos and the exuberantly baroque *Ayuntamiento,* or town hall, to the west, with the *Church of San Saturnino* adjacent. Other landmarks, including such churches as *San Nicolás, San Lorenzo* (with a chapel named for San Fermín, the patron saint in whose name the bulls are run annually), and *San Ignacio de Loyola,* are just south of Plaza Mayor in a central city that is eminently walkable.

Museo de Navarra (Plaza de Santa Ana) embraces a Renaissance church and hospital, with exhibits as well in the adjacent museum proper. There are remarkable remnants of the original Pamplona Cathedral, out of the Romanesque period. And mosaics of Roman Pamplona. But it is the work of later centuries that most evokes the Basque flavor of the city, especially paintings, mostly Renaissance, by artists of the old kingdom of Navarre, in an eye-filling suite of rooms duplicating a regal interior of that era.

Cathedral (Plaza de San José): The same Ventura Rodríguez who played a major role in the eighteenth-century reworking of the Basílica de Nuestra Señora del Pilar in Zaragoza (see the chapter on that city) was responsible for the present baroque façade of Pamplona Cathedral. It's deceptive, because the bulk of the rest of this giant is Gothic. And unexcitingly unadorned Gothic, at that. Go through the interior into the much more felicitous cloister, and from the cloister into the even handsomer *Capilla Barbazán*.

SETTLING IN
Hotel Tres Reyes is the traditional No. 1 house, interestingly placed at the edge of the park called *Jardines de la Taconera*, not far from Plaza Mayor. There are 170 attractive rooms and suites, top-category Enrique IV Restaurant, an inviting bar-lounge, and swimming pool. *Luxury.*

Hotel Maisonnave (Calle Nueva 20) is considerably more central than the Tres Reyes, albeit less elaborate. Still, there are 164 rooms with baths, and a restaurant. *First Class.*

Hotel Yoldi (Avenida de San Ignacio 11) is well-located, with half a hundred net rooms, many with private baths, and a dining room. *Moderate.*

DAILY BREAD
Josetxo (Plaza Príncipe de Vianal): Try the partridge with grapes or the champagne-sauced sole. *Luxury.*

Rodero (Arrieta 3) is a near-neighbor to Plaza de Toros, contemporary in look, and with an extraordinary kitchen. Order *merluza*—hake—prepared Navarre-style, with a bottle of crisp white wine. *Luxury.*

Hostal del Rey Noble (Paseo Sarasate 6) is heart-of-town, atmospheric, and—most important—with distinguished Basque cuisine, beginning with a noted vegetable soup and going on to lamb or crayfish. *First Class.*

Otano (Calle San Nicolás 5, up a flight) is convenient to Plaza Mayor, with tasty *menús del día. Moderate.*

INCIDENTAL INTELLIGENCE

Pamplona makes a worthwhile day's excursion from coastal San Sebastián, about 50 miles north. As in that city and other Basque towns, you'll encounter restaurant menus and other printed material in the Basque language, as well as Spanish. *Further information:* Oficina de Turismo de Pamplona, Calle Duque de Ahumada 3.

20

Salamanca
Spain's Sumptuous Sleeper

BACKGROUND BRIEFING

Madrid has the crown and the government, Barcelona the Mediterranean and commercial prowess, Seville the romance of its Andalusian setting, Granada the incomparable Alhambra, Toledo an immortality largely spurred by the canvasses of El Greco. Salamanca? It is Spain's best-kept secret—an utterly beautiful city with treasures of a remarkable past and a sense of style that belie its moderate size.

Even Salamanca's location—little more than 100 miles northwest of Madrid—appears not to work in its favor, touristically. It is just far enough away from the capital to be inconvenient as a one-day excursion destination, and, since it is not situated on the path to a major city to the north, it does not lend itself to service as a stopover point.

Its foreign inspectors are, as a consequence, relatively few in contrast to those flocking to the Big Five visitor-cities. But Spaniards come, drawn by the reputation of Salamanca's art and its architecture. Not to mention the university that made its name as one of the medieval centers of learning.

An early Roman colony, Salamanca fell to the Carthaginians' warrior-genius Hannibal a couple of hundred years before Christ. Later centuries saw it under the rule of Visigoths, who in turn lost out to Moorish conquerors from North Africa. The Moors were defeated by Leonese Christians in the late thirteenth century, almost 150 years before King Alfonso IX founded the University of Salamanca. His son, Alfonso X, aside from reuniting León with Castile, reorganized and strengthened the university, to the point where it came to be recognized throughout Europe, in a top-class with the Sorbonne, Oxford, and Italy's Bologna.

Powerful Renaissance families made Salamanca rich, and while on the one hand they created dissension as a consequence of internal feuds—Iberian counterparts of the Montagues and Capulets, or, to come closer to home, Hatfields and McCoys—their money attracted practitioners of the arts: architects to build sumptuous town houses, illustrators to paint portraits, sculptors and stonecutters to embellish public spaces.

ON SCENE

Lay of the Land: Start with the Tormes River. As did the Romans. They built a stone bridge—*Puente Romano*—over its waters that not only still stands, but still is in use. Walk over it to the south bank, to gain a bit of Salamanca perspective. The skyline is low-slung, but with verticals—towers of churches, mostly, and the splendid bulk of an unusual Salamanca treat: a pair of adjacent cathedrals.

Recross Puente Romano, traverse riverfront Paseo Rector Esperabe, and follow Calle Tentenecio to Plaza Episcopo. You have arrived at the cathedrals, to your right, with the ancient buildings of the university to your left. Rua Mayor—a principal thoroughfare—cuts between these two complexes, leading north past the fifteenth-century façade of shells of landmark *Casas de las Conchas* to a central square, Plaza Mayor, that has as its only peer the spectacular, similarly named square in Madrid. It was the work, largely, of the brothers Churriguera, for whom the peculiarly Spanish species of baroque architecture, Churrigueresque, is named. Like Madrid's, the square is enclosed on all four sides, with an arched opening on each side the means of access; the town hall—*Ayuntamiento*—and so-called Royal Pavilion are its grandest buildings. All about this heart-of-town area are mansion-lined streets, art-filled churches, convents that enclose superb cloisters. Walk about.

The Cathedrals (Plaza Episcopo) are, as I indicate earlier, two in number, one connected with the other. Both the so-called Old (*Vieja*) and New (*Nueva*) are entered through the latter, which is—to my taste—a case of the nicer of the pair coming second. The *Catedral Nueva* is soaring Gothic, of interest principally because of the strong and substantial scale of its façade. *Catedral Vieja* goes back some 800 years, is at once Romanesque (note its exquisitely detailed Gallow Tower and window arches) and Gothic (the high vaults of its nave). Proceed first to the high altar to marvel at half a hundred picture-panels. Then enter the cloister. End in the *Museo Diocesano*, a treasure trove of works by Salamanca masters like Juan de Flandes, Fernando Gallegos, and Pedro Bella.

Universidad de Salamanca (Plaza Anaya): Pause before you enter, at the façade of the principal university buildings. This intricately carved work is one of the best specimens in Spain of the distinctive Spanish Renaissance style, Plateresque, so called because it resembles the busily decorated silver pieces of that period. Then take in the library, filled with antique volumes; art-filled classrooms; chapel in which students for centuries have prayed for good grades; museum of fifteenth- and sixteenth-century paintings; and eye-filling Patio de las Escuelas.

Convento de la Clerecía (Plaza San Isidro) typifies Salamanca's exemplary ecclesiastical architecture, a baroque complex embracing the spectacular cloister of an originally Jesuit school, and an equally imposing church whose gilded high altar and complementary sculptures are stunners.

Convento de las Dueñas (Plaza Santo Domingo) ranks with Clerecía (above), thanks principally to its exceptional cloister—a two-level beauty out of the Renaissance. Resident nuns will let you have a look.

Convento de San Esteban (Plaza Santo Domingo) is an across-the-square neighbor of Las Dueñas that dazzles, at the outset, with the Plateresque façade of its church, and whose interior includes a high altar by José Churriguera and a painting by Claudio Coello, a ranking Spanish artist of the baroque period.

Colegio Fonseca (Plaza del Hospicio) is known also as *Los Irlandeses*, thanks to bands of Irish clerics who had populated it. Diego de Siloé, the sixteenth-century architect of other landmarks brought to your attention in other chapters of this book, was responsible for its patio and chapel.

Church of Las Agustinas (Calle Agustinas, opposite the monumental façade of landmark *Palacio Monterrey*) was an eighteenth-century project of the ducal—and neighboring—Monterrey family. What you want especially to observe are a painting of the Calvary by Italian master Bassano, and two paintings by Spanish great Ribera.

Museo de Bellas Artes (Calle Serranos) is eminently visitable: first, because its home—formally La Casa de los Doctores de la Reina—is a honey of a Gothic town house whose occupant had been *médico* to Queen Isabella in the course of her Salamanca visits; second, because it has been deftly transformed to house paintings of several epochs in a series of nine galleries that wrap themselves around a pretty patio. The ceiling of Gallery I is original Mudéjar. Note the period furniture, and paintings by mostly uncelebrated—albeit talented—artists, with works also by such known masters as Correggio, de Flandes, Luca Giordano, Guido Reni, and Hyacinthe Rigaud.

SETTLING IN
Gran Hotel (Plaza Poeta Iglesias 2) is just the ticket for an ideal Salamanca stay, centrally situated on the square adjacent to Plaza Mayor, with 100 traditional-style rooms and suites, bar-lounge, and the distinguished Restaurante Feudal, with *chuletones de ternera* (veal chops) and *pimientos rellenos* (stuffed peppers) among specialties. *Luxury.*

Hotel Monterrey (Calle Primo de Rivera 13), though not quite as central as the Gran (which shares the same owners), is not to be despised: some 90 agreeable rooms, restaurant-*cafetería*. *Luxury.*

Hotel Alfonso X (Calle de Toro 64) is next door to the Monterrey and, like the Gran, with the same landlord. There are 60-plus rooms with private bath. Guests are welcome in the restaurant of the Monterrey, adjacent. *First Class.*

Hotel Pasaje (Calle Espoz y Mina 23) is a near-neighbor to Plaza Mayor, with 70 rooms with bath. Restaurant. *Moderate.*

Hotel Condal (Plaza Santa Eulalia 2) is core-of-town with 70 neat rooms, most with baths. Breakfast only. *Moderate.*

Hotel Las Torres (Plaza Mayor 26) has the advantage of a smack-on-the-Plaza-Mayor location. This is a smallish house (a number of the 33 rooms have baths) with the bonus of a restaurant-café that's as ideal for a meal as for between-time coffee and a view of passersby. *Moderate.*

Parador Nacional de Salamanca (Teso de la Feria) is a welcome recent addition to the Salamanca hotel scene—one of the newest links of the nationwide chain of attractive—and attractively tabbed—inns. This is a modern 108-room house, with regional specialties served in its good-value restaurant, swimming pool, and an away-from-the-center location, the only reason why it is not at the head of my hotels group for this city. *First Class.*

DAILY BREAD
Candil Nuevo (Plaza de la Reina 2) is agreeable for a hearty lunch in the course of a day's exploration. Traditional-style decor, good-value *menú del día*. Order the lamb-and-sausage casserole specialty called *chanfaina*. *First Class.*

Venecia (Plaza del Mercado 5, upstairs) is another well-located spot; agreeable and tasty. *First Class.*

Altamira (Plaza Mayor 35) is a worth-knowing-about *cafetería* for casual meals. *Moderate.*

INCIDENTAL INTELLIGENCE

Oficina de Turismo de Salamanca, Calle de España 39.

21

San Sebastián

Faded Queen
of the North Coast

BACKGROUND BRIEFING

San Sebastián is Spain at its most bittersweet: sweet because of its extraordinary, peculiarly French-accented beauty, bitter because in recent years the terrorist tactics of a radical minority of Basques have succeeded with frightening effect in putting this elegant Bay of Biscay city out of the resort business. Or almost. The superb—and relatively recent—restoration of the beloved turn-of-the-century María Cristina Hotel by Italy-based Ciga Hotels has provided impetus for San Sebastián's comeback.

Some two million in number, with something like 100,000 across the frontier in France, Basques are believed to be the oldest surviving ethnic group on the continent of Europe, with a distinctive language[1], traditions, and culture, a facet of which is perfectly delicious food. No one will deny that proximity to France has had a positive effect on this gastronomic eminence, which manifests itself not only in superior restaurant food (Basques operate restaurants throughout Spain) but, on home ground, in cooking clubs, exclusively male, where the luckiest of visitors sample regional food at its most typical.

With a history no less ancient than that of much of the rest of

[1]In Basque, San Sebastián is Donostia, the Basque Country is Euskadi, and the Basque language—a co-official tongue in this region, along with Spanish—is Euskadia.

Spain, the Basques' principal resort city, San Sebastián, was mostly leveled in the complex early-nineteenth-century Peninsula War, when the British, under the 1st Duke of Wellington joined the Spaniards in an ultimately victorious anti-Napoleonic conflict. One may not, then, expect a rich store of antique architecture or art. Which is just as well, in the case of a resort town where the name of the game is relaxation and the enjoyment of the bounties of nature.

Set in a region of emerald-green mountains sweeping down to wide, white beaches, San Sebastián developed, as the nineteenth century evolved into the twentieth, into a small city of sufficient style to attract the Spanish court (and later, the Franco dictatorship), which made of it an unofficial capital during the warm-weather months.

ON SCENE

Lay of the Land: Four blessings of nature are San Sebastián standouts: a pair of peaks—Igueldo on the west, Urgull on the east—that constitute its backdrop; an extraordinarily lovely bay that is perfectly shell-shaped (Bahía la Concha by name), around which is wrapped a wide, white-sand beach; and a river—the Urumea—that intrudes through the very core of a compact downtown. The main street, Avenida de España, works its way west-east, from *Playa de la Concha*, to a bridge, *Puente de Santa Catalina*, that traverses the river, after which it becomes Calle Miracruz.

Walk a few blocks north of Avenida de España—in the direction of Monte Urgull—and you're in what remains of old San Sebastián: *La Parte Vieja*. It centers around Plaza del 18 de Julio and is dotted with good restaurants, not to mention old churches and the principal museum.

Walk south from Avenida de España along Calle Caribay and you reach the single spire of the *Cathedral*, on Calle San Martín. *Palacio de Miramar*, a rustic-look mock-Tudor mansion built in the late nineteenth century, served as the royal family's principal summer quarters through the 1930s and the reign of Alfonso XIII. It's at the west end of town, in a park overlooking Playa de la Concha. (Dictator Franco, during his San Sebastián summers, lived in another mini-palace dating from the turn of the century, *Ayete* by name.)

Take it all in from atop Monte Igueldo—ascendable via funicular—and then, between bouts of sun and surf on Playa de la Concha, concentrate on specifics.

Museo de San Telmo (Plaza de la Trinidad) is much more than San Sebastián's municipal museum. One goes as much for the setting—a Dominican convent founded under the patronage of a minister of Holy Roman Emperor Charles V—as for the exhibits. The convent is at its loveliest in its double-level cloister (the upper enclosed, the lower ringed by an open gallery) whose wall is hung with venerable carved-stone fragments. The Gothic-vaulted chapel is special, thanks in large part to frescoes portraying the history of the city and the surrounding province—tongue-twisting Guipúzcoa by name—by leading twentieth-century artist José María Sert. (Sert's sepia-toned frescoes are not unknown to Americans. They decorate the lobby of the office building at 30 Rockefeller Plaza, in New York's Rockefeller Center; and, until they were removed, another group was the principal decoration of the Waldorf-Astoria Hotel's subsequently renamed Sert Room restaurant.) Still other parts of the San Telmo complex display paintings (one is attributed to El Greco and a number are portraits of St. Sebastian) and sculpture.

Santa María and San Vicente churches are the old town's principal churches. Santa María (Calle Coro) welcomes with a resplendent baroque façade framed by a pair of small towers. San Vicente, a short walk away on Calle 31 de Agosto, is mellower—almost fortress-like Gothic.

The Cathedral (Calle de San Martín) is the newest in Spain—a late-nineteenth-century neo-Gothic work, of about the same period as New York's St. Patrick's and the Anglican Cathedral in England's Truro, but without the exquisite detailing of either of those structures. It is at its best from without: The central bell tower is graceful.

El Acuario (Paseo de José Antonio on Monte Urgull) is a worthy destination to learn of the marine life of the Bay of Biscay, the while listening to local small-fry exclaiming over the exhibits in their native Basque tongue.

Fuenterrabía on the coast, 14 miles east of San Sebastián, almost on the French frontier, is adjacent to the border town of Irún. Fuenterrabía, aside from being the site of the San Sebastián airport (see *Incidental Intelligence* below), holds its own as a fishing port with a substantial pedigree. The *Church of Santa María* is its showplace, originally Gothic, with additions appended in later centuries, mainly baroque. French tourists like to pay their respects, as why shouldn't they? Louis XIV was married within—if only by proxy, prior to a later ceremony—to a Spanish princess, all the way back in 1660.

SETTLING IN

Hotel María Cristina (Paseo República Argentina): I wrote, in an earlier edition of this book on the occasion of my first visit to the María Cristina some years back, that this *grande dame* had, rather sadly, deteriorated to the point where it was "only a shadow of what it must have been." I concluded thus: "Long may you reign, María Cristina!" My optimism was not unfounded. Ciga, the No. 1 Italian luxury chain (its hotels are of the caliber of Rome's Excelsior) took over a couple of years back, closed the hotel for a meticulous, multi-million-dollar, stem-to-stern renovation, and reopened to considerable acclaim in 1987. This is a historic house. It was opened in 1912 by the queen whose name it takes; she was the consort of Alfonso XII, regent after his death, mother of Alfonso XIII and great grandmother of the present king. María Cristina's son stayed in the hotel frequently after ascending the throne, as did many other royals. It is not difficult to see why, because the reopened hotel carefully employs the Beaux Arts motif of the original. The beautifully proportioned, high-ceilinged, chandeliered lobby has been returned to its original glory, as has the restaurant—once again the handsomest in town. The bar is at one and the same time elegant and relaxing. The 140 high-ceilinged, generous-size bedrooms and junior suites—no two of them quite alike—retain paneled walls, sumptuously draped windows (textiles throughout are a María Cristina highlight) and, wherever possible, original furnishings skillfully renewed. Bathrooms, though, have been completely replaced, with walls and floors of marble and broad counter sinks. Bravo, Ciga! *Luxury.*

Hotel de Londres y de Inglaterra (Calle Zubieta 2), though with no discernible link to either London or England despite its name, is a handsome house of some years that has modernized itself attractively. There are 175 rooms and suites of varying sizes and degrees of luxury, restaurant, café, bar, the town's casino (roulette, baccarat, and blackjack, but no slot machines), central situation overlooking Playa de la Concha. *Luxury.*

Hotel Orly (Plaza de Zaragoza 4) is a graceless, ugly, modern tower, well-situated and nicely staffed, with several score comfortable rooms with views, capacious lobby, *cafetería. First Class.*

Hotel Niza (Calle Zubieta 56) is no more reminiscent of Nice—for which it is named—than is the Hotel de Londres y de Inglaterra (above) of the United Kingdom. This is a small and cheerless but central house that has seen better days. Two score undersized rooms, many with baths, and those facing the sea with agreeable views. Breakfast only. *Moderate.*

Parador Nacional El Emperador (Plaza de Armas, in Fuenterrabía, 14 miles east of San Sebastián) occupies a castle as handsome as it is historic, in a fishing port that motorists might want to use as a headquarters for the area. Now a unit of the national chain of government-run inns, this stonewalled, tapestry-hung, fortress-like *castillo* (castle) was already half a millennium old when Holy Roman Emperor Charles V put it to rights—according to the taste of his time—in the sixteenth century. Just 16 no-two-alike rooms; striking dining and drinking parlors. *First Class.*

DAILY BREAD
Arzak (Calle Alto de Miracruz 21) is well worth the drive a few miles east of the center of town. This is a distinguished restaurant

and the ideal splurge spot for a grand Basque lunch or dinner. They have a way with seafood: *mero*, a form of sea bass, and *merluza*—hake—as well. *Luxury.*

Casa Nicolasa (Calle Aldamar 4) is up a flight from the street. Start with the crayfish and spinach appetizer—*cigalas con espinacas*—and if you're game for squid, next order *chipirones de anzuelo.* Good beef and lobster, too. Fine wines. *Luxury.*

Patxiku Kintana (Calle San Jerónimo 22) is an old-town house, traditional style, with specialties of *jamón* (the excellent local ham) and *cashuelitas* (the ubiquitous Basque casseroles) of varying combinations. *First Class.*

Juanito Kojua (Calle Puerto 14) is heart-of-the-old-town, with a cheerful ambience and straightforward fare, including fish soup and *lenguado*—the excellent local sole—*meunière.* Good-value *menú del día. Moderate.*

Dover (Avenida de España 21 and Calle Loyala 4) are *cafeterías*, central and ideal for casual meals. *Moderate.*

INCIDENTAL INTELLIGENCE

You may fly to San Sebastián, but there are caveats in this regard. The city's airport, as I indicate above, is at Fuenterrabía: 14 miles from town, and, please note, with what have to be the highest official airport–town taxi rates in Spain. The airline in this case is not Iberia but rather Aviaco. Should you want to fly Iberia, nearest airport is that of Bilbao, 60 miles west. To get from Bilbao Airport—surely the most congested in all Spain—to San Sebastián, you either rent a car, hire a cab (*very* pricey, this) or taxi into Bilbao, and hope that from its bus terminal you'll snag a seat on a bus to San Sebastián; travel time is less than an hour and a half. Going from San Sebastián to Bilbao Airport, you do well to reserve a bus seat in advance; departure is from the terminal on Calle Camino. Count on delays in departures from Bilbao Airport; bad weather is the usual reason given. San Sebastián has three railroad stations (Norte, Amara, and Tranvía). If you are departing the city by rail, ascertain from which one you will leave, in advance. Frontier point—if you are going to or coming from France—is Irún, with the French town of Bayonne (see *France at Its Best*) and the adjacent French resort of Biarritz not far distant. *Further information:* Oficina de Turismo de San Sebastián, Calle Reina Regente 13.

22

Santiago de Compostela
*La Coruña
and Pontevedra*

BACKGROUND BRIEFING

What happened was this: Thousands of devout medieval Europeans, over a period of half a millennium, tediously made their way over the high Pyrenees to an out-of-the-way city in Spain's verdant and often rain-soaked northwest corner. They went to pay their respects at the tomb of St. James—Santiago—the Apostle.

The reason for the pilgrimage site is at least as interesting as the phenomenon of the pilgrimages, which have not stopped to this day. As a consequence of a centuries-old papal decree, any year in which Santiago's feast day—July 25—falls on a Sunday becomes a Holy Year, so that this still-small city (some 75,000 population) has come to rank only after Rome and Jerusalem as a destination for Roman Catholic pilgrims, with foreign attendance at late twentieth-century Holy Years averaging two million.

Not that the pilgrimages' history is not a long one. It was all the way back in the ninth century when what was considered to be St. James's grave was found at this remote point. Beheaded in Palestine, his body was believed brought by sea to Galicia by a pious Asturian king—Alfonso II, or Alfonso the Chaste—who erected a church at the site. As the laity became attracted in increasing numbers to the saint's tomb, the town of Santiago de Compostela evolved, and with it, as the Dark Ages became the

Middle Ages, St. James became more widely venerated, to the point where a pilgrims' route—from France across the Pyrenees to Santiago—became well delineated by the Romanesque churches along the way, whose construction the shrine impelled, along with hostels and other layover facilities for the faithful.

(Two major cities on the route—Burgos and León—are accorded chapters in this book. The former is dotted with Romanesque churches, not to mention one of Europe's great cathedrals; in the latter, a monastery-turned-pilgrim's-hostel now serves as one of Spain's leading hotels. In still a third town, Astorga, suggested in another chapter as an excursion destination out of León, a bishop's palace has been turned into a museum of the lore of the Santiago-bound pilgrims.)

Travelers bound for Santiago were the world's first mass tourists. Their common goal—to pray at the tomb of a universally admired saint—transcended differences in nationality, language, culture. They might well be called the first internationalists. The city that was their destination has developed, as a result of their visits, into an extraordinary trove of riches—architectural, artistic, spiritual.

ON SCENE

Lay of the Land: This is a convenient, compact city. Once arrived, either by air or by rail (the train station is a taxi ride west of the historic center), there is little need for any transport other than shoe leather. And what a pleasure that can be—past the high and severe façades of enormous convents dating to the centuries of the earlier pilgrims, alongside legends carved in stone over the arched doorways of Romanesque churches, beneath granite-etched coats of arms framing entrances to town palaces of the gentry.

The skyline has remained close to the ground in deference to the *Cathedral*, remarkable in that it gives on to not one or even two plazas but a solid quartet of squares. The lot—beginning with the double-named Plaza del Obradoiro/Plaza de España at the front entrance, and the Plaza de la Inmaculada, Plaza de la Quintana, and Plaza de las Platerías at only somewhat lesser entrances—constitute the core of town. The first-mentioned, Plaza del Obradoiro, melds an all-star mix of architectural styles.

Besides the Cathedral façade in baroque, it includes—going clockwise—the Renaissance-front *Colegio Fonseca*, the Romanesque *Colegio de San Jerónimo*, the eighteenth-century neoclassic *Palacio de Rajoy* (which houses the *Ayuntamiento*, or town hall), and last, but hardly least, *Hotel de los Reyes Católicos*, built as a hospital for pilgrims by Ferdinand and Isabella (below).

Other landmarks are within easy reach of Plaza del Obradoiro. Go east, via Calle Fonseca, to shop-, café-, and mansion-lined streets like the Rua del Villar and Rua Nueva (proximity to Portugal manifests itself in the occasional use of the Portuguese word *rua* for street) and to the university in nearby Plaza Universidad. See the convent complexes like *San Francisco* (a short walk north of Plaza del Obradoiro), *San Martín Pinario*, even closer, and *San Pelayo*, directly east. Note, too, that Rua Nueva and Rua Vilar lead into the city's modern sector, with a number of hotels and restaurants, and shops based on its principal street, Calle Dr. Teijiro. *Simago*, the leading department store, is on Calle Montero Ríos.

The Cathedral (Plaza del Obradoiro) is worthy of more attention than any others in Spain save those of Toledo, Seville, and Burgos. You'll want to go back for a return visit or two: the wealth of detail is difficult to absorb on a single viewing. The site is that of the original tomb of St. James the Apostle, over which an earlier church went up some eleven centuries ago. The present Cathedral is special in that it is eleventh through thirteenth century Romanesque within—one of the greatest of all such style churches—*but* with a baroque shell appended in the eighteenth century.

To appreciate the exterior, walk about the entrances not only on Plaza del Obradoiro—with its elegant tracery and tall twin towers—but those giving on to Plazas de las Platerías, de la Quintana, and de la Inmaculada. Return, then, to the main entrance, halting in its vestibule. What one encounters at this point is the original Romanesque façade of the Cathedral. A wizard of a medieval sculptor—known simply as Maestro Mateo—single-handledly, carved into the arches surmounting the triple-door entranceway (accurately termed Pórtico de la Gloria) more than 100 groups of biblical figures, flanking Jesus and the Apostles—

including, of course, St. James—over the center arch. In short, one of Europe's superlative Romanesque art treasures.

Within, the high altar at the far end of a severe Romanesque nave is brilliantly baroque, centered about a statue of St. James. And just before it—at the wide and splendidly scaled transept—there occurs at least once daily (check on schedules, so as not to miss this show) a ritual that dates from pilgrim times, when the galleries of the Cathedral doubled as dorms and the air was foul. A giant incense-burner, attached to an ingenious pulley hanging from the ceiling, is ignited and swung by a traditionally costumed functionary—the Cathedral's scarlet-robed *buta-fumeiro*—the entire length of the transept, going higher and higher with each swing before it is lowered to the floor minutes later. It's quite a performance.

The tomb of Santiago, with relics of the saint, is in the crypt, adjacent to foundations of the original church on the site and beneath the high altar. The cloister—Gothic-vaulted—is one of the largest in a country dotted with cloisters. Then there are the Cathedral's museums. One is devoted to a collection of tapestries stitched to designs by Goya. Another, the treasury, is rich with metalwork: objects of gold and silver, jewel-embellished. In the library repose illuminated manuscripts. And the *Archeological Museum* displays bits and pieces of the Cathedral's architectural detail—sculpture, columns, and capitals among them. Adjacent to the Cathedral, with its own entrance, is *Palacio Gelmírez*, a remarkable example of civil Romanesque architecture.

Monasterio de San Pelayo de Anteltares (Vía Sacra) stuns, at first, with the broad expanse of its Plaza de la Quintana façade—broken only by the windows of cells on two upper levels. Within, silent Benedictine nuns show one through the *Museo de Arte Sacro*, resplendent with paintings and sculpture, crosses and reliquaries, documents and vestments. Lovely.

Monasterio de Santo Domingo (Plaza de Santo Domingo) scores on three counts. First is that it was established all the way back in the thirteenth century by St. Dominic as a result of his two recorded visits to Santiago de Compostela. Second is its baroque façade. And third is the interior, comprising a fine Roman-esque church, the *Museo del Pueblo Gallego* (with exhibits relat-ing to regional lore and history), the *Panteón Gallegos Ilustres* (honoring historic Galician figures) and *Escuela Taller* (pottery and crafts).

Monasterio de San Francisco (Plaza de San Francisco) is almost a city within a city, not surprisingly, since it was created after the visit to Santiago by St. Francis of Assisi somewhere around the year 1213. Little remains of the Gothic original, although the hall where Holy Roman Emperor Charles V received his court re-mains. The chapel is baroque, with a splendid high altar.

Monasterio de San Martín Pinario (Plaza de la Inmaculada) wraps itself around a trio of dazzling cloisters. This is a baroque beauty, with the high altar of its church in and of itself reason for a visit. Amble about.

Universidad de Santiago (Plaza Universidad): The university's eighteenth-century headquarters building warrants perusal. Go beyond its neoclassic façade to three destinations within. Ask in the library if you may see a few of the early books on Spanish America, and some medieval manuscripts. Second, take a peek at the nineteenth-century murals of the assembly hall. Then pop into the old *Church of La Compañia* adjacent.

Colegio Fonseca (Plaza Fonseca) beckons with a Plateresque façade—enough to draw one in, not to observe druggists in the making (this is the city's pharmacy college), but rather to see a two-level Renaissance patio from which the towers of the Cathe-dral form a memorable backdrop.

Hotel de los Reyes Católicos (Plaza del Obradoiro) was, as I in-dicate earlier, constructed as a hospital for pilgrims by Ferdinand and Isabella in the fifteenth century. It serves today as a hotel—about which more later—in which I very much hope you will headquarter. Should you not, I urge that you step beyond the in-tricately carved Plateresque façade, if only to have a look at the Gothic chapel (now used for art exhibitions and the like) and a quartet of no-two-alike patios. Santiago's sick convalesced in style.

Colegiata de Santa María del Sar is a 10- or 15-minute hope from the center of town. But you want to go. Certainly the core of the city is not without churches—mostly Romanesque ones like *Santa María Salomé* and *San Benito*. But Santa María del Sar is special. You go, in part, for the quiet cloister. But you go even more for the church interior. Buttresses appended to the outer walls centuries after the church was built have resulted in an interior that looks as it might upon inspection the morning after a heavy night in the pubs! Columns, vaults, and arches slant, veer, and topple. This is Spain's answer to the Leaning Tower of Pisa.

La Coruña: Look north on your map of Spain (not far north— the drive is under an hour) and your eye settles on La Coruña, an oddly under-appreciated, albeit significant, port settled by Celts, Phoenicians, Greeks and Romans (these last left a still-operating lighthouse, the only such extant in Europe) that is today a lively, lilting and lovely city deserving of better acquaintance and easily explored in the course of a day's outing (or better yet, an overnight excursion) from Santiago. And if it's summer take a swimsuit; no Spanish city of any size (population is about a quarter-million) has such a wealth of fine in-town beaches.

La Coruña's core is a stretch of territory flanked by one bay— *Ensenada del Orzán*—to the north (with its best-known beaches, *Riazor* and adjacent *Orzán*) and *Puerta de La Coruña* to the south (site of leading hotels, with more beaches and a plethora of pools). In between, facing the port, is the trademark thoroughfare—the windowed balconies of its houses are the city's most photographed aspect—called *Avenida de la Marina*, where, ideally, you position yourself at an outdoor table of a café (*Los Porches* is a nice one) for a bit of sustenance upon arrival, the while you get your bearings.

Start with Roman La Coruña: *Torre de Hércules*, on the northern tip of the peninsula delineating the city, as indeed it has been since the second century when it went up during the reign of Emperor Trajan. Despite restoration of outer walls a couple of hundred years back, it remains essentially as the Romans designed it, some 312 feet high, ascendable (by means of 242 steps) after a couple of millenia, still in operation.

Work your way south, then, to the originally sixteenth-century *Castello de San Antón*, hugging the shore, formidably walled and now seeing service as the city's *Museo Histórico-Arqueológico*, chockablock with ancient artifacts dating to Roman times, and with relatively recent Galician exhibits, an intact country kitchen and superb pottery collection, most especially. *Museo de Bellas Artes*, occupies a fine mansion on Plaza Pintor Sotomayor. You're not surprised to find paintings by Galician artists; treats are works by such Spanish greats as Velázquez, Murillo, and Goya, and such foreign masters as Veronese, Brueghel, Rubens and Tintoretto.

Take time out for lunch, concentrating in this harbor city on seafood, at one of a number of spots on Calle Estrella's Restaurant Row—*Coral*, perhaps, or such competitors as *El Rapido* or *Duna*. Afterwards, head to La Coruña's *Ciudad Vieja*, the old quarter in the west end, that remains an enchanting mix of serene squares, aged churches, and convents behind formidable walls. You want especially to take in cobbled *Plazuela de Santa Bárbara*, and the Romanesque chapel of its cloistered convent whose nuns pray from behind heavy grilles on a high balcony; the tiny, originally twelfth-century *Church of Santa María del Mar*, on the plaza taking its name and centered by a stone cross; and the contrastingly large *Church of Santo Domingo* (Plaza de Santo Domingo), severely Baroque, with the exception of the lavish altar in its side chapel.

Save time for a bit of shopping, in this wealthy city. *Calle Juan Flores* is lined with boutiques in which are sold trendy fashions—*El Pote* and *Zara* are but two. And bear in mind that the massive modern outlet of *El Corte Inglés*, the kingdom-wide department-store chain, is the only such in Galicia; its pizzeria and *cafetería* are on seven; porcelain, pottery and crystal are a floor below, while women's clothes are on one, men's duds are on two, children's wear is on three, and there's a *supermercado* in the basement.

That leaves beaches, ideally saved for a second La Coruña day. Overnight at *Hotel Riazor* (Calle Anden de Riazor, at Riazor Beach), with a *cafetería* and *Moderate*; *Hotel Atlantic* (Jardines de

Méndez Nuñez, with 200 full-facility rooms, the town's casino, near beaches and *First Class;* or—my preference hands down— *Hotel Finesterre* (Paseo del Parrote 20), a handsome 127-room house with restaurant and bar-lounge, overlooking a vast beach in which are embedded a quartet of swimming pools, with a pair of tennis courts, gym-sauna for good measure, and the category *First Class.*

Pontevedra and Galicia's coastal *rías:* Pontevedra—a delightful town amidst the region's Norway-like fjords, or *rías,* on the Atlantic coast, south of Santiago—hugs the inner fringe of its own fingerlike fjord, or *ría.* It is ancient, smallish (with a population of some 50,000), and, thanks to a location even more obscure than Santiago's, relatively little changed over the centuries. Head for heart-of-town Plaza de la Leña and the trio of eighteenth-century houses that embrace three-quarters of the *Museo de Pontevedra* complex. There are galleries of paintings, including Ribera, Murillo, Valdés Leal, and Zurbarán; altarpieces by such masters as Pedro de Berruguete and Juan de Borgoña, with foreigners—Brueghel and Teniers, Tiepolo and Giordano —represented too. Bonuses include furnished rooms representing various periods of recent centuries, and collections relating to the maritime history of this coastal town. It is an agreeable walk through Pontevedra's pretty *Zona Monumental* to the *Church of Santa María la Mayor.* You'll know when you've reached it: the Plateresque façade is among the more spectacular in Spain. You're in luck for lunch: *Parador Nacional Casa del Barón* (Calle Maceda), a link of the nationwide chain of inns, occupies an ancient stone mansion in a garden of no little charm.

Or lunch later, on the way to Santiago, at still another atmospheric *parador*—*Parador Nacional del Albariño*—in the sleepy coastal town of *Cambados,* whose venerable Plaza de Fefinañes and its *San Benito Church* are requisite inspectables in the course of the day's outing. En route back to Santiago, pause at *Padrón,* where the body of St. James was brought ashore, legend says, en route to Santiago. See the memorial, or *padrón,* on which the boat said to have carried the body was believed moored, at the village church. And consider an overnight stay at the nearby island of *La Toja*, site of the beautiful *Gran Hotel* (*Luxury*) and the smaller *Hotel Louxo* (*First Class*).

SETTLING IN

Hotel de los Reyes Católicos (Plaza del Obradoiro): At the risk of seeming a paid publicist for this remarkable remnant of the fifteenth century (see *On Scene*, above), let me repeat that it was built by Ferdinand and Isabella as a hospital for pilgrims. Its Plateresque façade was appended a century later, its Gothic chapel is now used as an exhibition/banquet hall (open for view when not in use), and its dramatically vaulted public space—lovely lobby, comfortable bar-lounge, breakfast room in which the day's first meal is served from a massive (and delicious) buffet, subterranean restaurant (evaluated on a later page)—surrounds no less than a quartet of architecturally masterful, no-two-alike patios (named San Marco, San Lucas, San Mateo and San Juan, after the Evangelists). There are 160 rooms of varying sizes, some quite small and plain, some with canopied beds, the priciest on the top floor leading from antiques-accented corridor-lounges, and all with good white-tile baths. Only a few accommodations—immense and splendid suites—face the square, as does a clutch of connected rooms used for parties and conventions. (They're worth inspecting, if you have the opportunity.) Alas, the unique qualities of this hotel are not a secret, as they were some years back when writers like myself began to sing its praises in print. The occupancy rate, contemporarily, is high, and a consequence is that staff smiles are severely rationed. Chilly ambience notwithstanding, headquartering here remains an opportunity hardly to be despised. Your host is Paradores de España. *Luxury*.

Hotel Araguaney (Calle Alfredo Brañas 5), with its friendly staff and commendable restaurants (see Daily Bread, below), is as good a reason as any to make one's acquaintance with the newer part of the city. With just under 60 traditional-style rooms (the doubles can be big and the baths are superb), pair of restaurants, capacious lobby, cocktail lounge-cum-entertainment, outdoor swimming pool, and subterranean disco, this is a hotel to be reckoned with. Very nice, indeed. *Luxury*.

Hotel Compostela (Calle Horreo 1) emulates the medieval architecture of the Old Town with its façade, but is, within, a relatively modern house, with close to 100 full-facility rooms, and agreeable public spaces that include a *cafetería* and bar. An easy walk to the historic core. *First Class.*

Hotel Gelmirez (Calle Horreo 92)—severely clean-lined—is good-sized (with just under 140 functional rooms with bath, *cafetería*, bar and a location close to the old town. *Moderate.*

Hotel Universal (Plaza Galicia 2) has half a hundred adequate rooms with bath and the virtue of being central. Breakfast only. *Moderate.*

Hotel Peregrino (Avenida Rosalía de Castro): Okay, if you have a car; otherwise, inconvenient. The Peregrino is a good distance from the center. Modern, with 150 rooms with bath, restaurant, bar, outdoor pool that's a plus in summer. *First Class.*

Hotel Los Tilos (Carretera de la Estrada) is, like the Peregrino (above), out of town. It is, however, modern and comfortable, with 84 not overlarge rooms with bath, restaurant, and bar. *First Class.*

Hotel Congreso (Carretera de la Estrada)—a neighbor of Los Tilos, above—is likewise suburban. There are 72 rooms (the doubles I have inspected are small but otherwise okay), restaurant, bar and a nightly folklore show. Groups are a specialty. *Moderate.*

DAILY BREAD
Hotel Reyes Católicos Restaurante (Plaza del Obradoiro): Santiago abounds in good—and for that matter, good-value—restaurants. (Indeed, I know of no town so heavily tourist-populated with so many really reasonably-priced places to eat.) Still, there is no denying that the dramatically barrel-vaulted, stone-walled subterranean space in the Reyes Católicos is the handsomest restaurant in the city. And with a satisfactory à la carte that runs to *entremeses variados* (assorted appetizers, mostly from the sea and including an excellent seafood salad),

hearty soups, and tasty entrées, including a scallop preparation wherein the mollusks are served, appropriately enough, in a scallop shell—the symbol of St. James in this, his city—and combined with Serrano ham. Order Albaraino, the favored Galician white wine, to accompany. And if you've a sweet tooth, this is a good place to indulge it. But expect neither smiles nor small talk from the serving staff. *Luxury.*

Araguaney Hotel Restaurante (Calle Alfredo Brañas 5), illuminated by crystal chandeliers, emulates the style of Louis XVI, with brocaded rose silk inserted in wall panels and upholstering chairs at its tables. Daily specials are a good bet—oysters on the half-shell or vichysoisse to start, sole *meunière* or the Spanish steak masterwork, *solomillo* as entrées, perhaps house-made lemon sherbet to conclude. (Bear in mind, too, that the Araguaney's rustic *Taverna* has a temptingly-tabbed three-course menu that might run to fish soup, veal steak and house wine.) Both have friendly staffs. The restaurant is *Luxury;* the *Taverna, Moderate.*

Alameda (Avenida de Figueroa 15): Take a table by the window of this long-on-scene, up-a-flight restaurant, ordering either the daily menu (opening perhaps with *caldo gallego,* the nourishing standby soup of the region; with grilled fish, veal filet, or an *empanada,* a meat-filled turnover, as an entrée; concluding with *flan* or fruit). Or select from the extensive à la carte, with an extraordinary range of fish and seafood appetizers and entrées—oysters, fresh sardines, octopus, shrimp and trout among them. Good wines, too. *First Class.*

Vilas (Calle Rosalía de Castro 88) and *Anexo Vilas* (nearby at Avenida de Villagarcía 21) share a management reputed for its expertise at seafood. Both are in the newer part of the city. Galician-style hake—served in an earthenware casserole with potatoes, peas, sweet peppers, onions and garlic—is a specialty, but you may have the day's catch simply grilled. *Tarta de Santiago,* almond-filled, is indicated for dessert. *First Class.*

La Cigala d'Oro (Calle del Franco 10) is, in my experience, the best of the myriad restaurants lining Calle del Franco, Rua del Vilar, and other streets in the core of the old town. It is also the most attractive, with leather-back chairs surrounding tables set in white linen in a room illuminated by wrought-iron chandeliers, and with a terrace for warm-weather service. The prix-fixe menu is well-priced (although not as cheap as those of simpler neighborhood eateries), but you do well to order à la carte so that your entrée will be *cocido gallego*, the utterly delicious seafood stew of the region. Lovely service. *First Class.*

Carbelleira (Rua del Villar 41): I am often leary of restaurants next-door to city tourist offices for the obvious reason: they become too touristy. Not so, Carbelleira. Its prix-fixe is offered at a rock-bottom tab, and might run to *cocido gallego* or a seafood appetizer to open, grilled hake or roast veal, fresh fruit and a glass of the local Ribeiro white wine, with good coarse bread accompanying, crisp white paper tablecloths and napkins, and spirited service. *Moderate.*

Monroy (Plazuela de Fonseca) is another of the many good-value budget eateries in the old town, with a menu that includes the day's soup, roast or fish, fresh fruit, bread and wine. Paper tablecloths, of course, but service is cordial. *Moderate.*

Los Caracoles (Calle Raiña 14), another of the bargain beaneries, offers as part of its three-course menu a *paella marinara* with more *mariscos* (actually, tiny clams in shells the size of your thumb) than rice, to the point where it could actually do with more of the latter. Withal it's tasty, and the Gonzalez family-members who serve you are gracious. Fun. *Moderate.*

Mesón a Charca (Calle del Franco 32) is core-of-town, reasonable and reasonably attractive, albeit the least cordial of the Santiago restaurants in which I've lunched or dined. Withal, an à la carte meal embracing soup or an omelet, grilled chicken or a chop, with Paternina wine accompanying, proves satisfactory. *Moderate.*

Zürich (Rue del Vilar 45), surely the only café in Spain named for a Swiss city, is called to your attention because its outdoor tables are inviting, if you would pause for coffee or a cold drink, in the course of old town exploration. *Moderate.*

INCIDENTAL INTELLIGENCE

Santiago is linked directly with New York via Iberia, which makes summer flights. It is also, of course, on Iberia's domestic route, so that you may fly up from Madrid or Barcelona; the airport is seven scenic miles from the center. Do not under any circumstances arrive without umbrella and raincoat. *Further information:* Oficina de Turismo de Santiago de Compostela, Rua del Villar 43; Oficina de Turismo de La Coruña, Dársena de la Marina; Oficina de Turismo de Pontevedra, Calle de General Mola 3.

23

Segovia
The Romanticist's Castile

BACKGROUND BRIEFING
Segovia, atop a rocky eminence over a valley delineated by a pair of rivers, is the very essence of Old Castile. Consider this setting: A skyline pierced by the needle-like towers of a fortified palace, contrasting with a chunky cathedral belfry and the steeples of a cluster of Romanesque masterworks, while lower down, the arches of a still-working aqueduct dating to Roman times create a lacy silhouette against a backdrop of snowy peaks.

The Romans settled in first. The city they built on the plateau above the confluence of the Clamores and Eresma rivers thrived until the Visigoths' occupation in the fifth century. Later, Moors, during their on-again, off-again periods of control between the eighth and eleventh centuries, achieved prosperity.

The aggressive warrior-king Alfonso VI conquered Islamic Segovia in 1079, and ere long it became a favorite royal residence. It was at Segovia, in the original Alcázar (still standing albeit much restored), that Isabella I was proclaimed queen of what was to become, after her marriage to Ferdinand of Aragón, a united Spain. The following century—the sixteenth—saw Segovia a focal point in the wars of the *Comunidades*: uprising by Spanish gentry antagonized by the increasing power and pan-Spanish designs of Holy Roman Emperor Charles V.

The Renaissance was not a great Segovia period. But with the Bourbon dynasty of the eighteenth century, a rococo Segovia flourished as a result of the Bourbon kings' country palaces—still-visitable La Granja and Riofrío—constructed as emulations of Versailles by Philip V and Charles III.

ON SCENE

Lay of the Land: The pinnacles of the *Alcázar* form the western-most landmark of substance, while the double-tiered Roman aqueduct marks Segovia's eastern flank, in the neighborhood of the railway station. The old town—*Ciudad Vieja*—centers around Plaza Mayor, set off by the massive Cathedral. Plaza San Esteban, due west, is dominated by the steeple of the *Church of San Esteban*, which gives on to Calle Victoria, becoming Calle Doctor Loguna just before it leads to the old palace now seeing service as the *Museo Provincial de Bellas Artes*. Plaza San Martín, just east of the center, is a core of walking territory, centered by the church whose name it takes and surrounded by equally venerable town houses.

Alcázar (Plaza del Alcázar): Its romantic silhouette is the Alcázar at its best, even though, much restored, it's more artifice than reality. Still, one wants to pay one's respects at the palace where Isabella I was named queen of Castile in 1474 and where Philip II married his fourth and last wife, Anne of Austria, almost a century later. State chambers include throne room, king's bedroom, and chapel—all stage-setty—and a small artillery museum.

Cathedral: Last Gothic cathedral built in Spain, this is an extraordinarily powerful structure. Without, one most admires its massive, box-like tower and the felicitous wedding-cake tiers of its apse. Within, principal lures are a well-scaled and vaulted central nave and a beautifully detailed cloister. Add to these half a dozen chapels brimming with treasures and a museum of painted altars, with Renaissance tapestries reposing in the chapterhouse.

A trio of Romanesque churches: All central, these constitute a remarkable group, the lot from the early Middle Ages. *San Millán* (Calle Fernández Ladreda) is a nine-century-old beauty: compact, with a trio of naves, a quartet of apses, and a pair of lovely porches. Note the carved capitals supporting its windows. *San Esteban* (Plaza San Esteban) impresses with the vigor of its multilevel tower, the arches of its porch, and a thirteenth-century crucifix within. *San Martín's* (Plaza San Martín) masterfully carved doors want attention, as one enters, and so do the treasures— sculpture especially—within the chapel-dotted interior.

Museo Provincial de Bellas Artes (Calle de San Agustín) is a sixteenth-century mansion, a perfect foil for a charming collection of art objects, largely from no-longer-operating Segovia churches, and including paintings, drawings, and sculpture, with occasional surprises for the careful viewer, such as engravings by both Rembrandt and Dürer.

Acueducto Romano (Plaza Acueducto) is the double-level marvel of the Roman colonists that is unsurpassed by any other Roman remnant in Spain: approximately 2,700 feet long, 92 feet high, and as graceful as it is—to this very day—functional.

Museo Zuloaga (Plaza Comenares) occupies the desanctified Romanesque *Church of San Juan de los Caballeros*—triple-apsed and intricately designed. It was taken over by painter Daniel Zuloaga at the turn of the present century for use as a studio, and to display his work and that of other artists.

A trio of out-of-town monasteries: *San Antonio del Real,* just south of town, is fifteenth century, at its most extraordinary in the chapel, whose Mudéjar ceiling is intricately paneled in the geometric style of the Moors. The sisters show you other beautiful ceilings in their refectory. *El Portal,* on the north side of town, is a Gothic-Renaissance meld with its church's high altar—a towering giant of a six-level triptych. *Carmelitas Descalzas,* also south of town, was a joint undertaking of the remarkable team of sixteenth-century saints, Teresa of Ávila and John of the Cross. St. John of the Cross was a prior of the convent, and both his tombs are there: a simple one made immediately after his death, and an elaborate one on the high altar, to mark his sainthood.

The Bourbon country palaces: The first of the French-origin Bourbon dynasty, Philip V built *La Granja* (at Ildefonso, seven miles south of town) with grandpapa Louis XIV's Versailles at the back of his mind. It is not, of course, anything like a copy. But it is very grand, embodying the peculiarly Spanish branch of rococo that never—in any of the royal palaces of Spain—achieves the brilliance of French or even Italian rococo, even when nationals of those two lands have been involved in the design. The fountain-filled and sculpture-embellished gardens of La Granja are superb, and there are some smart salons within, most notably the king's capacious office, a properly opulent—but not coarse—throne room in gold and scarlet, and the *salón de los espejos*, gallery of mirrors, nothing like that of Versailles but exemplary in its own right. There are two bonuses. One is a museum of tapestries, mostly Flemish out of the sixteenth century, and high-caliber. The other—far more spectacular—is the group of 26 fountains in the gardens—attached to sculptures, in ponds, adjacent to cascades, as geyser-like *jets d'eau*—which are turned on several afternoons each week, traditionally Thursday, Saturday, and Sunday at 2 P.M., late spring through early autumn. Time your visit, if you can, for the show. Riofrío, second of the Bourbon palace pair, is smaller than La Granja. It's the work of Philip V's widow, Queen Isabella Farnese. I like the elegant pink façade, and the well-restored rooms within: reception salons, dining room, royal bedrooms. This palace was used well into the 1920s reign of Alfonso XIII. It has two special features: a vast gallery of eighteenth-century paintings depicting scenes from the life of Christ, and what the French would call a *musée de la chasse*, with hunters and hunted birds and animals its theme.

SETTLING IN
Hotel Los Linajes (Calle Dr. Velasco 9) is nicely located on the fringe of the Ciudad Vieja, in traditional style and with 55 rooms with baths. Breakfast only. *First Class.*

Hotel Los Arcos (Paseo Ezequiel Gonzáles 24) opened in 1987 and is, to understate, full-facility, with close to 60 attractive rooms, atmospheric *La Cocina de Segovia* Restaurant, bar-lounge, and a state-of-the-art conference center than can accommodate

as many as 500 persons. With a giant disco—its name is Yuppy—
that packs in 500 dancers. Affiliated with Best Western.
Luxury.

Hotel Acueducto (Avenida del Padre Claret 10) is within view of
the monument whose name it takes, fairly convenient to the center. There are close to 80 adequate rooms with private facilities.
Restaurant. *Moderate.*

Parador Nacional de Segovia (Carretera 601, about two miles
from town) is a modern link in the nationwide chain of
government-run inns. There are 80 agreeable rooms with baths,
lounge-cum-bar, indoor-outdoor pools, and reliable restaurant.
Ideal if you have a car. *First Class.*

DAILY BREAD
Mesón de Cándido (Plaza Asoguejo 7): If you go for lunch, consider the afternoon dissipated. A meal takes time here. Better, if
sightseeing time is limited, to go in the evening. The fare is
sumptuous, the traditional ambience inviting, the hospitality
gracious. Specialty is *cochinillo asado*, the roast suckling pig that
Segovianos consider their major gastronomic accomplishment.
Open with the also-special Castilian soup. *Luxury.*

Duque (Calle Cervantes 12) is an atmospheric, typically Segovian restaurant, with delicious dishes, such as roast lamb and
tender veal, prepared in a number of ways. *First Class.*

La Taurina (Plaza Mayor 8) is heart-of-town, and appropriate
for lunch in the course of a day's exploration. Decor is traditional
and so is the cooking. *Moderate.*

Oficina (Calle Cronista Lecea 10) is conveniently close to Plaza
Mayor, with a Segovian look and a Segovian menu. *Moderate.*

INCIDENTAL INTELLIGENCE ══════════

Too many of Segovia's visitors are day-trippers out of Madrid, some 50 miles south. Try to do better by this city; stay a couple of days. *Further information:* Oficina de Turismo de Segovia, Plaza Mayor 8.

24

Seville

Carmen's Town Is a Winner

BACKGROUND BRIEFING

Take an informal poll of your friends, as I have in this connection, and the city that evokes Spain at its most positive—castanets to cathedrals, guitars to gazpacho—will be Seville. (With Madrid tying, Toledo and Granada not far behind.) And let me say at the outset of this chapter: Polled friends, I'm with you all the way.

No single city on the peninsula is an easier, more enjoyable, more immediately perceivable lesson in Spain—its history as well as its romance. With souvenirs of all the major epochs of its past still on scene, the better to bring the remarkable Seville story into sharp focus.

Take a mild climate. Combine it with southern location. Add a river (the Guadalquivir) that is able to accommodate even modern ocean-going vessels and flows into the Atlantic. And it's not difficult to perceive why there have been Sevillians of many origins over many centuries. The earliest Seville styled itself Hispalis, and was not unknown to seafaring Phoenicians, who settled in, to be followed by Greeks from the Aegean, Carthaginians from the southern shore of the Mediterranean, and, just three centuries before Christ, the Romans.

Their colony—substantial and sophisticated like so much of Roman Spain—still is to be seen, albeit in ruined state, at nearby Itálica. (Not one but a pair of emperors were Itálica-born: the famous Hadrian and the almost-as-celebrated Trajan.)

In the usual peninsular order of things, there came, later, the unwelcome Vandals, who were displaced by Germanic Christian Visigoths; their labors to reestablish the cultural eminence of Roman times were successful. Moors, following in the year 712, were hardly less diligent. They came on in full force, not only politically and militarily, but as architects and builders, artists and merchants, mathematicians and astronomers.

In the eleventh century, when the long-powerful caliphate of nearby Córdoba fell, Seville came into its own as an independent monarchy under emirs of a trio of alliteratively-easy-to-recall dynasties: Abbadids, Almoravids, Almohads. All this while, Christian kings of outlying realms coveted Moslem Spain. In 1248, Castile's Ferdinand III—who had already united the kingdoms of Castile and León, and conquered Córdoba—seized the key city of Seville. By so doing he virtually completed the Christian reconquest of Spain; only Granada remained Moslem, and even it became a vassal state of the Christians. (The church was not unmindful of Ferdinand's victories in its name. Some four centuries after he died, he was canonized.)

St. Ferdinand was the first but by no means the last of the Christian kings to live in Seville. Its Alcázar, the fortress-palace of the Moslem sovereigns, was built upon, added to, refurbished in part to suit the needs of the Moors' successors, and in the Moorish—or Mudéjar—style. The city's great mosque was razed for its even greater Cathedral, but only partially. Its patio and tower—La Giralda, still Seville's trademark-landmark—remain as a part of the Cathedral complex.

Seville's Golden Age approached. As a royal seat, its commercial and cultural eminence peaked. Or seemed to. But the end was not in sight. New World settlement saw Seville become principal port in the rich commerce with Spanish America. (It remained so until the early eighteenth century, when Cádiz—directly on the Atlantic—succeeded it.) One has only to visit the Cuarto del Almirante, or Admiral's Room, of the Alcázar, to appreciate Seville's connection with the Americas; it was there that Queen Isabella welcomed Columbus home from his second voyage, and where numerous other historic journeys, including those by Balboa and Magellan, were planned and documented.

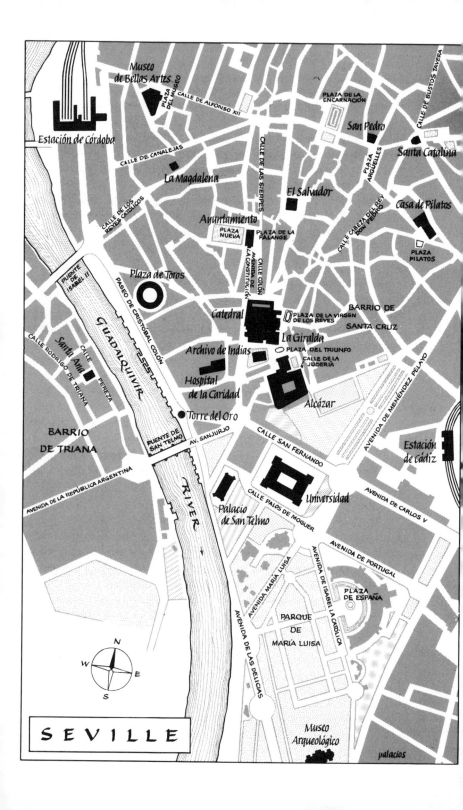

Wealth has a way of attracting and encouraging artists. Spain's greatest painter, Velázquez, was Seville-born (although he made his reputation in Madrid as Philip IV's court painter); Zurbarán, though born in Extremadura (see the chapter on that region), studied and thrived in Seville; Valdés Leal, though lesser known beyond Spain, is hardly to be underestimated in the Seville painting school. And matchless Murillo was born—and worked prodigiously—in the city.

Now Spain's fourth largest urban center (only Madrid, Barcelona, and Valencia are bigger) with a population exceeding a half-million, Seville has not lost its distinctive flavor. Whitewashed houses line winding streets in the old Santa Cruz quarter, intersected by small squares of extraordinary beauty. Churches and convents are dotted about, in the Mudéjar style of post-Islamic Christians who adapted designs of the Moors of later baroque brilliance. Other noteworthy structures include the neoclassic buildings of the eighteenth century (the elegant cigarette factory where the Merimée-Bizet *Carmen* toiled is now the University of Seville) and the still-grand international exposition buildings of Plaza de España, a souvenir of the 1920s.

ON SCENE
Lay of the Land: Seville clusters itself mostly on the east bank of the meandering Guadalquivir River. *Puente de San Telmo*, one of three bridges spanning the river, is adjacent to the Moorish-built landmark tower, *Torre del Oro*, and connects the main part of town with the smaller *Triana* quarter across the water. There are a pair of railway stations: Estación de Córdoba is riverfront, at the western edge of downtown, while Estación de Cádiz is across town, on its eastern fringe. Core of the city lies between these terminals, with the *Giralda tower* of the *Cathedral*—between Plaza de la Virgen de los Reyes and Plaza del Triunfo—the classic central landmark. Main Street is narrow, café- and shop-lined Calle de las Sierpes, for pedestrians only, running north from the Cathedral complex, from which it is briefly separated by a pair of parallel streets, Calle Colón and Avenida de la Constitución leading to Plaza de San Francisco, which marks Calle de las Sierpes's southern extremity. Plaza Nueva, with its principal monument the *Ayuntamiento*, or city hall, is just west of Plaza de

San Francisco and nearby Plaza del Duque is flanked by a trio of department stores.

Parque de María Luisa, south of downtown, is important for two destinations. One is crescent-shaped Plaza de España and the buildings bordering it, which were built for Seville's international exposition of 1929; the other is the esteemed *Museo Arqueológico.* The *Plaza de Toros,* one of Spain's preeminent bullrings, is on Paseo de Cristóbal Colón, a riverview promenade with the earlier-mentioned Moorish-origin Torre del Oro at its southern tip, near Puente de San Telmo.

Barrio de Santa Cruz, the ancient ghetto just east of the Cathedral, conveniently entered via Calle de Judería, is today Seville's most romantic—and most pleasantly walkable—quarter, a jumble of lane-like streets bordered by immaculately whitewashed patio-centered houses, with eye-filling plazas (especially Plaza de Santa Cruz) providing additional aesthetic excitement.

The Cathedral (Plaza de la Virgen de Los Reyes) is one of Christendom's most spectacular. The queue for admission tickets (no Spanish cathedral is more expensive to enter) is invariably long. But worth every peseta, and every minute of your wait. Only Rome's St. Peter's and London's St. Paul's are larger. But this church has more than scale. When the later-sainted King Ferdinand III wrested Seville from the Moslems in the thirteenth century, Spain had become a virtually Christian land. The idea, when the Cathedral started to rise more than 100 years later, was to make a strong visual impact to commemorate so consequential a victory for the Christian cause.

Europe's largest Gothic cathedral, it is built astride foundations of an ancient mosque. This is a cross-shaped structure, its iron-grille-enclosed choir blocking the central nave in the peculiar tradition of Spanish cathedrals. The main altar is 65 feet high, with exquisitely sculpted panels—some two score of them—depicting easily identifiable moments in the lives of Jesus and the Virgin Mary. Note, too, paintings by native sons Murillo and Valdés Leal and others by Zurbarán, Goya, and Murillo in the two sacristies; St. Ferdinand III's sword—among other glittering exhibits—in the treasury; an entire ring of art-filled chapels; and two principal remnants of the pre-Christian mosque:

Patio de los Naranjos, the capacious and elegant courtyard, and the *Giralda* (separately entered at an additional fee), which was originally a minaret.

The Alcázar (Plaza del Triunfo)—though it appears to be essentially Moorish—is actually more Mudéjar: built in the centuries following the expulsion of the Moors, sometimes by Moors who remained, sometimes by Christians utilizing the Moorish style. There are bits and pieces (a patio especially) from the original Moslem period, but essentially this palace-fortress is mid-fourteenth century with embellishments of later centuries.

Foreign visitors tend to slight the Alcázar in favor of the more celebrated Cathedral just next door. But Spaniards don't. They know it's been a royal residence from the time of King Peter the Cruel—its original Mudéjar patron—through those of Ferdinand and Isabella (they received Columbus in the Alcázar), Holy Roman Emperor Charles V, and later sovereigns like the nineteenth century's Isabella II.

State apartments of later residents—of the last century and the current one—are, disconcertingly, closed more often than not. Never mind, it's the pavilions that one most wants to amble through, not so much for furnishings, of which there are precious few, as for the scale and detail of the architecture: arched galleries of tiled patios, and intricate stuccowork in the walls, ceilings, cupolas, and niches of the royal apartments. Pause in the Cuarto del Almirante, the so-called Admiral's Apartments where *Los Reyes Católicos*, Ferdinand and Isabella, operated the agency called Casa de Contratación, through which the Spanish crown's New World enterprises were coordinated. Columbus himself is painted into an altarpiece, the *Virgen de los Mareantes*, and a model of one of his ships, the *Santa María*, is to be seen. But there's more: Isabella's bedrooms, the Renaissance-era apartments of Emperor Charles V (look up at the coffered ceiling), and the Salón de Embajadores, for invited ambassadors, with a gilded honeycomb of a ceiling cupola, possibly the single most beautiful detail of the Alcázar.

Museo de Bellas Artes (Plaza del Museo): The operative word is gorgeous. You're not going to find an art museum in a more resplendent setting. Seville bills Bellas Artes as Spain's No. 2, with only the Prado preceding it. There are, to be sure, first-rank works, even if only a fraction of the Prado's in number. It's the environment—a baroque convent enclosing a pair of cloisters with a chapel surmounted by a painted cupola and a monumental stairway—that makes you especially glad you went.

The Spaniards, for starters: Zurbarán (who spent much of his career in Seville) is at his most unusual and likable in a study of a half-dozen cuddly *conejos y cuinas*—rabbits and mice—against a stark black ground, not to mention portraits of more typically Zurbarán saints and white-robed monks. There are luminous works by Seville-born Murillo, most memorably his *Virgen de la Servilleta*, notable as much for the Virgin as for a wide-eyed baby Jesus. Native-son Valdés Leal is well-represented too, especially by his *Temptation of St. Jerome*. So, for that matter, are Velázquez (still another Sevillian), by a kneeling *St. Ildefonso*; Goya, by a black-robed priest reading a scarlet-bound missal; and El Greco, the artist's painter son, as interpreted by his father, with pallette and brushes.

Foreigners are unusually strong: Brueghel and Teniers, Lorrain and Caravaggio, Cranach and David, Veronese and Bassano. With splendid specimens of medieval sculpture and Renaissance furniture, not to mention silver and tiles.

Archivo de Indias (Plaza del Triunfo) is so close a neighbor of the Cathedral and Alcázar and so imposing a Renaissance building that you will want to go in. You're not going to see many of the nearly 40,000 documents having to do with the discovery and colonization of the Americas, among which—to give you an idea of their caliber—is a diary, kept in his own hand, of Columbus. Still, a sampling of the archives is generally on view in eye-level glass cases.

Hospital de la Caridad (Calle Temprano) is an often-bypassed, heart-of-town treasure—architectural and artistic both—of the seventeenth century. Look first at the lushly planted patio, then at the chapel's surprisingly rich cache of paintings by a pair of Sevillian painters, Murillo and Valdés Leal. Those of Murillo—

including an *Annunciation, St. John of God, Moses Receiving the Ten Commandments*—are exceptional, no less so their setting.

Casa de Pilatos (Plaza Pilatos) is representative of a substantial number of Sevillian town palaces. This one—sixteenth century—is to be entered primarily for its patio, sculpture-filled. Still another palace, *San Telmo* (Avenida de Roma), is visit-worthy for the baroque carving that frames its front door. A third, *Casa de las Dueñas* (Calle de las Dueñas), embraces three architectural epochs: Gothic (its chapel), Mudéjar (chapel's ceiling), Plateresque (patio).

Museo Arqueológico (Plaza de América in Parque de María Luisa) glitters with prehistoric gold jewelry—bracelets, necklaces, a score-plus pieces all told—discovered in the 1950s at nearby Carrámbolo. There are also souvenirs—a Venus, a Diana, a Mercury—of Roman Seville, from the still-visitable ruins of suburban Itálica (below). And other exhibits, Spanish all the way back to Phoenician.

Museo de Arte Contemporáneo (Calle Santa Tomás 5, near the Alcázar): Well, it is unlikely that you're going to know the artists' names—sculptors like Torner, abstract painters like Gerrero, of-this-era Sevillians like Cortijo—but you cannot help but be impressed with the caliber of the modern work in this exceptionally good-looking multi-level environment, with the arched ceilings quite as impressive as the marble floors.

Ayuntamiento (Plaza Nueva): Spanish city halls are invariably visit-worthy. The uniformed chaps guarding them hospitably pass curious visitors right along to whatever it is that should be inspected. In Seville's case—after admiring the carved-stone Plateresque façade—one wants to see the gold ceiling of the Sala Capitular (now a library) and the upper floor, which includes the archives, packed with extraordinary documents and the chandelier-hung Salón de Colón.

Church of El Salvador (Plaza Salvador, near Calle de las Sierpes) is a triumph of the rococo of the eighteenth century, triple-naved, with a dome surmounting its transept, a shining high altar, and figures of Christ by master sculptors.

Capilla de San José (Calle Jovellanos) is a chapel smaller than Salvador (above), but no less joyous rococo; enter to marvel at the lavishly gilded altar that covers the rear wall.

Church of Santa María Magdalena (Calle de San Pablo): For starters note the transept paintings, the baroque-era statue of St. Mary Magdalene, and the memorial to a Spanish colonial priest for his devotion to New World Indians.

Church of San Antonio Abad (Calle Alfonso XII): You'll pass by this Baroque beauty en route to or from Museo de Bellas Artes (above). Pop in to note its pair of lavishly gilded altars.

Universidad de Sevilla (Calle de San Fernando) is a case of an ancient structure being built for one purpose and, in its advancing years, being converted to quite another function. By that I mean that the cigarette factory where the celebrated principal of the Merimée-Bizet opera, *Carmen*, toiled—later to be fatally stabbed by her lover, Don José—is now home to the University of Seville. Both the building and the university date to the eighteenth century; the latter was in quarters elsewhere until taking over the onetime factory just a couple of decades back. And would that contemporary factories looked so good. This one is a massive square, classical-style, with an inner maze-like design incorporating more than 100 courtyards, the lot constituting the largest area of any aged Spanish building complex, the Escorial excepted.

Torre del Oro (Paseo de Cristóbal Colón) is the principal on-scene representation of Islamic Seville, if one excepts the foundations of the Alcázar and the built-upon Giralda tower of the Cathedral. Torre del Oro (the Golden Tower) is thirteenth century; its original purpose was more than decorative. Moors of the time controlled Guadalquivir River traffic by means of a vast chain extending from the Torre del Oro to a now-defunct twin tower across the water. When a ship sailed into view, up went the chain, so that the vessel would have to stop and pay tolls. It's nice that the tower remains, because it is special, architecturally: not octagonal as one assumes at first glance, but 12-sided. And yes, you may enter. At least if the little *Museo Naval* is open.

Itálica (4 miles northwest of Seville on Route 630, near the village of Santiponce): Though not perhaps as celebrated as Tarragona (Chapter 25), the onetime Roman city of Itálica—wherein Seville had its beginnings—is hardly to be overlooked by antiquities buffs. It was, after all, the birthplace of a pair of Roman emperors (Hadrian and Trajan) and is hardly without spectacular remnants of Roman-era glory, an immense amphitheater most especially, but mosaics and capitals, baths and buildings, streets and sculpture, as well. With an on-sight museum that nicely complements the Itálica exhibits in Seville's *Museo Arqueológico* (above).

Holy Week in Seville: My philosophy of travel, with respect to timing, has always been simple: go when you can, regardless of weather or of special events that you may—or may not—miss. That said, let me make clear that Holy Week—*Semana Santa*—in Seville is an experience worth building an entire itinerary around. The week is celebrated throughout the south, but nowhere quite like in Seville. Every night, Palm Sunday to Good Friday, the costumed members of some 60 religious brotherhoods—*cofradías* the are called—move through the city, led by a pair of gigantic golden floats, one to honor Christ, the other the Virgin Mary, and each massed with flowers and lighted tapers, with several dozen men serving as volunteer carriers of these litters, whose weight averages 6,000 pounds.

Thousands of hooded penitents march behind, in each procession, many under the weight of heavy wooden crosses. Their in-town destination is Seville Cathedral, and the streets are lined with mobs of the faithful—Spaniards come from other regions of the kingdom, and visitors from abroad who have booked hotel space well in advance—lining the route, to cries of *Olé*—the same term of approbation used at bullfights and flamenco performances—for the best floats.

SETTLING IN

Hotel Alfonso XIII (Calle San Fernando 2) is a Seville tradition, an extraordinary leftover from the same 1929 international fair that gave the city its Plaza España complex (above). Like the Plaza España buildings, it is unabashedly mock-Moorish, in the exuberant manner of movie palaces of the same genre built at the same time in large United States cities, and now, more's the pity, mostly extinct. The Alfonso "tray-thay"—to give it phonetic pronunciation—was named for the then reigning, last pre-Franco king, who came down from Madrid to dedicate it. It closed for five years in the 1970s for a multi-million-peseta refurbishing, and when it reopened in 1979, Alfonso's grandson, King Juan Carlos, was on hand to rededicate it. (Lobby plaques attest to both royal visits.) There are just under 150 rooms and suites in this vast pile; they're large, luxurious, and still with hand-embroidered white bedspreads, as from the early days. The public spaces flank a central lobby-court encircling a glass-roofed, fountain-centered patio. The main restaurant is nothing less than one of the handsomest in the kingdom (on an esthetic par with those of Madrid's Ritz and San Sebastián's María Cristina, and reviewed on a later page) and there's nothing to beat a dip in the swimming pool (located in the big garden, a veritable orange grove) after a hot day of Seville exploration. Your hosts are Ciga Hotels, Italy's leading luxury chain, and with a Spanish network, as well. *Luxury.*

Hotel Doña María (Calle Don Remondo 19) is an enchanter. Start with location: It's a stone's throw from the Giralda tower and Cathedral. Go on from there to an antiques-accented lobby; three score rooms, no two alike, each with modern bath and ancient charm; a swimming pool with bar that's a joy in summer. Breakfast only. *First Class.*

Hotel Colón (Calle Canalejas 1) is late-Twenties, like the Alfonso XIII (above), but without its distinctive style. Which is hardly to be critical. This 262-room, central-as-can-be house is a pleasure, starting with the circular glass dome-covered lobby, on through to attractive accommodations. There are two restaurants—one special enough to warrant attention in a later paragraph—and a busy, buzzy bar. Don't be surprised if you bump into a *toreador* in the lobby; this is visiting bullfighters' traditional headquarters. *First Class.*

Hotel Inglaterra (Plaza Nueva 10): This is a low-key modern house with 120 welcoming—if not over-large—rooms, some with balconies and smashing Cathedral views. The lobby is big and rambling, there's a bar-lounge, and the restaurant overlooks action-packed Plaza Nueva. I like. Best Western. *First Class.*

Sevilla Sol Hotel (Avenida de la Borbolla 3) is clean-lined contemporary (it's one of the city's newest), with just over 400 well-equipped rooms and suites, trio of restaurants and as many bars, and a fairly central location overlooking Plaza de España and adjacent Parque María Luisa. *First Class.*

Pasarela Hotel (Avenida de la Borbolla 11) is a near-neighbor of the Sevilla Sol (above), albeit considerably smaller (there are just over 80 rooms) and with a gym-sauna. Breakfast only. *First Class.*

América Hotel (Plaza del Duque) is conveniently heart-of-town, up-to-the-minute with respect to amenities. There are 100 full-facility rooms (a third of them singles), *cafetería* and bar. *Moderate.*

Fernando III Hotel (Calle San Jose 21) is at once central and comfortable. Many of its 159 rooms are terraced, all are with bath. Amenities include a bar, solarium and swimming pool. Breakfast only. *Moderate.*

Murillo Hotel (Calle Lope de Rueda 7) is just the ticket if you would be content with a budget-tabbed house in one of Seville's most romantic quarters; location is Barrio de Santa Cruz. There are just over 60 bath-equipped rooms and an agreeable lounge. Breakfast only. *Moderate.*

Parador Nacional Alcázar del Rey Don Pedro (Carmona, 20 miles northeast of Seville) is worth knowing about it you're motoring. This is an atmospheric link of the national chain of *paradores,* traditional in style, with an elevated situation that makes possible fabulous views of the countryside from its terrace and many of the 60-plus rooms, all with tiled bath. Public spaces are handsome, the bar is relaxing and the restaurant features regional specialties. *First Class.*

Hotel Bécquer (Calle Reyes Católicos 4) is worth knowing about because it offers good value. It's modern, with a spacious lobby, off of which there's a lounge that doubles as a drinks-spot and breakfast room. (There's no proper restaurant.) The 126 bedrooms are good-sized, with baths, and, if they're high enough up and facing southeast, with vistas of the Cathedral—a 10-minute walk away. *Moderate.*

Hotel Venecia (Calle Trajano 31) is contemporary and charmless, but with a couple of dozen spotless and comfortable rooms with baths. Breakfast only. *Moderate.*

Hotel La Rábida (Calle Castelar 24) is faded and elderly but not without the flavor of Seville in its patio-like lobby, beamed-ceiling restaurant, popular bar, and garden. There are 90 rooms with baths or showers, but—mind, here—you do well to ask specifically for those of the top category; even then, be prepared for thin mattresses. Clientele is delightfully international. Central. *Moderate.*

Hotel Simón (Calle García de Vinuesa 19) is a find, if it's ambience (this is an old town house) and value one seeks. Mattresses are slim and baths attached only to double rooms. No matter: The main lounge—chandelier-hung, with venerable paintings, tiled walls, antique furnishings—is a pleasure, the lobby high-ceilinged, the restaurant likewise. Near the Cathedral. *Moderate.*

Hotel Montecarlo (Calle Gravina 51) is an interesting choice if it's the west bank of the Guadalquivir that appeals. This is steps from the bridge that leads to downtown. Twenty-six rooms, all with baths or showers. Breakfast only. *Moderate.*

DAILY BREAD

San Marco (Calle Cuna 6) occupies a pair of contiguous ground-floor rooms in an eighteenth-century core-of-town mansion that constitutes one of Seville's handsomest—and, it develops, most delicious—restaurant environments. Take your choice of the forward chamber, dominated by a great Murano chandelier, and with trellised windows, or of the even more dramatic atrium, framed by a massive glass cupola embellished by sculpture in its *faux-marbre* niches. Host Angelo Ansano is invariably on hand to greet and seat guests, and make suggestions from an extensive à la carte. A meal might commence with a delicate crayfish bisque, or fresh salmon salad, as preludes to such superlative entrées as *confit* of duck served with cèpes and *pommes gratinois*, or *entrecôte* in tandem with an authentic *marchand-du-vin* sauce. Accompanying vegetables are fresh and flavorful and sweets—including house-made sherbets, a rich and rewarding profiterole au chocolat, the chef's own cakes and hot soufflés—do not disappoint. And service is at once alert and engaging. An exceptional restaurant. *Luxury.*

Itálica (Alfonso XIII Hotel, Calle San Fernando 2) is arguably—along with the restaurant of Madrid's Ritz—the quintessential grand-hotel dining room, a meticulously restored throwback to the period between the World Wars when high coffered ceilings, veritable networks of crystal chandeliers, frescoed walls, richly draped windows, amply spaced tables set with bowls of professionally-arranged flowers, and attentive, tail-coated captains, was the accepted rule in luxury hotels. Itálica is at its best in the soft light of the evening. There's a three-course menu and an extensive grouping of daily specials ranging from properly chilled vichysoisse and subtly flavored house terrines through entrées like grilled lobster, roast pheasant, or, if you like, *Kansas Tibone à la Brasa*—a sure winner. As indeed are the house's pastries and ice creams. And wines from a vast cellar. *Luxury.*

La Judería (Calle Cano y Cueto 13): You want to have at least one meal in the historic Santa Cruz quarter, and you could do worse than to have it at La Judería. The look is properly Sevillian—brick walls, arched ceilings, ladderback chairs at immaculately set tables. Waiters are kindly and old-school, fare is hearty and typical. Andalusia-origin gazpacho—Spain's famed chilled, tomato-base soup—is nowhere more refreshing. It's ladled from a tureen, and you yourself embellish it, as the waiter presents bowls of chopped onion, diced hard-cooked egg, cubed tomatoes, sliced green peppers, crisp cucumber bits, and croutons. Broiled steak Spanish style—*solomillo parillada*—nicely garnished, is excellent here. So is seafood and so are salads. And the bread is crusty and commendable, not always the case with Spanish restaurants. There's an à la carte, but your best buy is the day's menu. *First Class.*

Casa Senra (Calle de Bécquer 45) attracts locals as well as visitors, first because it is congenial—the look is unpretentious but comfortable—and second, because the Andalusian cuisine is so corking good. Salads are as good as you'll find in Spain, gazpacho special, and the fish—sole, especially—prepared with sherry, delicious. Interesting desserts and—never unimportant, at least to me—coarse and crusty country bread. *First Class.*

Enrique Becerra (Calle de Gamaza 2) is for hearty meals in an attractive setting—a nicely furnished antique house, core of the city. Meat is excellent here—with the stew of *ternera*, or veal, especially tasty. But the fish—fresh and well sauced—is commendable, too. And so are the *tapas*, bite-size nibbles that accompany pre-meal aperitifs at the busy bar. *First Class.*

Mesón del Moro (Calle Mesón del Moro 6) is indeed a Moor's house, or might well have been. This is a handsome environment. Tables are set in a yellow-walled four-story-high patio, awning-roofed, with plants suspended from upper galleries. One lunches or dines on rattan chairs, ideally ordering the *menú del día* and a house wine. *First Class.*

Río Grande (Calle Betis 70) is as good an excuse as I know for crossing the Guadalquivir, to its west bank. The walk, over Puente de San Telmo, is scenic, no less so than a table on this restaurant's riverfront terrace, in full view of the Torre del Oro across the water. Gazpacho here is exemplary, as are *huevos* *revueltos*—eggs scrambled with asparagus—and *pollo con ajo,* masterfully fried chicken chunks, garlic-flavored. Drink the house wine, served in pitchers. *First Class.*

Hostería del Laurel (Plaza de los Venerables 5) is indicated as a splurge spot for lunch or dinner. In venerable Barrio de Santa Cruz, this is a loaded-with-atmosphere eighteenth-century house, with the bar on the main floor (start there with *tapas*— appetizers—and a sherry) and the restaurant up a flight. The roasts, from a slowly turning spit, are delicious. *First Class.*

El Burladero (Hotel Colón, Calle Canalejas) is the stylish, purposely understated grill of Hotel Colón, not to be confused with its more prosaic main restaurant. Clientele here—well-heeled Sevillians, visiting Spaniards with expense accounts, affluent international diners—tend to order à la carte, from waiters who are more skilled than cordial. No matter: The food, be it paella or a grilled steak, is absolutely delicious. Try the properly aged and crumbly *manchego* cheese for dessert; not many restaurants in Spain have it. *Luxury.*

La Isla (Calle Arfe 25) is worth knowing about because it is central and—if you order the three-course menu which might be based on *paella* or filet of veal—reasonably priced. Look is spotless-functional, service cooly efficient if hardly gracious (at least in the case of foreign visitors; Sevillian regulars are warmly welcomed). Insist on a table downstairs; the upper dining room is Siberia. *Moderate/First Class.*

Ochoa (Calle las Sierpes 45) is a *cafetería,* brought to your attention principally because it is conveniently located on the main shopping street. You might want to drop in for coffee, a snack or a casual lunch. *Moderate.*

Robles (Calle Alvarez Quintero 58) lies between the Cathedral and Barrio de Santa Cruz. It's modern, spotless, cheery, with tasty fare and good house wines. You want to order the attractively priced *menú del día. Moderate.*

Mesón El Tenorio (Calle Mesón del Moro 16) occupies an antique house. Specialties—fish, lamb, pork. *Moderate.*

El Caserío Vasco (Calle Santas Patronas at Calle Reyes Católicos) is unpretentious but with Basque flair to its fare, as the name suggests. Delicious casseroles. *Moderate.*

Cueva del Pez Espada (Calle Rodrigo Caro 18) is small and noted for its seafood specialties. With charm as a bonus. In Barrio de Santa Cruz. *Moderate.*

Los Alcázares (Calle Miguel de Mañara 10) is worth knowing about if it's a simple meal you fancy in a traditional setting and you'd like it in the historic core, near, say, the Alcázar. *Moderate.*

Nairobi (Calle Moratin 10) is no more Kenyan than the city in which it's situated. This is a near-Plaza Nueva *cafetería*, self-service, and convenient for casual meals or snacks. *Moderate.*

Galerías Preciados (Plaza de Magdalena): The Seville outpost of this Spain-wide department-store empire is a sound source of sustenance. Head for the *cafetería* on the second floor of the main building. At lunch, consider the generous three-course *menú del día*; it's a buy. And in the afternoon, why not an *escrín-soda* (as the menu lists it)? They bring a tall glass with a double scoop of the flavor of ice cream you've selected, and a glob of *nata*, or whipped cream, together with a bottle of soda, from which you pour your own; delicious. *Moderate.*

SHOPPER'S SEVILLE

Plaza del Duque, heart of town, is fringed by three department stores—*Simago, Lubre* and, most significant of the trio, the Seville outlet of *El Corte Inglés*, with a big *supermercado* and shoe-repair in the basement, such departments as perfume-cologne (Spanish brands can be good buys), a sandwich counter and souvenirs on main, men's and women's shoes on one, men's clothing on two, women's and children's clothing on three, porcelain, glass, home furnishings, women's hairdresser and men's barbershop on four, and restaurant-*cafetería* on five. *Galerías*

Preciados, the other big department-store chain, occupies two buildings on Plaza de Magdalena, with men's, women's and kids' clothing and a *cafetería* (above recommended) in the main building. Calle de las Sierpes, the main pedestrian street, abounds in smaller stores, including both *Martian* and *Sevillarte* (ceramics), *Pascual Lázaro* (books, with an English-language section), *Danielos* (chocolates), *Victor & Luccino* (smart women's clothing), *Paños* (men's custom duds), *Nicolás* (men's and women's shoes) and *La Campana*, an *heladería*, wherein house-made ice cream (scooped into *conos*, if you like) has been vended for well over a century. (My flavor suggestion: half lemon, half chocolate.)

INCIDENTAL INTELLIGENCE

Seville is my favorite bullfight city. First, because the sport is no more a part of the culture anywhere else in Spain—even Granada. Second, because the location of the *Plaza de Toros*, here called Maestranza, on Paseo de Cristóbal Colón at Calle Adriano, is so central you can walk, if your hotel is likewise central, obviating public transportation or a taxi, which is necessary in such cities as Madrid. And third, because the ring is at once immense and historic, dating originally to the eighteenth century. Along with Madrid, Granada, and Córdoba, this is a center for flamenco dancing. Ask your hotel concierge for a currently acceptable locale; the rule—as with *tablao flamenco* performances Spain-wide—is that the fairly steep entrance tab includes a first drink. Again, as throughout Spain, caliber of the dancers can disappoint. Iberia flies to Seville from Madrid and other Spanish cities; Aeropuerto de San Pablo is nine miles from the center. *Further information:* Oficina de Turismo de Sevilla, Avenida de la Constitución 21.

25

Tarragona

*The Glory of
Roman Spain*

BACKGROUND BRIEFING

No matter its lack of contemporary eminence, Tarragona can look back—way, way back, to be sure—to when, as Tarraco, it was capital of imposingly named *Colonia Juli Urbi Triumphalis Tarraconensis*: the Roman empire's thriving Spanish domain and, as such, a Mediterranean port of consequence, and a commercial entrepôt to be reckoned with.

Founded originally by prehistoric Iberians, Tarragona fell to Rome in the third pre-Christian century, in a battle led by a pair of warrior brothers of the fighting Scipio clan. And it knew other eminent Romans. Julius Caesar himself was its first major builder. His grandnephew, Augustus, liked it so much on a visit that he settled in for two years. And Pontius Pilate, whose immortality came in later years in another outpost of the empire, was born in Tarraco.

Not unlike still another relatively obscure European city (Germany's Trier, which had been a major Roman empire outpost with emperors resident), Tarragona, in the post-Roman centuries, became increasingly less important in the then international scheme of things when aggressive, Germanic—and at the time still pagan—Visigoths, in the course of their conquest of Spain, took control.

Later peninsular invaders—the Moors out of North Africa—conquered the city. By the time of the Christian hegemony in

Spain, economics had played a major part in Tarragona's regression. Competing cities along the Mediterranean coast, Barcelona to the north and Valencia to the south, ascended the maritime scale as top ports.

Today's Tarragona is compact (the population hovers at about 100,000), with a fairly busy and very modern harbor, and a certain political clout that comes to it as a provincial seat of government. More important, to the visitor at least, are remnants of a remarkable past. In no other Spanish city is the early presence of Rome more vividly re-created. And, if it's summer, bring your swimsuit; there are wide white-sand beaches in town, and to the north and south.

ON SCENE
Lay of the Land: Tarragona straddles the sea, with the railway station and a wide Mediterranean in-town beach—*Playa del Milagro*—near the foot of tree-centered, boulevard-like Rambla Nova, principal street of its modern quarter and not unlike the similarly attractive Ramblas of neighboring Barcelona. A series of thoroughfares running perpendicular to Rambla Nova—Calle San Francisco in particular—lead inland to the increasingly elevated part of town, past still another rambla to the major in-town monuments, centered around the square variously called Llano de la Catedral and Llano de la Seo. Mind, though, you can't walk everywhere, once arrived at this focal point. Other requisite destinations are along Paseo Arqueológico, high above town; in other central quarters; and beyond the city, as well.

Cathedral (Llano de la Catedral): The Cathedral does not, of course, typify Tarragona's great Roman era. I still consider it the ideal Tarragona starting point, because its considerable bulk provides the newcomer with a sense of focus for the city. It is a felicitous Romanesque-Gothic meld, capacious and high-walled, with an octagonal bell tower the dominant feature. Principal masterwork within is a spectacular altarpiece of Santa Tecla, the city's patron saint, by a fifteenth-century sculptor called Pedro Juan. Have a look at the ring of chapels: Gothic, Renaissance (Plateresque), and baroque (Churrigueresque). The best comes last: an enormous cloister that's one of Europe's most superlative. It is mostly late twelfth-century Romanesque, but, like the rest of the Cathedral, with later work—Gothic and Mudéjar. Detail throughout—carving on the arches, capitals, vaults, and niches—warrants study.

Museo Diocesano, a part of the Cathedral, is to be surveyed mostly for its rich and ravishing tapestries, more than half a hundred, with the oldest—from the Middle Ages—telling the most interesting stories. But there's more: Iberian and roman pottery, and illuminated manuscripts, especially.

Antiguo Hospital de la Ciudad (Calle Caldereros) is a near-neighbor to the Cathedral, to its left as you look toward Llano de la Catedral. Amble over if only to appreciate its elegant Gothic façade.

San Pablo and Santa Tecla chapels (Calle San Pablo) are the pair of lovely little churches just behind the Cathedral. The former is Romanesque-Gothic; the latter surprises with a front door that's a copy of a ceremonial Roman gateway, and, within, a mass of ancient tombs.

Paseo Arqueológico, above and behind the Cathedral complex, is a kind of Roman way, in a garden beneath the fantastically thick (as much as five feet) Roman ramparts that go back some 22 centuries. There are grottoes, towers, and sculptures, not to mention fine vistas.

Museo Arqueológico and Praetorium (Calle Pescadería Solegario, going toward downtown, near Rambla San Carlos): Close-up evidence of the glory that was Roman Tarragona, including exquisitely carved pedestals and cornices, busts and medallions, a doll fashioned of marble, coins of the ancient realm, and memorable mosaics, a head of Medusa without any doubt the star of the whole show. Bonus: a just-next-door tower—Praetorium by name—that goes back to a century before Christ, and is said to be the birthplace of Pontius Pilate.

Museo Paleo Cristiano is worth the taxi hop a mile south of town, at least if one would see the remarkable collection within, of tombs—simple tiled ones through to elaborate sarcophagi—of early Tarragona Christians. An ancient necropolis, or cemetery, in connection.

Acueducto Romano, a magnificent feat of Roman engineering that ranks with the Roman aqueduct in Segovia (see the chapter on that city), is a bit more distant than the museum (above): on the highway to Lérida. Nicknamed *El Puente del Diablo*—Devil's Bridge—it embraces two perfect levels of arches, extending a length of 400 feet. And if you're game for a drive of an additional 10 miles, you may take in *Arco de Barâ*, a gem of a second-century triumphal arch.

SETTLING IN
Hotel Imperial Tarraco (Rambla Vella 2) bears the name of Roman Tarragona and is excellently situated, between the Cathedral area and Rambla Nova. This is an all-the-comforts house, even including an outdoor pool (a pleasure at the end of a summer day of sightseeing), tennis court, and garden, with 170 comfortable rooms with baths, restaurant, bar-lounge. *Luxury.*

Hotel Lauria (Rambla Nova 20) is center-of-the-action, on the favored principal Rambla and near the beach. There are some 70 rooms with baths, and an outdoor pool. Breakfast only. *First Class.*

Hotel Urbis (Calle Reding 20, near Plaza Corsini) is a couple of blocks below Rambla Nova, but still reasonably central. Close to 60 rooms, many with private bathrooms. Breakfast only. *Moderate.*

DAILY BREAD
Náutico (Puerto) is away from the center, to be sure. But this harborview spot is an ideal choice for a solid seafood lunch or dinner in a properly maritime setting. Order a *zarzuela*—or casserole—of the day's catch. And the house white wine, a crisp Tarragona. *First Class.*

Lauria 2 (Rambla Nova 20, upstairs) is an apt downtown choice. Hopefully, *colcotado*—a local meat and sausage specialty—will be on the day's menu. *Moderate.*

La Puda (Muelle Pescadores 25) is another possibility for seafood, at the harbor. Order grilled fish with *romesco*, a local peppery sauce. *Moderate.*

INCIDENTAL INTELLIGENCE

Tarragona is about two hours south of Barcelona by train; there is frequent service—often on good equipment—between the two cities. Pressed for time, you can explore quite a bit in the course of a day's excursion from Barcelona. But an overnight stay is recommended. You might want to stop off, going or coming, at Sitges, a popular beach resort town lying between the pair of cities. *Further information:* Oficina de Información y Turismo de Tarragona, Calle Fortuny 4.

26

Toledo

Europe's Greatest
Small City

BACKGROUND BRIEFING
There's not a small city in all Europe that can match this town of 50,000 when it comes to really substantial historic significance, matchless art and architecture, evocative ambience, and an utterly smashing natural setting.

What one wants so much to say is, Day-trippers out of Madrid, keep your distance! This is—or at least should be—a destination for the curious traveler willing to at least take in a bit of its fascination by remaining a night or two. Toledo is, after all, the city from which were shaped the destinies of Spain over a thousand-year span, from the sixth to the sixteenth centuries.

Capital for a millennium, Toledo was not inconsequential even before that time. Take its name. Long in advance of the Romans—they settled in as colonists in the second century before Christ—it had been called Toletum, from which the present Hispanic name derives. In the fifth century, Visigoths out of Germany conquered the Iberian peninsula—it had known something like a century of the barbaric Vandals—and made Toledo their principal seat. The Visigoths lavished effort upon the town, with palaces, schools, and churches (they were, of course, Christian). A good deal of what the world has come to accept as the culture of Spain evolved and developed amidst the crosscurrents of this stimulating early Toledan environment.

The Moors contributed mightily, too. They brought the Is-

.its rich concomitant culture with them in force
.rrica in the early eighth century. They also dis-
.ostantial chunk of Toledo's populace, which moved
.ner regions of the peninsula—especially Asturias in the
.nwest—and later organized the Christian reconquest.

But the interim Moorish centuries in Toledo are not to be underappreciated. First the court of an emirate, later the capital of a kingdom, Toledo evolved as a distillate of cultures of its Arabic, Jewish, and Christian peoples; contributions of the first two groups—too often forgotten—were to have lasting effects in the pan-Spanish scheme of things.

El Cid, most romantic of the Spanish heroes, drove the Moors from Toledo in the late eleventh century, to be succeeded by a dynasty of Castilian monarchs, one of whom—Isabella I—paved the way for the unification of Spain with her marriage, in 1469, to Ferdinand of Aragón. Ferdinand and Isabella, known to Spaniards simply as *Los Reyes Católicos*, jointly presided over Spain's Golden Age. In the latter decades of the fifteenth century, their Toledo-centered monarchy united Spain, ousted Moors as well as Jews, led the dreaded Inquisition, the while inspiring a flowering of the arts, and indeed of artisanship. Toledo's repute spread—as much for the strength of its sword blades as its prowess in painting.

It was from Toledo, too, that the crown of Spain and the crown of the vast Holy Roman Empire became one and the same. That happened when Ferdinand and Isabella's daughter Juana—later to become mentally ill and known in history as Juana la Loca—married a Hapsburg prince, Philip the Handsome. Their son, the trimly bearded Charles (immortal, thanks in part to masterful Titian portraits) became both king of Spain (as Charles I) and Holy Roman Emperor (as Charles V).

Charles V's death in 1558 was to result in the demise of Toledo as the capital. His son, Philip II—like his father, painted by Titian—up and moved the court to what then could accurately be called upstart Madrid, not yet a proper city, even for its time. And so Toledo was shorn of its political power. Its only official eminence, in the intervening centuries, has been as headquarters for the Catholic archbishop who serves as primate of Spain, No. 1 among the clerics controlling the kingdom's many dioceses.

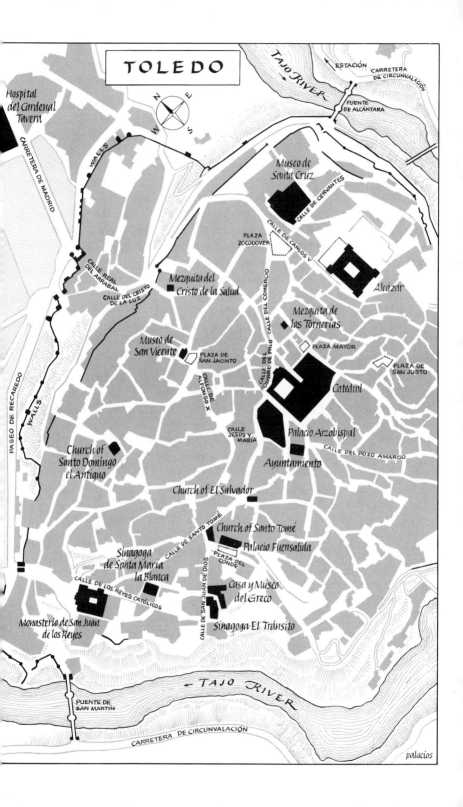

ON SCENE

Lay of the Land: Toledo is quite as it was when El Greco painted it: perched atop a craggy tableland that could be a stage set, what with a gorge of the Tagus River enclosing three of its four sides.

Center of town is a jumble of squares. Plaza de Zocodover, the most ancient, is where sovereigns were proclaimed, heretics denounced, and markets held—the last of which still is the case every Tuesday. Plaza Mayor is the smallest, dwarfed by the massive adjacent Cathedral. A maze of charming streets links the squares, with Calle del Comercio—the main business thoroughfare—extending west from Plaza de Zocodover, changing its name to Calle Hombre de Polo before it reaches the Cathedral. Sights and sensations of the historic core present themselves on streets with names like Alfonso X and Jesús y María, and such squares as San Vicente and San Justo. The trick is simply one of time: staying long enough to savor the most consistently rushed-through of Spanish cities.

The Cathedral (Calle del Arco del Palacio Arzobispo) wants to be regarded as both a church and a museums-complex; it warrants the kind of time reserved for big league counterparts like the cathedrals of Burgos, Santiago de Compostela, and Seville. The pity is that there is not enough open space, without, to afford sufficient perspective of what represents one of Europe's great Gothic achievements, dating from the thirteenth century (the east façade) to the fifteenth (the main façade), with later appendages including an oddly incongruous little dome whose seventeenth-century designer was a son of the painter whose name is synonymous with Toledo—El Greco.

Glance down the central nave, past the choir, which, as is the custom in Spanish cathedrals, blocks the aisle leading to the high altar. Then concentrate on specifics. The choir comprises multilevel walnut stalls, whose Renaissance carving is exceptional in a kingdom brimming with lovely choirs; its wrought-iron grille is an all-Spain standout, too.

At the high altar, Christ's life is delineated in half a hundred individually framed panels. The cloister has two levels, each serene and handsome. The treasury is not misnamed; it abounds in ecclesiastical objects—monstrances, reliquaries, and crowns embedded with precious stones—the lot under a sumptuous ceiling in the geometric Mudéjar style. Still another Mudéjar ceiling is to be found in the Sala Capitular where, among rows of archbishops' portraits, are two by Goya. I leave contents of the chapels—totaling two dozen—for you to discover. And I end with the Cathedral's biggest surprise: an Old Masters gallery that overflows from the sacristy into an adjacent hall. To be seen? Well, a cache of El Grecos, including a series of 13—one is of Christ and the remainder are of the Apostles. There are, as well, works by Spaniards including Goya and Juan de Borgoña; by Flemings like Rubens and Van Dyck; by Italians like Bellini and Bassano. I don't know of a more important collection of paintings in any cathedral, anywhere.

Museo de Santa Cruz (Calle de Cervantes 3), although a near-neighbor to central Plaza de Zocodover, remains one of Spain's most bypassed museums of consequence. The setting is a jewel of Renaissance/Mudéjar design begun by a fifteenth-century archbishop as a hospital, and completed after his death by Queen Isabella. Santa Cruz, fronted by a Plateresque portal, embraces two crucifix-shaped floors connected by an extraordinary stairway. The wide, high galleries of each are surmounted by Mudéjar ceilings of such magnificence that they conflict with the art objects on display. These include a generous group of El Grecos, with some especially moving works among these, including an *Assumption*, a *Coronation of the Virgin*, an *Annunciation* like no other you've seen, and a *St. Joseph* with Jesus a gowned toddler at his side. Other Spanish painters are represented, too: Ribera and Goya, for example. With two bonuses: an architectural museum in connection, and an especially graceful patio.

Casa y Museo del Greco (Calle de San Juan de Dios) unites a pair of contiguous core-of-town houses, one the only remaining part of the complex of mansions in which El Greco lived, the other a neighboring residence restored and rebuilt in the early years of this century for exhibits. Crete-born El Greco went as a young man to study in Italy, moving along some years later to Toledo, where he remained, painting prolifically, until he died.

The house-museum is as interesting for its portrayal of bourgeois life in Renaissance Spain as it is for insight into the Greco genius. One goes as much for authentically furnished rooms of the period as for paintings. The former include a patio, living room, dining room, bedrooms, and tiled kitchen. The second floor is a gallery of Grecos—especially noteworthy is his *View of Toledo* (of which Madrid's Prado and New York's Metropolitan Museum have counterparts, the Met's being the better-known *Storm over Toledo*), which is exciting to see on home ground. Among other Grecos are a set of 13 paintings of Christ and the Apostles, similar to that I mention earlier, on display in the Cathedral. Coming as a delightful surprise are works of such other Spaniards as Zurbarán, Valdés Leal, and Luis Tristan, who studied with the master of the house.

A pair of former synagogues— El Tránsito (Calle de San Juan de Dios) and *Santa María la Blanca* (Calle de los Jacintos)—indicate how handsome were the environments in which Toledo's substantial Jewish community worshiped during the Moorish domination, and moreover, how the Jews used the architectural style of the Moslems in their synagogues. El Tránsito, next-door neighbor to the Casa y Museo del Greco, and the newer of the two, is fourteenth century. It is a simple oblong of a hall, made brilliant by its Mudéjar decor. An intricate carved-wood ceiling shelters half a hundred delicately framed windows. The name comes from that of the church that the building housed after the expulsion of the Jews; wisely, the Hebrew characters carved into the alabaster have been allowed to remain all these centuries. Santa María Blanca—the name of the church that followed in the wake of this older synagogue—is something else again: a mosque-like hall dominated by rows of pillars that serve as the bases for extraordinarily striking horseshoe-shaped arches.

Monasterio de San Juan de los Reyes (Calle de los Reyes Católicos): The kings—*los Reyes*—of the title were Ferdinand and Isabella, who built it as an act of thanksgiving for winning a battle, the same reason their greatgrandson, Philip II, was to use for erecting El Escorial. This is worth the trip from downtown to the west side: an intact specimen of late Spanish Gothic, with fine Plateresque carving where broad expanses of the choir permit it. And the ceilings of the perfectly beautiful two-story cloister are wood-embellished Mudéjar.

Church of Santo Tomé (Calle de Santo Tomé): The point of a visit here is not the church itself, a respectable Renaissance structure with a slim Mudéjar-style bell tower, but rather to see a celebrated El Greco painting, *El Entierro del Conde de Orgaz.* This massive fresco is beloved of Toledans because all of the nonbiblical figures it portrays—attending the burial of a local count—were of the city. (The painter himself is believed to be the sixth gent from the left.)

Hospital del Cardenal Tavera (Carretera de Madrid) is, more often than not, passed over by Toledo visitors. Its location—at the northern edge of town on the Madrid road—is one reason; stiff competition from in-town destinations is another. Neither holds any water. A pilgrimage here pays off. The sixteenth-century building, project of a powerful cardinal for whom it is named, was a collaborative effort of more than one Renaissance master. El Greco was one, along with the architect Bustamente and the sculptor Alonso Berruguete; they worked under the aegis of Toledo's last resident ruler, Emperor Charles V.

Tavera, at least that part of it not operating as an orphanage, remains brimful of treasures. What one encounters is a sumptuous suite of rooms, furnished with Renaissance pieces, and embellished with extraordinary works of art. There are El Grecos of the founder-cardinal, among others, along with a high altar in the hospital's domed chapel, gained by means of a stroll through a pair of connected patios. And so much more, including a Titian of Charles V; works by other Italians including Tintoretto and Giordano; and by other Spaniards, among them Ribera and Coello.

Palacio de Fuensalida (Plaza del Conde): Royal palaces of the Renaissance are not all that easy to come by, even in Spain. Here's one, heart-of-town. The patio is elegant Mudéjar, and within, one inspects, among others, the opulently decorated room in which Emperor Charles V's wife died in childbirth.

Church of Cristo de la Luz (Calle del Cristo de la Luz) is Toledo's only remaining vestige of the period before the Christian reconquest. It was built as a Christian church during the time of the Germanic Visigoths, probably as early as the seventh century. A few hundred years later, the Moslems fashioned a mosque on its ruins, utilizing a quartet of extant columns to support nine cupolas. The look is not unlike the mosque-cathedral in Córdoba, believed to have been its inspiration.

Church of Santiago del Arrabal (Calle Real del Arrabal) is a gem of Mudéjar. You might want to take it in en route to Hospital de Tavera, north of the center.

SETTLING IN
Hostal del Cardenal (Paseo de Recaredo 24): Built to house an eighteenth-century archbishop, it fronts a luxuriant garden, shielded from the street by a medieval wall dating to the eleventh century. Public spaces are museum-caliber—a fountain-centered patio, vaulted lounges, antique-accented corridors, restaurant exemplary enough to warrant later comment—and not quite 30 rooms, no two alike, each a period piece of considerable charm. And central. In a word: one of Spain's best smaller houses. *Luxury.*

Parador Nacional Conde de Orgaz (Cerro del Emperador): Named for the very same count whose funeral is immortalized in an El Greco painting in a downtown church, this link in the government-operated chain of inns is contemporary as regards age, traditional in design. Handsome, rambling, with not quite two dozen inviting rooms, ravishing views of the city from the front ones and the public spaces, and a distinguished restaurant, of which more later. A hitch, though: The elevated, above-town setting is away from the center. You'll need a car or taxi for to-and-fro bouts of exploration. *First Class.*

Hotel Alfonso VI (Calle General Moscardó 2) is a comfortable, core-of-town house, full-facility with 80 sprightly rooms with bath, restaurant, bar-lounge. *First Class.*

Hotel Carlos V (Plaza Horno Magdalena 1): Not far from the Cathedral and other central monuments, the Carlos V has private baths in its more than half a hundred rooms. Restaurant. *First Class.*

Hotel Maravilla (Calle Barrio Rey 7) is a worth-knowing-about small house—a score of rooms with bath—a bit north of the Cathedral. Restaurant. *Moderate.*

Hotel Imperio (Calle Cárdenas 7) is a centrally situated house of modest pretensions, in the same neighborhood as the Maravilla (above). Breakfast only. *Moderate.*

DAILY BREAD
Hostal del Cardenal (Paseo de Recaredo 24) rates No. 1 with me as a hotel (above). Ditto as a restaurant. Meal service moves from the Mudéjar-ceilinged dining room to the patio in warm weather. Alfresco or otherwise, you eat very well. Ask for stewed partridge, a Toledo specialty. Or a roast. Or grilled fish. Desserts rate a separate *carta de postres*; if you're going to order baked Alaska—*tortilla Alaska*—in Spain, this is the place. Fine wines. *Luxury.*

Parador Nacional Conde de Orgaz (Cerro del Emperador): The atmospheric traditional-look restaurant of this inn (see above) is indicated for lunch—the three-course prix fixe—when you've a hearty appetite. Start with the assorted *entremeses*—a score of appetizers, each in its own dish, the lot on a massive tray—and go on to the main course (often a local specialty), and the sweet. Regional wines. *First Class.*

Chirón (Paseo Recaredo 1) abuts the western edge of town, affording breathtaking vistas of the valley below. Within are a modish setting and tasty fare. Try the *menú del día. First Class.*

Aurelio (Plaza del Ayuntamiento 8) is convenient for a lunch pause in the course of a day's exploration. Traditional decor, typical dishes, appealing tabs, near the Cathedral. *Moderate.*

Plácido (Calle Santo Tomé 6) is a longtime favorite, at once heart-of-town, humming, and with a top-value *menú del día*. *Moderate.*

INCIDENTAL INTELLIGENCE

Those pricey one-day tour-bus excursions out of Madrid are the coward's way of seeing Toledo. If you insist on allotting this major destination but a single day, come on your own from the capital, leaving early, staying late, spending less, and seeing more. Better yet—much better—settle in overnight. *Further information:* Oficina de Turismo de Toledo, Puerta de Bisagra.

27

Valencia

Culture, Charm and Paella

BACKGROUND BRIEFING

When we think about Valencia, which is not very often, we acknowledge its association with oranges and the rice masterwork called paella. And go on to other matters. Well, there are worse associations, to be sure. Still, one cannot help but relate Valencia's relative obscurity—in the contemporary scheme of things—with a location on the Mediterranean midway between Barcelona to the north and the Andalusia-Costa del Sol regions to the south that is just far enough away from principal visitor areas to be considered skippable.

Spain's No. 3 city? The newcomer to the kingdom is not so much surprised at this intelligence as indifferent. A pity, for what turns out to be a city sprightly and buoyant, bright and sun-dappled, with a core that brings to life prouder centuries when it was the nerve center of a kingdom to be reckoned with, and, for that matter, of earlier, equally consequential eras. Valencia's city fathers said it all in 1962 when they officially proclaimed the city's two-thousandth birthday—and had a year-long party. There had been earlier settlements in the region: by prehistoric Iberians, Carthaginians, even Greeks. Still, the first proper Valencians—colonists come from Rome—settled in 138 years before Christ; the town's name then, *Valentia*, was just about what it is today. Souvenirs of the progressive Roman centuries remain. There are fewer reminders of the succeeding Christian Visigoths, out of Germany.

But the Moors, who came and conquered in the eighth century, made contributions that were to endure. A vast and fertile plain—*la huerta*, it is called—surrounding the city and flanking the Mediterranean was first put to use by the North African-origin Moslems, for cultivation of the oranges and rice which to this day are staples of the Valencia region.

The Moors were more than farmers. They were the first Valencians to set up a sovereign government, in their case a caliphate ultimately independent of the pan-Spanish one in Córdoba. That period—a millennium back—was one of interminable Moorish-Christian fighting. The celebrated Moor-fighter, El Cid, gained control of Valencia for a remarkable half-decade (1094–1099), ruling until he died on the scene, with his strong-willed widow, Jimena, carrying on for three valiant years thereafter, finally surrendering to the Moors in 1102.

It was not until 1238, well over a century later, that Valencia reverted to Christian control, with the conquest of James I. Though allied with the larger kingdom of Aragón, James in his way emulated the earlier Moorish emirs of Valencia, creating self-governing Valencian kingdoms within the Aragonese framework. The city became seat of a sovereign state for the second time in its history. And it became great.

As a maritime power, it competed with stronger Barcelona, up the coast. Its merchants—trading with the bountiful agriculture of the region—became rich. With wealth came cultural achievement. The University of Valencia opened in 1501. A Valencian school of painting (specimens of its work are to be seen in the Museo de Bellas Artes) flourished. Architects graced the city with works both civil and ecclesiastical. And artisans came into their own, as potters (it is not for nothing that Valencia is the seat of Spain's national ceramics museum), silversmiths and goldsmiths, and makers of fans and long-fringed *mantillas*, eternal symbols of the romance of Spain.

ON SCENE
Lay of the Land: The lovely part about this substantial city of some three-quarters of a million population is that, size notwith-

standing, it is agreeably walkable. The ancient core, instead of being relegated to lesser status as in some cities, remains the vital center, ringed by a modern city, with the Turia River flanking it to the north, and the railway station signaling the southern frontier. Beaches and port are about three miles from the center, to the east, the airport several miles to the west.

Center of Valencia action, graced by greenery and sculpture and the play of waters in its great fountain, is elliptical Plaza del País Valenciano. Fringed by hotels, restaurants, cafés, and shop-lined streets, that square is a short walk south—along Avenida María Cristina—of the city's principal monuments. These mostly extend as far west as Plaza del Mercado, east to Plaza Tetuán, with the important Cathedral district due north, around Plaza de Zaragoza. Still other requisite destinations lie across Puente Trinidad, a bridge spanning the Turia River, leading to a surprise-filled park called Viveros Municipales.

Museo Nacional de Cerámica (Rinconada García Sánchez) is accorded pride of place because it's Spain's only nationally oper-ated museum devoted exclusively to the art of ceramics. Look sharp, even before entering. The museum is quartered in an eighteenth-century palace—*Palacio de Dos Aguas*—whose ro-coco façade, especially the exuberant, larger-than-life carved al-abaster figures framing the front door, in and of itself makes a Valencia visit worthwhile. Within, the palace is more nineteenth century than eighteenth—two floor of elaborate, high-ceilinged rooms give on to a charming patio. The flamboyant decor at times fights with the exhibits. But no matter. This is a remarkable collection of ceramics, running the gamut of centuries of Spanish regional variations. What one wants most to concentrate on is the local work from the nearby villages of Manises and Paterna (the former still has open-to-the-public potteries). Single most spectacular exhibit is an absolute smasher of a kitchen in which one doesn't know what to admire most, the tiles of the floor, the tiles of the walls, the tile-backed ovens, the ceramic plaques em-bedded in the walls, or the exquisite pieces on the wall shelves. There are foreign ceramics, as well—notably Italian Della Robbia. And other treats, including a roomful of Valencian fans, and the opulently embellished carriage—three centuries old—of the palace's builder, Marqués de Dos Aguas.

Museo de Bellas Artes (Calle de San Pío V) occupies a somber seventeenth-century palace, named after the sainted Pope Pius V (Palacio de San Pío V), that fringes Viveros Park, across the Turia. It's the most distant from the core of our selected Valencia destinations, ranking just after galleries of Madrid, Barcelona, and Seville. One wants, first, to become acquainted, on home ground, with the Valencian school that flourished half a millennium back, during the city's Golden Age. Its works take the form, mostly, of oversized altarpieces, three-dimensional, richly colored and gilded, and surprisingly detailed. If you don't know Valencians' names before you go, you'll remember them after seeing their work: Miguel Alcañiz, Fray Bonifacio Ferrer, Maestro de Perea, Juan Silvera, to cite a quartet. See, as well, the small but special representation of other Spanish masters: a riveting self-portrait of the young Velázquez; a black-gowned young lady with fan and dog by Goya; El Greco's *San Juan Bautista*; a Ribera *San Sebastián*. With bonuses of sculpture and mosaics from Valencia's early Roman centuries. Exiting the museum, take a stroll through the adjacent park, whose special treat (aside from a mini-zoo and an excellent restaurant, about which more later) are the gardens—*Jardines del Real*—with an offbeat collection of architectural elements saved from razed city churches, convents, and palaces. Doors and entranceways, mostly, they're charming souvenirs of baroque and Renaissance Valencia.

Colegio del Patriarca (Calle de la Nave 1) is Valencia's most extraordinary single building-complex. Originally a seminary, dating to the Renaissance, it abounds in beauty. Look first at its cloister, comprising two levels, each gracefully arched. Move along to the intimate *Capilla de la Purísima*, to see not only its frescoed ceiling and gilded Virgin, but the half dozen five-century-old Brussels tapestries (their themes are vice and virtue) surfacing its walls. Then visit the larger *Capilla de Corpus Cristi*, sumptuously frescoed, with a Ribera *Last Supper* on the altar. End in the museum, almost on a par with the Bellas Artes, as you'll perceive at the sight of a trio of El Grecos, a *Virgin and*

Child by Juan de Juanes, and an early Flemish *Calvary*—to give you an idea.

La Lonja (Plaza del Mercado) represents medieval Spain's civil architecture at its most sublime. This was where Valencia's merchants negotiated, schemed, and strutted, the while enriching themselves and their city. Its central hall, in which four rows of slim and fluted columns support a magnificently vaulted ceiling, is one of the memorable interiors of the kingdom. The coffered ceiling—gold-leaf surfacing its intricate designs—of the adjacent *Consulado Marítimo* is almost equally stunning.

Mercado Central (Plaza del Mercado): If you're going to visit a single all-purpose market anywhere in Spain, make it Valencia's. An across-the-square neighbor of *La Lonja* (above), this steel-girded pavilion is high, wide, and spotless. Take in row after row of stalls wherein are vended all manner of Spanish comestibles—sausages and seafood, meat and poultry, fruits and vegetables, wines and sweets. Fun.

Church of Santos Juanes (Plaza del Mercado): The market district is not without its share of churches. This one has the distinction of being named for both St. John the Apostle and St. John the Baptist. But it's known, popularly, as San Juan del Mercado. The façade is broad and bold and beautiful baroque, striking enough so as to make the interior—despite a lovely frescoed dome—almost anticlimactic.

Church of San Nicolás (Calle Valenciano) is a five-minute walk along venerable Calle Calatrava, through the oldest part of town, from Plaza del Mercado. And worth the trek, as much for the atmospheric terrain en route as for its interior: a masterwork of the Spanish species of baroque called Churrigueresque. Not a cubic centimeter of St. Nick's has been left unembellished. Sculpted angels top the capitals of the columns supporting the arched ceiling, every bit of which is gloriously frescoed. High altar and chapels are art-filled, too, with masters like de Juanes among the painters. No doubt about it: Valencia's No. 1 church.

Convento de Santo Domingo (Plaza de Tetuán) is now seat of the regional army brass. Happily, they allow visitors in for quick peeps. Give the army credit for good taste. This is a Gothic beauty spot. The onetime Sala Capitular still is used for weddings, and the cloister, its lower gallery dating to the thirteenth century, is extraordinary.

The Cathedral (Plaza de Zaragoza) is at its best from without. Take a look from the far end of Plaza de Zaragoza, the better to afford perspective, at a left-to-right trio of silhouettes. First the tall, octagonal, and unusual tower—El Miguelete, it is called— that dates to the Middle Ages. Then, center, the main spire, a fanciful baroque conceit, three-tiered and elaborate. At right, the squat Sala Capitular section of the complex, topped by a pretty Gothic tower. There is, as well, a fourth Cathedral exterior, its oldest Gothic entrance. It's in front of this doorway that you want to position yourself, should you be in town on a Thursday midday. Then, at noon, as it has every week for a thousand years, a tribunal—its half dozen members traditionally black-robed— meets alfresco to adjudicate land disputes among farmers of the *huerta*, the rich agricultural region surrounding the city that has for centuries been watered by a network of eight canals. Losers pay by forfeiting water rights for whatever period the judges— whose decisions are final—decree. It's quite a show.

Within, the Cathedral, a pastiche of architectural epochs, Gothic through baroque, disappoints, offering severity unrelieved by a sense of style, with the appendage of a museum whose exhibits mostly leave one cold.

Basílica de la Virgen de los Desamparados (Plaza de la Virgen) translates as Virgin of the Forsaken. At the rear of the Cathedral, the basilica is named for a statue of the Virgin—gilded, pearl-studded, and Valencia's patron saint. The church itself is less elaborate, a neoclassic oval, with its only jarring notes a cluster of fussy crystal chandeliers.

Church of Santa Catalina (Plaza de Zaragoza) is still another neighbor to the Cathedral, on the southern flank of the square on which it stands. Of our trio of churches in this area, this is the standout: single-nave Gothic, whose massive vaults frame a setting at once somber and moving.

Ayuntamiento (Plaza del País Valenciano) bespeaks the mid-nineteenth-century wealth of Valencia. This is the city hall, broad-stroked in its grandeur, a maze of high-ceilinged halls, several of which—up a ceremonial stairway—constitute a museum of Valenciana. Go in—and up.

Beaches: Sun and a swim? Valencia's wide, white-sand beaches flank the city, a few miles—via bus, taxi, or car—from the center. *Playa Nazaret* is a favorite to the south of town; *Playa Malvarrosa* to the north.

SETTLING IN
Hotel Astoria Palace (Plaza Rodrigo Botet 5) is one of Spain's most striking urban hotels: a traditional-style house, with 230 perfectly lovely rooms and baths, top-rank restaurant, convivial cocktail lounge (full of gossipy locals at the end of the day), even a disco. The staff is skilled and obliging. And the location, just off Plaza del País Valenciano, adjacent to the historic Church of San Juan de Dios, is central. *Luxury.*

Hotel Reina Victoria (Calle Barcas 4) occupies a richly detailed turn-of-century building, just off Plaza del País Valenciano. This is a handsome house, with Louis XV-style furnishings in its small lobby, paneled bar (beloved of locals), and attractive restaurant. Rooms are period-style, smartly papered, but with baths that could be better. *Luxury.*

Hotel Inglés (Calle Marqués de Dos Aguas 6) is a period piece, well over a century in age, just opposite the dazzling rococo façade of Museo Nacional de Cerámica (above). Nothing English about this hotel save its name. The ambience is nineteenth-century Valencia, façade through lobby-lounge, brass-chandeliered restaurant, cozy bar, and three-score attractive rooms with baths. With a mostly long-on-the-scene staff that cares. *First Class.*

Hotel Excelsior (Calle Barcelonina 5) is a heart-of-town inn, a step from Plaza del País Valenciano. The look is sprightly, a nice mix of contemporary with antique accents, in a series of lounges and the bar. There are 100 full-facility rooms and suites. Breakfast and snacks only. *First Class.*

Hotel Oltra (Plaza del País Valenciano 4) is smack on Valencia's busiest square. Beyond the tiny lobby and larger lounge with TV and bar, there's a *cafetería* and some 90 comfortable rooms-cum-baths. If street noises don't bother you, ask for front accommodations (higher up, the quieter), the better for vistas of the ebullient fountain-centered plaza. *Moderate.*

Hotel Bristol (Calle Abadía San Martín 3) is a small, simple house, with the advantage of a central situation, near the Ceramics Museum. Tiny lobby. Some 50 neat rooms with baths or showers. Breakfast only. *Moderate.*

Hotel Continental (Calle Correos 8) has the virtue of location (central, near Plaza del País Valenciano), and price (cheap). Some 40 rooms, many with baths. Breakfast only. *Moderate.*

DAILY BREAD

Viveros (Jardines del Real, in Viveros Park, across the Turia River) is a restaurant of consequence: eye-filling and spacious, with a welcoming staff. Walls of the dining rooms beyond the lobby are wood-paneled. Chairs are Louis XV, plates silver, flowers fresh roses, waiters tuxedoed—and fare extraordinary. Open with *huevos Godart*, eggs scrambled with mushrooms. Go on to the city's own invention, *paella Valenciana*. Here, the saffron-colored rice is heaped with both meat and poultry, as well as snails. For dessert: a pair of Valencia oranges, masterfully sliced, and doused with Grand Marnier. Or a beaker of tart, made-on-premises lemon sherbet. Order wines of the region—red Utiels, white Turis, most especially. *Luxury.*

Hotel Astoria Palace Restaurante (Plaza Rodrigo Botet 5): High-ceilinged, with pink linen on the widely spaced tables, this is a comfortable setting for the steak you may crave, *lenguado* (the excellent Spanish sole), or the well-priced *menú del día*. Depending on what you order: *first Class/Luxury*.

Mesón del Marisquero (Calle Felix Pizcueta 7) first tempts with atmosphere: the look is of old. But the fare—roasts, seafood casseroles, delicious desserts, area wines—is exceptional, too. *First Class.*

Alcázar (Calle Mosén Fermades 12) is one of a number of temptingly tabbed restaurants whose tables spill out (in good weather at least) onto the pavement of this venerable and narrow street, heart-of-town. Alcázar's fare is hearty—a huge paella with snails, chicken, string beans, and artichokes, preceded by a Valencian variation of a French *salade Niçoise* (tuna, hard-cooked eggs, tomatoes, with cold mussels a local addition), and, for dessert, the custard called *flan*. With a bottle of local Val de San Jaume. And the tab is *Moderate.*

Mesón Mosén (Calle Mosén Fermades 15) is still another Restaurante Row choice (see above) with the fare and ambience not unlike those of its neighbors. Difference, at least as regards those tables placed on the pavement, centers on color of the tablecloths. Mesón Mosén's are red-and-white check, in contrast to pale blue at Alcázar and varying colors at the tables of the others. Because they border each other, this way you know whose restaurant your table belongs to. So do the waiters! *Moderate.*

Ateneo (Plaza del País Valenciano 18) confuses, with a single entrance from which doors to the right lead to a *cafetería* and other doors, to the left, to a proper restaurant. The latter is fussy and unfriendly. The former is so inexpensive that you don't mind the disagreeable waiters, given the tasty paella and the sound house wine. For a meal at the *cafetería: Moderate.*

El Corte Inglés (Plaza Sorolla) is the Valencia outpost of one of the pair of Spain-wide department-store chains. Take the escalator to six, where you've a choice of restaurants. One offers service (including hot dishes and wines) at a counter. Another is exclusively for a groaning buffet, hot and cold, and a wise choice if you're famished. The third—my preference—is a sit-down, waitress-service restaurant with gold-colored linen and well-priced *menús del día* that include *pollo con ajo*: delicious fried chicken, disjointed and garlic-accented. *Moderate.*

Lerma (Calle Paza 18) is an aged and elegant *pastelería*—pastry shop—that also creates candies and ice cream, and serves whatever you order at a cluster of little tables. Buy a bagful of whatever suits your fancy, to go; or tarry and enjoy a snack on the spot, with tea or coffee. *Moderate.*

INCIDENTAL INTELLIGENCE

Iberia flies to Valencia from major Spanish mainland cities as well as from Majorca and Ibiza. The airport is near the earlier-mentioned pottery-making village of Manises, five miles from town. Passenger ships sail regularly for Majorca and Ibiza, as well as the Canary Islands. Valencia's classic-style *Teatro Principal* is the scene of an annual April-June opera season, with companies both Spanish and foreign, and ballet as well; concerts, too. Musicals, revues, and plays are performed at the Alcázar and Princesa theaters. The *Plaza de Toros* is one of the biggest in Spain; frequent bullfights. *Further information:* Oficina de Turismo de Valencia, Ayuntamiento, Plaza del País Valenciano.

28

Valladolid

Sophistication,
Northern-Style

BACKGROUND BRIEFING

You like the name (*va-ya-dough-leed*). And you learn, from a bit of digging, there are three theories as to its origin. One school holds that it derives from the underappreciated name of a landholding Moor (*Olit*) who owned the valley (*valle*) upon which this north-central city was later built. A second guess centers around olive cultivation, from the Latin *vallis olivetum*, and the third takes us back to the early Roman period, when the colonists are believed to have called their settlement *Valle Tolitum*, valley of waters.

Romans, Germanic Visigoths, North African-origin Moors: Valladolid, like so much of Spain, knew them all. Christian forces reconquered the city a thousand years ago, with a single noble family—Ansúrez by name—taking control for something like 200 years. By which time the monarchs of Castile got the word, and began to use Valladolid as a principal residence.

Before long, the city became a center of the action. Interesting things soon were to take place there. Ferdinand and Isabella picked Valladolid as the site of what proved to be a political union of planetary significance: their wedding. It was in Valladolid, also, that they set up the machinery for what came to be the dreaded Inquisition.

Columbus died in Valladolid. Emperor Charles V was often in Valladolid, and his son, Philip II, was born there (you may still see in what is now the town hall the window through which, legend says, the infant Philip was handed for baptism).

The adult Philip II moved the royal court to Madrid. But his son, Philip III, moved it back to Valladolid for a brief seventeenth-century half-decade. All those royals on scene for so substantial a period did Valladolid no harm either culturally or, for that matter, architecturally.

It is today a lively metropolis of a quarter-million, mostly concerned with industry and commerce, far enough away from Madrid to stand quite on its own as a regional center of consequence, and sophistication. However, enough of its regal heyday period—the centuries when it was a kind of co-capital with Toledo, to the south—remains to warrant the curious visitor's settling in and having a look.

ON SCENE

Lay of the Land: With the Pisuerga River a natural western frontier and the railway station as good a delineation of its southern extremity as any, central Valladolid comprises a network of arteries connecting a quartet of principal squares. First is Plaza de España, which Calle Gamazo connects with the railway station and from which one proceeds along Calle Duque de la Victoria to arcaded Plaza Mayor, the second of our plazas, and the *Ayuntamiento*, or town hall. From Plaza Mayor head south along shop- and café-lined Calle de Santiago to a third square, fountain-centered Plaza de Zorilla, which fringes the park called Campo Grande. Again from Plaza Mayor, the direction might be east into the historic core, along Calle Francisco Ferrari, to a group of ancillary churches and the university. Fourth of our quartet of squares, Plaza de San Pablo, to the north, is named for an adjacent church with its neighbor a palace housing a museum that, though operated by the Spanish government, is among the most underappreciated of any such in the kingdom, and among the most beautiful in Europe. Which is why I lead off with it, below.

Museo Nacional de Escultura (Plaza de San Pablo): Spain's national sculpture museum dates to the 1930s when the government took over Colegio de San Gregorio, built, in the same decade Columbus discovered America, by Fray Alonso de Burgos, Queen Isabella's confessor. It's a magnificent building in the Isabelline style. The carved-stone façade over the door is a work of art. And then, within: a two-level patio, whose decorated columns and arches are no less sublime than the façade; a chapel that ranks, as regards both its art and architecture, with the best in a city full of fine churches; and a score and a half of galleries—some with carved-wood and gilded-geometric-design ceilings in the Mudéjar style—sheltering an extraordinary collection of sculpted objects. These include polychromed saints, gilded altarpieces, multichair walnut choirs taken intact from medieval and Renaissance churches and monasteries: a collection that, taken in toto, is unique. And note: Each gallery has been designed as a separate entity, boldly and dramatically. An Alonso Berruguete *Calvary* is set, alone, against a deep blue wall. A Renaissance Saint Anne reposes against a background of vivid scarlet. Two elongated rows of stalls out of nearby *San Benito Church* line a severe rectangle of a room, with the background stark white. A black-robed Saint Teresa dominates a long gilded wall of a gallery. Three salons are devoted to Alonso Berruguete. Juan de Juni has a whole room, as do equally reputed Renaissance sculptors like Gregorio Fernández and Pompeo Leoni. You may never before have given a damn about the sculpture of Spain's Golden Age. You will, after a visit to Colegio de San Gregorio.

Church of San Pablo (Plaza de San Pablo): San Pablo, like neighboring Colegio de San Gregorio, is fronted by a massive carved-stone façade. Except that the church's is even bigger and grander than the museum's. Within, admire the choir and polychromatic sculpture.

The Cathedral (Plaza de la Universidad) has impeccable credentials: Its initial designer was the same Juan de Herrera who was co-architect of Philip II's El Escorial. And it had the very same royal patron. The façade is in the neoclassic style Herrera employed at El Escorial, if not so severe. Within, lures are an altar by de Juni and the Museo Diocesano occupying an adjacent Gothic chapel filled with lovely things.

Cathedral-area churches that you'll want to take in, after the Cathedral, include *El Salvador* (Calle Galera), a Gothic beauty with a Flemish altar that may or may not be the work of Quentin Metsys, but is magnificent, withal; *Santa María la Antigua* (Plaza Redondo), with a near-skyscraper of a Romanesque bell tower and a long, Gothic-vaulted nave; and *Las Angustias* (Calle Angustias), whose baroque interior is a kind of mini-museum of sculpture.

Casa Museo de Colón (Calle de Colón) is the house in which Christopher Columbus is believed to have lived prior to his death in Valladolid in 1506, with a museum of Columbus documents within that is of interest to New Worlders.

Church of La Magdalena (Calle de Colón) is easily taken in, in tandem with Casa de Colón, its immediate neighbor. A massively embellished coat of arms of the bishop who founded it makes up the façade. There are a pair of glittering altars and the founding bishop's marble tomb within. If you can get into adjacent *Convento de las Huelgas*, do so, if only to see the sculptures of its chapel, including some by de Juni.

Museo Arqueológico Provincial (Calle Expósitos): A somber Renaissance palace shelters a score of galleries enclosing both upper and lower levels of a tranquil patio. There are souvenirs of ancient Valladolid, Roman busts among them. But it is the Renaissance paintings—a Virgin at prayer, a luminous Pietà, a richly detailed Nativity—that stand out.

Convento de Santa Ana (Plaza de Santa Ana) has associations with two important kings and a major painter. The former are Philip II, who was its original patron, and Charles III, most enlightened of the eighteenth-century Bourbon kings, who had it rebuilt in the classic style of his era, with its chapel elegantly elliptical. The latter is Goya, for the convent is the site of a trio of his paintings, each of a different saint: *José, Bernardo, Ludgarda*.

SETTLING IN
Hotel Olid Meliá (Plaza San Miguel 10) is a looker of a mod house, with some 240 smartly understated rooms and suites, and—off a capacious lobby—a range of rooms for dining and drinking, including a top-rank restaurant (of which more later) and an inexpensive *cafetería*. Excellent location. *Luxury.*

Hotel Felipe IV (Calle Gamazo 16) is a modern house, with 130 comfortable rooms, proper restaurant, casual *cafetería*, bar-lounge. Not quite as central as the Olid Meliá. *Luxury.*

Hotel Roma (Calle Héroes del Alcázar de Toledo 8): A hotel with a mouthful of a street address like the Roma's has to be paid some attention. This is an agreeable smaller place, not far from Plaza Mayor, with 40 rooms—many with baths—and a restaurant. *Moderate.*

Hotel Enara (Plaza de España 5) has an easy-to-find situation on a major square, not far from the Cathedral. Just 25 rooms with bath. Breakfast only. *Moderate.*

DAILY BREAD
Mesón La Fragua (Paseo de Zorrilla 10), with its hearty traditional decor, looks more casual than it is. Make no mistake: This is a restaurant that takes food seriously, especially regional specialties like *sopa Castellana* and roast suckling pig, known locally as *lechazo* rather than *cochinillo*. A brochette of sole and shrimp is tasty. So are the grilled veal chops. Exceptional wine list, with the local Bachs—red and white—good buys. Among the best restaurants in Spain. *First Class.*

Mesón Cervantes (Calle El Rastro 6) is not to be confused with the neighboring Casa Cervantes, a house in which the writer is said to have lived, but which is open so spasmodically as a museum that I do not recommend it. The restaurant—or *mesón*—is something else again: A handsome period piece that *does* maintain regular hours of opening, serving local and all-Spain specialties. *First Class.*

Machaquito (Calle Calixto Fernández de la Torre 5) is another worth-knowing-about spot near Plaza Mayor. Decibel count is high—albeit agreeably so—thanks, for the most part, to the patronage of local business types. *First Class.*

Hotel Olid Meliá Restaurante (Plaza San Miguel 10): In a bright contemporary environment, the Meliá chefs prepare a delicious full-course *menú del día*—a grilled trout to start, chicken en brochette following, with fresh fruit cup for dessert, for example—that is one of the best buys in town. Skilled service. *Moderate.*

Chicote (Plaza Leones de Castilla 7) is well-located, not far from Plaza Mayor, with tasty fare—select the *menú del día*—temptingly tabbed. *Moderate.*

Oscar (Calle Ferrari 1) is for on-the-run lunches and snacks or a proper meal; more *cafetería* than restaurant. *Moderate.*

INCIDENTAL INTELLIGENCE

You can, for reasons known only to Iberia, fly that airline to Valladolid from Barcelona but not from Madrid. The airport is seven miles from the center. *Further information:* Oficina de Turismo de Valladolid, Plaza de Zorrilla 3.

29

Zamora

Romanesque Treasure Trove

BACKGROUND BRIEFING

Zamora does not come on strong. It is something of an exaggeration to term it a sleepy town; it is, to be sure, a low-key one. But refreshingly so, especially if encountered, say, in the course of a motor journey from central Spain northwest to Galicia. And one would be wrong to assume that far earlier travelers have not come upon the place, for this Duero River city played a disproportionately large role in Spanish history. Its proximity to Portugal has been, politically and militarily, a minus as well as a plus, for armies under one banner or other tended to consider it strategic.

It is old, too. Roman colonists were by no means its first residents; they followed earlier Iberian peoples, were ultimately succeeded by Moors, who were later ousted by Christians (legend says the great Moor-fighter El Cid was knighted in a still-standing Zamora church). These last, as the Middle Ages became the Renaissance, took to fighting among themselves—the forces of León against those of Castile—until eventually Castilians were the victors, with the town and province of Zamora absorbed into a united Spain.

Zamora knew battle and dissension, but it achieved wealth and commercial eminence, both of which engendered a medieval building boom, resulting in one of the most remarkable ensembles of Romanesque architecture in Spain.

ON SCENE

Lay of the Land: Not unlike bigger, richer, more stylish Salamanca to the south (see the chapter on the city), Zamora's center is pierced by a still-in-use Roman-built bridge. Again, not unlike in Salamanca, I suggest you gain a perspective of the town by crossing *Puente Romano* to the south bank of the Duero, and taking in a skyline that has remained intact for centuries, embracing the steeples of a dozen churches, the unusual dome of the *Cathedral*—dead center—standing out. Regain the city, then, via Calle Arcos to Plaza Santa Lucía and the church for which it is named, and neighboring *San Cipriano Church* with still another landmark: the Renaissance mansion that is the city's leading hostelry (see *Settling In*).

Exit this square and you're on Calle Ramos, heart of town. A little to the east, and you've reached Zamora's Plaza Mayor. Walk west and you pass landmark churches like *San Ildefonso* and *La Magdalena*, with the Cathedral just beyond. What remains of the city's fortifications looms over the Cathedral, most especially Traitor's Gate, where—nearly a thousand years ago—Castilian King Sancho II was assassinated by the forces of his sister, Princess Urraca.

The Cathedral (Plaza de la Catedral): You want first to consider the dome. Take a look at the unusual tiles surfacing its central area as well as the half-dozen-odd smaller domes; the technique is called fishtail—which it resembles—and it was not uncommon in twelfth-century Romanesque works. The front door and its arch (a Renaissance addition) excepted, the look is of the east; Zamora Cathedral puts one in mind of a Byzantine church, with its high altar by Fernando Gallego and a marvelously carved choir. Cross through the quiet cloister to the museum, a jumble of ecclesiastical art, including Flemish tapestries half a millennium in age.

A quartet of Romanesque churches: San Cipriano (Plaza Santa Lucía) is at once central, venerable (it went up in 1025), and atmospheric. *La Magdalena* (Rua de los Notarios) is high-walled, and with an especially grand façade. *Santa María de la Orta* (Calle Plata) stands out because of its chunky bell tower and handsomely scaled nave. Last of our group, *Santiago de los Caballeros*, is up beyond the old walls and the earlier-described Traitor's Gate. It is a case of big things coming in small packages: a tiny Romanesque gem, at whose altar El Cid, the Spanish medieval hero and Moor-battler, is said to have been knighted.

Museo de Bellas Artes (Calle Santa Clara 17) is a tempting hodgepodge of Old Zamora in a properly atmospheric setting. No pieces of global repute, to be sure, but paintings, drawings, weathered documents, furniture, and accessories, the lot delineating a not uneventful local history.

Museo de la Santa Semana (Plaza de Santa María la Nueva): Holy Week is hardly inconsequential anywhere in Spain, least of all in little Zamora, with elaborate processions through the core of town—*pasos*, they are called—the highlights. This museum, chockablock with the impedimenta of the ceremonials, is as good a place as any in Spain to absorb the essence of these annual spring rites. To be combined with across-the-plaza *Church of Santa María la Nueva* for an inspection of its own Holy Week regalia and an extraordinary sculpted Christ.

SETTLING IN

Parador Nacional Condes de Alba y Aliste (Plaza de Cánovas): I can't imagine anyone overnighting in Zamora and staying elsewhere, unless the *parador* is fully booked, which is, of course, a possibility; it has but 27 rooms. Each is virtually stadium-sized, for this is a palace out of the Renaissance built around one of the finest patios—a different personality carved in a stone medallion over each pillar of its two levels—in the kingdom. With interior public spaces to match, bar-lounge, and restaurant that's an all-Zamora leader. Take snuggies if your visit is a nonsummer one; tiny radiators—one in each of the enormous bedrooms—can't begin to do a proper heating job. But if it's summer, have a swimsuit; there's a pool. *First Class.*

Hotel Dos Infantas (Calle Dortinas de San Miguel 3) is distinctly No. 2, with close to 70 rooms with bath, and a *cafetería. Moderate.*

DAILY BREAD

París (Avenida de Portugal 14) is on the wide street dividing the center of town from a pretty park on its east flank. Spiffy-looking, with spiffy fare, including local delights like deliciously roasted veal, and grilled fish out of nearby waters. Toro wines—regional reds—are indicated. *First Class.*

La Rueda (Ronda de la Feria 19) is a nice walk north of Plaza Mayor, central city. This is a looker, in traditional style, with the food as inviting as the decor. *Moderate/First Class.*

INCIDENTAL INTELLIGENCE

Oficia de Turismo de Zamora, Calle Santa Clara 20.

30

Zaragoza
Ancient Aragón, Updated

BACKGROUND BRIEFING
There are several points worth making about Zaragoza. The first, as a matter of practicality, is that it's sometimes spelled Saragossa in English. The second is that, of the two "Z" cities accorded chapters in this book, it's by far the larger and more consequential. With its half-million-plus population, it's more than 10 times the size of Zamora, to the west; indeed, only Madrid, Barcelona, Valencia, and Seville are larger. The third is that, though touristically overlooked more often than not (at least in the general all-Spain scheme of such matters), its location is worth noting: about midway on the northern route between the Big Two towns, Madrid and Barcelona.

More contemporarily noted for commerce than culture, Zaragoza need not hide its head as regards souvenirs of an extraordinary past. It was the seat of ancient Aragón, a name that in itself conjures up armored knights and massive battles and Moorish invasions.

Not without good reason. Zaragoza goes back to the Roman occupation, when Emperor Augustus dubbed it part after himself, part after another emperor; the original name was Caesarea Augusta. German-origin Goths remained until the eighth century, when the Moors out of North Africa not only settled in but designated Zaragoza capital of a self-governing caliphate; it was so strong that not even Charlemagne could conquer it, try as he did.

Not until the twelfth century did the city become Christian, and capital of the same kingdom of Aragón that was later to play a major role in the creation of a unified Spain when it joined forces with Castile, under Aragón's Ferdinand and Castile's Isabella.

Those epochs of derring-do and later heroic periods— especially early nineteenth-century resistance to the French— left their mark. The past mingles with a perky contemporary pace. End of the alphabet notwithstanding, Zaragoza merits the traveler's acquaintance.

ON SCENE
Lay of the Land: Geography is a relatively uncomplicated matter. The four towers of *Basílica del Pilar*, on a plaza by that name, constitute a major and easily identifiable landmark. The city's Cathedral, *La Seo*, is almost next door. And the *Ayuntamiento*, or town hall, separates this pair. Move into town along humming Calle Alfonso I until you gain the greenery of Plaza de España. Continue along Paseo de la Independencia to the Plateresque façade of the *Church of Santa Engracia*. An additional major monument—a Moorish fortress-palace, the *Aljafería*—remains; it's considerably to the west on Calle Castillo, a near-neighbor to the railway station.

Basílica de Nuestra Señora del Pilar (Plaza de Nuestra Señora del Pilar) is Zaragoza's most distinctive building, an all-Spain one-of-a-kind, thanks to a quartet of widely separated bell towers, one at each of its corners, with the ensemble framing a cluster of lower domes, the lot creating a spectacular effect that constitutes one of the great works of Spanish baroque. The designer, renowned Francisco de Herrera, had intended a baroque interior as well, but his successor on the project had other ideas, based on more somber neoclassic principles, with a surprise feature the linings of some of the cupolas taking the form of frescoes by Goya. Look up as you amble.

La Seo (Plaza de la Seo), the older of the pair of Cathedrals (see

Pilar above), yields to no other in Spain in the variety of its architectural styles. It is substantially—but by no means entirely—Gothic. The apse's exterior is Moorish-influence Mudéjar. The façade is Plateresque. The main altar is Gothic, and one finds Spanish baroque—or Churrigueresque—in the chapels. There are a pair of museums, one devoted to an unusually opulent collection of Flemish tapestries, and the other, El Tesoro, indeed filled with treasures: gold and ivory and precious stones.

La Lonja (Plaza de Nuestra Señora del Pilar) is conveniently midway between the Cathedrals. This Renaissance monument reflects the wealth of the merchants of that era who did their business within. Look up to see their coats of arms in the vaults of a splendid ceiling. Zaragoza's *Ayuntamiento*, or city hall, is in connection.

Museo Provincial de Bellas Artes (Plaza de José Antonio) is not to be overlooked in the course of a Zaragoza visit, what with canvasses by El Greco, Claudio Coello, José de Ribera, and Goya. There are, as well, remnants of Roman Zaragoza, mosaics being the most memorable of these.

Castillo de la Aljafería (Calle Castillo) puts one in mind of the inimitable mosque-cathedral in Córdoba. It is, of course, on a much smaller scale. But the mazes of delicate Moorish arches delight, quite as they do in Andalusian counterparts, and one can understand why Christian kings moved in after the Moors were ousted. There are two floors in this thousand-year-old complex—a mosque highlights the first—with later Gothic quarters (throne room most definitely included) of the rulers of Aragón upstairs.

Church of San Pablo (Calle de San Pablo) is, along with churches like *Santa Engracia, La Magdalena,* and *San Carlos,* a leader among ecclesiastical monuments. Without, admire its eight-sided tower, a Mudéjar masterwork. Then go in to see the Plateresque intricacies of the main altar.

SETTLING IN

Hotel Corona de Aragón Sol (Avenida Cesar Augusto 13) has the advantage of a central situation, 250 pastel-hued, thoughtfully equipped rooms (a cluster of which are on a premium-rate, extra-amenity Executive Floor), trio of restaurants (El Bearn is the poshest) as well as a late-hours disco, convenient *cafetería*, busy bar and rooftop swimming pool—a joy in summer. *Luxury.*

Gran Hotel (Calle Joaquín Costa 5) is full-facility, with 170 rooms, restaurant, bar-lounge. Very comfortable and quite central. *First Class.*

Hotel Rey Alfonso I (Calle Coso 17, and the "I" is pronounced "Primero") is well-situated, well-equipped, and welcoming, with 120 rooms and a restaurant. *Moderate.*

Hotel Conde Blanco (Calle Predicadores 84) is nicely located near the Ebro River, just opposite the municipal tourist office, and not far from the cathedrals. There are 80 rooms, many with baths, and a *cafetería. Moderate.*

DAILY BREAD

Savoy (Calle Coso 42, upstairs), popular with the locals, is where one wants to sample the chicken specialty *pollo a la chilindrón*, or *lomo a la Zaragozana*, a pork dish. Logroño, principal city for the Rioja wine industry, is nearby, so you'll want to order either a red or a white of this species, Spain's finest. *First Class.*

Costa Vasca (Calle Coronel Valenzuela 13) is heart-of-town, with delicious specialties from the Basque country to the near-north. *First Class.*

Las Palomas (Plaza del Pilar 16) is indicated for lunch after a morning in the Cathedrals adjacent. Regional dishes, all-Spain favorites, with carafes of good Rioja. *Moderate.*

INCIDENTAL INTELLIGENCE ══════════════

Zaragoza is on Iberia's domestic network; fly from either Madrid or Barcelona. The airport is five miles from the center. *Further information:* Oficina de Turismo de Zaragoza, Glorieta Pio XII.

Acknowledgments

Many good friends, on both sides of the Atlantic, have been helpful in connection with the research for this revised edition of *Spain at Its Best*. I am especially indebted to two longtime Spanish friends. The first is Pilar Vico, crack public relations director for the National Tourist Office of Spain in North America, based in New York—a veritable encyclopedia of matters Spanish, ever supportive, and never too busy to extend the expert helping hand of a good friend. The second is Antonio Alonso, whom I first came to admire during his tenure as press chief at the Spanish tourist office, when he made many good friends for Spain among the American travel press, and who has since become Número Uno expert, in the U.S., on the Spanish hotel scene, as president of Marketing Ahead, Inc., in New York. I am grateful to Pilar and Antonio, as well as to my research editor, Max Drechsler, like myself a longtime Spain enthusiast; and, as well, to these colleagues whom I want to thank, alphabetically, for their personal kindness and professional cooperation:

María Luisa Albacar, Eugenio Expósito Alburquerque, Angelo Ansano, Beatriz Zuazo Aramburu, Cesar Perez Araque, Victoria Ayuso, Rev. Juan L. Barrera, O.F.M., Juan J. Bergés, Jose M. Bermejo, Mercedes Bernal, Manual Mártinez Cornejo, Maribel Romero Caravajal, Enza Cirrincione, María Muriel Clemente, Jose Luis Estevez, Antonio Hernangómez Fernández, Dr. Ferdando Conde Fernández, Carlos Gonzales, Michael Kuh, Linda Gwinn, Asunción Iglesias, Virginia Kelly, Juan Carlos Morales Lavería, John S. Macedo, Evelyn Mariperisena, Encana Martín, Luis Merino, Inmaculada Sánchez Miñambras, Victoriano Perez Muñoz, Miguel Paradela, Rev. F. Tomás Patero, O.F.M., Giorgio Petracco, Geraldo Quintana, Jesús Pardo Quiroga, Carmen Rey, Miguel Sánchez, Ernesto Santos, Bob Schaeffer, Francisco Gerón Tena, and Florencia Vivancos.

Last, but hardly least, special appreciation to Mark Pattis, vice president/business manager of National Textbook Co., parent corporation of Passport Books; S. William Pattis, NTC's president; Leonard I. Fiddle, executive vice president/editorial director; and my skilled editor, Michael Ross; as well as to my agent, Anita Diamant, and her associate, Robin Rue.

R.S.K.

Index

Descalzas Reales, Monasterio de las, 192
Diocesano, Museo: in Málaga, 103, 104; in Majorca, 223–24; in Salamanca, 240; in Tarragona, 290
Diocesano de Arte Sacro, Museo, 64
Diputación, in Barcelona, 35
Diputados, Palacio de los, 186–87
Don Juan, 15, 178
Dos Aguas, Palacio de, 305
Drach, 222
Dress, Museum of Court, 21–22
Driving, 5
Dueñas, Convento de las, 240

E

Ejército, Museo del, 191
Electric current, 5–6
Elena, Princess 16
Elizabeth I, 131, 175
Elizabeth of Valois, 131
Emeritus Augustus, 136–137
Empresa Nacional de Artesanía, 5
Encarnación, Convent of the, 25
Encarnación, Monasterio de la: in Ávila, 26; in Madrid, 192
Ensenada del Orzán, 256
Episcopal, Palacio, 104
ESCORIAL, EL, 19, 130; geography, 132; history, 130–31; hotels, 134; restaurants, 134; sightseeing, 132–33; travel information, 134
Escultura, Museo Nacional de, 314–15
Esperanza, Church of, 85
Espíritu Santo, Church of, 108
EXTREMADURA, 135; geography, 136; history, 135–36; hotels, 141–44; restaurants, 144–47; sightseeing, 136–41; travel information, 147

F

Facial tissue, 6
Felipe, Prince, 16
Ferdinand of Aragón, 54, 62, 264, 294

Ferdinand II, 8, 57
Ferdinand III, 75
Ferdinand VI, 132, 133
Ferdinand VIII, 9, 20
Figueras, 87
Flamenco dancing, 6; in Córdoba, 287; in Costa del Sol, 124; in Granada, 287; in Madrid, 218; in Seville, 287
Foods, 6–7; breakfast, 1–2. *See also* Restaurants
Francisco de Asís, 21
Franco, Francisco, 9, 15
Fuego, Montañas del, 67
Fuensalida, Palacio de, 299
Fuenterrabía, 247

G

Galerías Preciados, 5
Galicia, 258
Gaudí, Museo, 38–39
Gaudí, Antonio, 36
Gelmírez, Palacio, 254
Generalife, 151
Geography, 7–8
Gerona, 82, 84–85, 91; hotels, 87; sightseeing, 84–85
Gibralfaro, Castillo, 105
Gibraltar, 97–98
Gil de Siloé, 58
Government, 8
Goya, 9
GRANADA, 2, 3; geography, 149; history, 148–49; hotels, 155–57; restaurants, 157–59; sightseeing, 149–55; travel information, 159
Gran Canaria Island, 63–65; hotels, 67; restaurants, 71
Granja, La, 267
Greco, Casa y Museo del, 297–98
Guadalupe, 136, 140–41; hotels, 143–44; restaurants, 146–47
Guadalupe, Monasterio de, 140–41
Guernica, 178